SPEAKING OUT

SPEAKING OUT

Women's economic empowerment in South Asia

Edited by MARILYN CARR, MARTHA CHEN
and RENANA JHABVALA

IT PUBLICATIONS
on behalf of
AGA KHAN FOUNDATION CANADA and
UNITED NATIONS DEVELOPMENT FUND
FOR WOMEN (UNIFEM)
1996

Intermediate Technology Publications Ltd,
103–105 Southampton Row, London WC1B 4HH, UK

© Aga Khan Foundation Canada 1996

A CIP catalogue for this book is available from the British Library

ISBN 1 85339 382 7

Typeset by Dorwyn Ltd, Rowlands Castle, Hants
Printed in UK by SRP Exeter

CONTENTS

v

Preface

NAZEER AZIZ LADHANI

From the Northern Areas of Pakistan to Hambantota District in southern Sri Lanka, women in South Asia have been organizing to gain access to credit, training, technologies and other inputs necessary for successful enterprises. These women have gained more than just increased income from participating in women's organizations – they have increased their bargaining power in the marketplace and have overcome many barriers to women's participation in economic development.

In 1994 Aga Khan Foundation Canada launched the South Asian NGO Development Research Programme to draw out, distil, analyse and disseminate lessons from successful NGOs and successful NGO projects in South Asia. As part of this programme, the Foundation in collaboration with UNIFEM initiated a research project on NGO Experience in Organizing Women for Economic Empowerment to better understand and document the strategies and organizing principles for bringing about women's economic empowerment.

The project was designed to contribute to the following three objectives: enabling South Asian NGOs to learn from each other's experiences in promoting women's economic empowerment; strengthening the capacity of NGOs to undertake further gender research and evaluation alone or jointly; and creating a more favourable environment in which programmes and projects to further women's economic empowerment can be undertaken.

This book is just one element of a strategy to disseminate the experience of the organizations detailed in the following pages with other NGOs and governmental bodies within and outside South Asia. Through workshops and seminars in South Asia and Canada, we hope to build the capacity of NGOs to conduct research and to inform policymakers and practitioners of the means for achieving women's economic empowerment in differing circumstances. These activities build on the Foundation's ongoing efforts to promote documentation and dialogue on gender and development issues.

The Foundation wishes to thank the organizations that collaborated with us on this project. We very much appreciate the time and effort staff members and researchers dedicated to writing the case studies. The members of these organizations participated in the research process through interviews and focus group sessions, and we thank them for sharing their experiences.

We would like to extend our sincere thanks to Marilyn Carr, Martha Chen and Renana Jhabvala for their tireless work and dedication to this research project. This volume is infused with their intellect and energy. Thanks must also be extended to UNIFEM, the Harvard Institute for International Development and SEWA for allowing these individuals the time to work on this project.

In particular, working with UNIFEM on this project has been a special honour for Aga Khan Foundation Canada. We thank UNIFEM for its support of the project and look forward to future opportunities for collaboration.

Finally, we thank the Canadian International Development Agency for its generous assistance.

Nazeer Aziz Ladhani
Chief Executive Officer
Aga Khan Foundation Canada

Preface

NOELEEN HEYZER

IN SEPTEMBER 1995, some 50 000 women from all parts of the world came together in Beijing to participate in the Fourth World Conference on Women (FWCW). Women demanded many things of their governments. Among them was a call for an agenda for development that will empower people, eradicate poverty, create sustainable livelihoods, build stable lives in healthy communities, and promote peace on a long-term basis.

We at the United Nations Development Fund for Women (UNIFEM) played an important role in supporting women in their preparations for and during the UN Conference and NGO Forum, and came away from it with a strengthened mandate to support women's economic and political empowerment. In fulfilling this mandate we will need to work closely with all sections of society – governments, NGOs and with women themselves – and will continue with our role of promoting concern for women's empowerment within the rest of the UN system.

In the Beijing Declaration, the preface to the Platform for Action adopted by the FWCW, it is recognized that 'progress has been uneven, inequalities between men and women have persisted, and major obstacles remain, with serious consequences for the well-being of all people' and also that 'women's empowerment and their full participation on the basis of equality in all spheres of society . . . are fundamental for the achievement of equality, development, and peace'.

Few people concerned with world development would disagree with such statements, but often a willingness on the part of policy makers and practitioners to make changes fails to be translated into action because of a lack of practical ideas and information on how to proceed. As such, UNIFEM sees one of its critical roles as feeding relevant field-level experiences to those who have the power and ability to effect change. It also seeks to feed information to women themselves so that they can better organize for their own empowerment.

Within this context, the current book – on organizing women's economic empowerment in South Asia – is particularly timely. Not only does it give a wealth of new insights based on primary research, it also gives cause for optimism by showing that – given an appropriate enabling environment – women's empowerment is happening on a significant scale and that this in turn is having a noticeable impact on levels of poverty and well-being.

What is of particular interest to us at UNIFEM is the way in which the thousands of women's neighbourhood groups – established by the many well- and lesser-known NGOs in the sub-continent – are growing in strength, federating among themselves and becoming independent and self-sufficient entities in their own right. As is rightly stated in the introduction to the book 'people owning and managing their own organizations are more empowered than those who are beneficiaries of someone else's organization'.

While the literature on the empowerment approach to development is beginning to grow, much of this is still at the level of theory. By speaking from field experience and putting forward the voices of women themselves – and those of the people who work directly with them – we believe that this book will add considerably to the understanding of what women's empowerment means, how it can best be achieved under different circumstances, and how it translates into increased well-being for society as a whole.

UNIFEM has welcomed and enjoyed collaborating with Aga Khan Foundation Canada on this project and looks forward to taking the work forward in ways which will further empower women in South Asia and elsewhere. It has also very much appreciated the close working relationship with the seven major South Asian organizations that participated in the research. Without their vast accumulated experience in this field, and their willingness to share it with others, this book would not have been possible.

Finally, UNIFEM wishes to acknowledge the generous contribution of the Government of Japan, the Osaka Prefectural Government and the Japanese Committee for UNIFEM towards the undertaking of the research.

Noeleen Heyzer
Director
United Nations Development Fund For Women (UNIFEM)

ACKNOWLEDGEMENTS

THE EDITORS WOULD like to acknowledge the assistance of the many people who were involved in putting together a volume of this nature. In particular, we would like to thank Marcia Nation, Research Officer, Gender and Development, Aga Khan Foundation Canada for the excellent work she did in providing logistical support to the initial research workshop held in Dhaka in January 1995 and to the subsequent research programme. We also gratefully acknowledge her substantive involvement in the editing of several of the individual case studies in the book.

Laila Salim, Programme Officer, Aga Khan Foundation (Pakistan) assisted with the running of the Dhaka workshop and helped with the monitoring of research in Pakistan and Sri Lanka. Sophie Lam worked on the preparations for the research project until she left Aga Khan Foundation Canada in 1995 but continued her involvement from her base at Harvard University – where she is a graduate student – through the production of an annotated bibliography for inclusion in the current book.

We would like to acknowledge Nazeer Aziz Ladhani, Chief Executive Officer, Aga Khan Foundation Canada, for his constant support for the research project and the subsequent production of this volume. Chandni Joshi, UNIFEM's Regional Programme Advisor for South Asia, also gave support throughout and was especially helpful to us during the final editing process in New Delhi during January of this year. Aga Khan Foundation (Bangladesh) gave welcome logistical support to the 1995 workshop.

The case study authors would like to thank the organizations involved in the research for their support of and assistance to this project. They sincerely thank the many women who they interviewed during the preparation of their case studies.

We would also like to thank those who have allowed their photographs to be included with the case study material. These include: Jean-Luc Ray and Shehzad Noorain (cover); Jean-Luc Ray (pages 20 and 142); Shehzad Noorani (page 44); Faris Ahmed (page 126); and Martha Chen (pages 66, 84, 104 and 166).

The Sri Lanka–Canada Development Fund assisted with co-ordinating the Sri Lankan research.

Finally, we would like to thank all of the research teams – as well as everyone in the organizations who participated in this project – for their hard work and thoughtful contributions. Thanks to all of you for bearing with us and dealing so patiently with our numerous enquiries during the process of editing this volume. We enjoyed working with you all.

Marilyn Carr, Martha Chen, Renana Jhabvala

Introduction

MARILYN CARR, MARTHA CHEN, RENANA JHABVALA

Women and Poverty in South Asia

ACCORDING TO THE 1995 *Human Development Report*, there are 1.3 billion people living in poverty, of whom almost one-half are in South Asia. Seventy per cent of the poor are female, and the situation is getting worse, with the number of rural women living in absolute poverty rising by 50 per cent (as opposed to 30 per cent for men) over the last two decades (UNDP, 1995).

The consequences of women's poverty are easy to see. In a region where 300 million people do not have enough to eat, women and girls bear the brunt of the hunger, with predictable effects on their health and well-being. South Asia is the only region in the world in which, in countries such as Bangladesh, female life expectancy is lower than male life expectancy. About 80 per cent of pregnant women suffer from anaemia – the highest rate in the world – and about one-third of newborn babies are underweight (UNDP, 1995).

This book is not about women's poverty in South Asia. Rather, it is about the ways in which non-governmental organizations, women's organizations and village and community groups of women themselves have been attempting to overcome it. However, to understand properly the programmes and processes described in the book, it is important to set them within the context of women's poverty and its underlying causes. In particular, it is important to understand the linkages between women's lack of power at all levels and the poverty experienced by themselves, their families and communities.

The causes of women's poverty and absolute poverty fall into two categories: those which result from belonging to families that are poor; and those which relate to women's subordination within the family, the community, and the wider economic and political spheres.

An underlying cause of poverty both for women and men in South Asia is that of entrenched traditional structures: notably class and caste hierarchies; ethnic or religious discrimination; and unequal land distribution. All of these add up to a lack of access to economic resources and a lack of power on the part of the masses of the population, which limits their ability to take control of their lives and improve their well-being. In many cases, these long-term structural causes are being compounded by recent trends

1

in the world economy, including globalization and economic restructuring, which often are responsible for the loss of livelihoods in the public and private sectors. In some areas and for some groups, natural disasters and internal strife further contribute to the deepening of poverty.

In addition to these generic forces, women from low-income groups face gender-specific causes of disempowerment which stem from a patriarchal kinship system that is in force throughout most of the region. To begin with, there are strong norms of female seclusion which, if rigidly enforced – as among Hindu upper castes in northern India and among most Muslim groups in northern India, Bangladesh and Pakistan – deny women the right to gainful employment outside the home. These norms, in their turn, are reflected in two gender divisions of labour: the gender division of tasks within the home and family farm or firm; and the gender division or segmentation of labour markets outside the home. For example, the 1995 edition of *The World's Women* (UN, 1995) reveals that in both Bangladesh and India, while women on average work for longer hours than men (53 hours per week as opposed to 46 hours for men in Bangladesh, and 69 hours as opposed to 57 hours for men in India), most of this is classified as housework and is unpaid, or is subsistence-level economic activity which brings little remuneration (UN, 1995). Then there is the system of patrilineal inheritance whereby daughters, wives and widows are entitled to smaller shares (if any) than sons, husbands and widowers.

The net impact of these traditional cultural forces is, firstly, that most women in South Asia have less direct independent access than men to capital, property, markets and extension services. For example, women have very restricted access to credit because of their lack of collateral in the form of property or other assets. A study of 38 branches of major banks in India found that only 11 per cent of the borrowers were women (UNDP, 1995). And in most Indian States, women farmers are not included among extension beneficiaries, even though an estimated 48 per cent of self-employed cultivators are women (UNDP, 1995).

Secondly, many women have limited geographic mobility, economic independence, or personal autonomy, and as a result remain economically dependent on male kin (father, husband or son depending on their stage in the female life-cycle). Finally, because of their perceived liabilities and their limited bargaining power, women and girls often receive less health care, education, and training than men and boys. For example, although female literacy rates have increased over the past two decades, two-thirds of adult women in South Asia are still illiterate (as opposed to less than 40 per cent of men). Similarly, while combined primary and secondary school enrolment of girls has risen to 55 per cent in South Asia, this is lower than anywhere other than sub-Saharan Africa and lags significantly behind that for boys (UN, 1995).

2

To compound their traditional sources of disempowerment, there are specific implications of globalization and economic restructuring for women. To begin with, many women cannot take advantage of new opportunities because they are not allowed to participate in the paid labour force or, when they do, they do so with relatively few skills and little experience. In particular, many women cannot take advantage of new technologies or technology-based employment because they have been denied technical training. Even when they *can* take advantage of new opportunities, women are often employed in workplaces, such as export processing zones, where they cannot bargain for fair wages or worker benefits. Further, with the privatization and deregulation that accompanies economic restructuring, women in the informal sector often face increased competition due to overcrowding (as former public sector employees enter the informal sector) and women in the modern wage sector face the risk of being forced to work at home for a piece rate (Mitter and Rowbotham, 1995; Ng and Kua, 1994).

Approaches to Women's Empowerment

Any strategy which aims to deal with the empowerment of the poor, and with women's empowerment in particular, must be based on an understanding of, and ability to overcome, the causes of the lack of power which lie behind it. While the logic behind this is clear, and the term 'empowerment' is now in widespread use in development circles, it is still a relatively recent development concept and remains relatively underdefined.

A review of the literature suggests that while there is much debate at the theoretical level as to what empowerment comprises and how it best can be achieved, there has been little primary research at the grassroots level to contribute to our understanding of what empowerment means in everyday terms. Annotations of some of the more relevant recent studies are at the back of the book, and a brief overview of major issues raised in these is given below in order to place our own research in context.

A central question that theorists interested in empowerment seek to answer is: What are the causes of the subordination or oppression of a specific powerless group (in this case, of women)? One approach to thinking about women's powerlessness focuses on patriarchy as an overarching gender (or kinship) system which determines women's roles and relationships. A second approach focuses on a single (or primary) domain of women's powerlessness, the most common being the household or the workplace, giving rise to a focus on women's reproductive or productive roles respectively. A third approach assumes that women experience subordination or powerlessness in multiple domains (either simultaneously or sequentially). As we shall see, the various approaches to women's empowerment documented in this book – although distinct in many regards –

3

all assume that women experience powerlessness in (and through the inter-action of) multiple social, political, and economic institutions (not just the household).

The central challenge that practitioners interested in empowering dis-advantaged groups seek to address is: how best to overcome or transform the causes of the subordination or oppression of a specific powerless group (in this case, of women)? Of course, the empowerment practitioner must first answer the empowerment theorist's question (either implicitly or explicitly): what are the causes of subordination or oppression to be addressed?

In her study of the empowerment of women in South Asia, Srilatha Batliwala (1994) distinguishes between three different non-governmental organization (NGO) approaches: the integrated development approach, the economic approach, and the consciousness raising cum organizing approach.[1] According to Batliwala, those who promote women's empowerment through integrated rural development programmes ascribe women's disempowerment to their lack of education, low economic status, lack of access to resources and low decision-making power; those who promote women's empowerment through economic interventions see women's disempowerment as stemming from their low economic status (and consequent dependence) and their lack of decision-making power; and those who promote women's empowerment through awareness building and organizing women see women's disempower-ment as stemming from a complex interplay of factors – historical, cultural, social, economic and political.

As the case studies documented in this book show – and as Batliwala also observes – the distinctions between these approaches can only be made con-ceptually. In practice, these distinctions often get blurred. Indeed, most de-velopment programmes – including those documented in this book – combine some mix of these approaches. Under Batliwala's typology, the experiences documented here would be classified as integrated rural development or econ-omic approaches. However, all of them build upon an initial underlying base of consciousness-raising and organizing. And all of them, either explicitly or implicitly, attribute women's disempowerment to multiple factors.

In their study on empowerment of women in rural Bangladesh, Sydney Schuler and Syed Hashemi (1993) focus on empowerment as envisioned and experienced by women members of the Bangladesh Rural Advance-ment Committee (BRAC) and Grameen Bank, both of which have been characterized as adopting individualistic economic approaches. From their discussions and interviews with women who belong to both programmes,

---

[1] Batliwala also describes a fourth approach – the training, research, and resource agency approach – adopted by some NGOs which do not directly operate at the grassroots level.

Other observers distinguish between two broad approaches: the economic (or econom-istic) approach and the socio-political approach (Omvedt, 1986). Still others distinguish between the market approach to women's micro-enterprise development and the em-powerment approach (Mayoux, 1995).

4

Schuler and Hashemi argue that there are six specific components to female empowerment in Bangladesh: sense of self and vision of a future; mobility and visibility; economic security; status and decision-making power within the household; ability to interact effectively in the public sphere; and participation in non-family groups. Among the examples of collective empowerment and action, they report cases of women's groups taking action against the husbands of group members who either beat or divorce their wives, of women's groups taking part in local judicials (*shalish*), of women's groups fielding their own candidates and voting with their own minds in local elections. Clearly, even individualistic economic approaches can have collective political effects.

In her study of the women's movement in India, Leslie Calman sees two major ideological and organizational tendencies within the movement: one, largely urban-based, which focuses on issues of rights and equality; the other, both rural and urban based, which emphasizes empowerment and liberation. According to Calman the women's rights advocates see women's concerns as issues of civil and political rights – the rights of women as equal citizens with men – and aim for equality under the law (Calman, 1992). The women's empowerment advocates, on the other hand, see women's concerns as issues of economic and social rights – the right to a livelihood and to determine one's own future – and aim at the personal and community empowerment of poor women.

As observed by Calman, those women's organizations which seek to empower women focus on the material conditions to which women are subject and make 'conscientization' central to their organizing. The first step in organizing for empowerment is to get groups of women to analyse their common problems and then collectively to seek solutions. Based on their common understanding of a given situation, the women's group then sets the agenda for action. Under Calman's classification, the Self Employed Women's Association (SEWA) is a leading example of an empowerment organization. Given their focus on the material conditions of women's lives and on organizing and conscientizing women, all of the case studies in this volume would be classified as empowerment organizations by Calman.

As noted earlier, the current research was set up in such a way as to contribute to the debate on the nature and definition of women's empowerment and the best ways to achieve this under differing circumstances. Given that many of the most successful and stable organizations in the region have, over the years, come to the conclusion that promoting women's empowerment in their economic lives is the best base for achieving overall empowerment, a major purpose of the research was to see what concrete evidence could be found to this effect. Thus, the organizations involved in the study have all focused for some time on women's economic empowerment and believe that, as a result of this, they have achieved considerable headway in promoting women's empowerment overall.

5

In addition to examining the linkages between economic and political empowerment and the most appropriate strategies for promoting women's overall empowerment, it is hoped that this book will contribute to the on-going debates on women's empowerment, both at the theoretical level – by bringing in women's voices and perspectives – and at the practical level – by documenting different approaches to women's empowerment as well as the experience of specific NGOs and women's organizations in the region.

Experiences of NGOs and POs in Working with Women

There are vast numbers of NGOs in South Asia which now have many years of experience in working with the rural and urban poor (and especially women) in an attempt to alleviate poverty. These NGOs are of varying origins, purpose, size and structure, and they adopt varying approaches to their work. It was the purpose of the current research to document a cross-section of these experiences within the context of women's organizing strategies for empowerment. These case studies form the basis of the main section of the book, but again, to give context to the research, it is useful first to indicate generally the nature of the wider population from which our cases were selected.

With respect to *origins*, many NGOs have been founded by committed middle class, educated people or professionals who want to do something about poverty alleviation. Many of the most successful of these NGOs have helped to promote people's organizations (POs) and women's organizations (WOs) at the community level which operate with varying degrees of autonomy from the parent NGO. Others are NGOs which have been founded by POs to serve their membership. Still others are outgrowths of the trade union movement and are not really NGOs at all in the normal sense of the word. The difference between NGOs and POs/WOs is important in the South Asian context, where both types of organization exist and have various relationships with each other. As the case studies show, the distinction is particularly important if we are interested in women's empowerment (rather than simply in service delivery mechanisms) since, by definition, people owning and managing their own organization are more empowered than those who are beneficiaries of someone else's organization. That is, people making decisions themselves are more empowered than those who have their decisions made by others; people's own organizations are more empowering for the people than are NGOs.

The great majority of Asian NGOs/POs/WOs state their major *purpose* as poverty alleviation. However, it is clear that what exactly is involved in this is viewed differently by different organizations. Some see poverty alleviation in terms of giving welfare assistance to women, and concentrate on women's social needs and domestic responsibilities. Others see the need as being one of women's ability to earn money, and are concerned solely

6

with income-generation or women's increased participation in the labour force. Many feel that the root of poverty is the subordination of, and discrimination against, women and see their role as one of fighting for women's equal rights or of organizing women to advocate for their own rights. Still others believe that the root cause of women's poverty is lack of power in the economic and political spheres and see their purpose as one of promoting women's overall economic and political empowerment. As we shall see, while many of the more successful and stable NGOs/POs/WOs may have started off with welfare approaches or by organizing women for income-generation or advocacy activities, they have all tended over the years to move towards a more comprehensive approach to women's empowerment which has economic empowerment as its starting point.

Perhaps the most striking thing about the South Asian NGOs/POs/WOs is the variation in their size and structure. NGOs vary from mature, well-established, well-funded and well-known organizations employing thousands of people, to small ones with only a handful of people and little means of support. POs and WOs can be small, village-level organizations, or larger district ones, or even national in scope. They may be unregistered, or have complex legal forms such as co-operatives. They can hire or involve professionals or may be completely run by the community. NGOs and POs may concentrate solely on women, or may deal with the community as a whole and have women's programmes or sections devoted to women, or specific quotas for women's involvement. As we shall see in the main section of the book, organizations which are concerned with women's empowerment have learned through experience that this can only happen if special attention is given to women's needs, at least until such time as they are more able to hold their own within their family and community structures.

Finally, as elsewhere in the world, the approaches and strategies of South Asian organizations have changed over the years as the socio-economic and political context has changed and as lessons have been learned from experience. While it is difficult to generalize, there does seem to have been a trend away from welfare approaches and those which concentrate solely on income generation or solely on organizing women for advocacy purposes towards more comprehensive development-focused approaches which aim at organizing women for overall economic and political empowerment.

There are a variety of reasons for this trend. Organizations have learned that economic change through income generation for women or women's increased participation in the labour force does not lead to economic and political empowerment. Furthermore, they have recognized the limitations of strategies that focus on organizing women for advocacy purposes without paying attention to economic empowerment (Farrington, 1993). The case studies in this book document and add to this evidence.

7

While much has been written about the experiences of NGOs in South Asia, particularly with respect to poverty alleviation and women's access to credit, training and other resources, this has been largely of a descriptive nature and has tended to put forward the voice of the people running the NGO, rather than the voice of the women who are the intended beneficiaries of their programmes. In addition, there has been concentration on the parent NGO itself, rather than on any women's organizations it has promoted, and on the linkages and changing relationships between the two. Even less is known about those people's or women's organizations which do not owe their existence to an NGO. As a consequence, our ability to learn from the considerable experiences of organizing for women's empowerment in the region has been limited.

The Purpose of the Research

In light of this, the research undertaken in the preparation of this book had three major purposes. First, it aimed to provide NGOs and WOs in the region with the opportunity to examine their experiences of organizing for women's empowerment within a common analytical framework and to help them, and the development community at large, to understand better the range of strategies adopted and which ones work best under which circumstances. Thus, the research was undertaken not by outside consultants, but by people who actually work for the organizations involved, assisted by local researchers of their own choosing. The range of organizing forms involved was made as wide as possible (including associations, cooperatives, trade unions, thrift and credit groups, producer groups, women's banks) so as to enrich learning experiences.

Second, given the increased emphasis placed by NGOs on the promotion of people's and women's organizations, the phenomenal growth and development of such organizations, and the apparent linkages between these and the ability of the parent NGO to promote women's empowerment successfully, the research concentrated on the women's groups themselves, rather than on the parent NGO, and carefully examined the nature of, and the changing relationships between, the two. People's and women's organizations which did not owe their origins to an NGO are also included in the study.

Third, the research was set up in such a way as to contribute to the current debate on the nature and definition of women's empowerment and the best ways to achieve this under differing circumstances. In particular, it set out to examine the linkages between economic and political empowerment and to determine the most appropriate or efficient entry point for organizations wanting to promote women's overall empowerment. In doing this it placed great emphasis on women's own definitions of empowerment in terms of themselves as individuals, as members of families

8

and communities, as members of their own local organizations, and within the larger economic and political sphere.

The Research Project

The research project commenced with a workshop held in Dhaka, Bangladesh in January 1995 which brought together a senior representative and a chosen local researcher from each of nine organizations in the region. The senior representative and the researcher composed the research team for each case study.

The purpose of the workshop was to share experiences in organizing for women's empowerment (using economic empowerment as an entry point); to identify key issues in need of research; and to develop and agree upon a common methodology for the research and content of case studies. The workshop was informed by materials developed by members of the project's steering committee who also acted as facilitators.

Research Questions

With respect to issues in need of research, it was agreed that the overall key research task was:

> to explore the linkages between economic and overall empowerment of women and the best strategies and organizing principles for bringing about economic empowerment of women under differing circumstances.

More specific research questions fell into four categories:

- ○ Women's disempowerment
  - What are the sources or determinants of women's disempowerment?
  - How critical is economic disempowerment to women's disempowerment overall?
  - How critical is political empowerment to women's disempowerment overall?

- ○ Organizing principles and practices
  - Is organizing women necessary to overcome women's economic constraints?
  - If so, what types of women's organizations/organizing strategies have been developed, and why?
  - What are the major constraints to organizing and to organizational growth, autonomy, and sustainability?

- ○ Strategies
  - What types of strategies other than organizing – e.g. legal interventions, policy reforms, delivery of credit, training, technology and

9

other services – are needed to address the economic constraints of women?

- What mix of interventions has been found to be needed for different economic and political circumstances?
- To what extent are women's groups/organizations which were started by an NGO becoming able to handle members' needs independently of the NGO which brought them together?

○ Economic empowerment

- What types of economic changes have been experienced by the individual women, the women's households and communities, and the women's organizations?
- Has women's bargaining power in economic relationships increased?
- Have structural changes taken place which will sustain women's ability to exert power in the economic sphere?
- What have been the linkages between economic and political empowerment of women?
- Has women's economic empowerment led to overall empowerment, and how?

Methodology
Various methods of undertaking research for the case studies were discussed at the workshop. It was decided that the following guidelines should be followed:

○ researcher to spend time at the organization's headquarters to read existing documentation on policy programme approaches and results/impact;
○ researcher/senior representative (research team) to spend time with all relevant people working for the organization to gain understanding of how decisions regarding approaches to women's economic empowerment were made over time, and why;
○ on basis of reading and discussions, research team to choose field site(s);
○ field visit(s) undertaken by research team using the following techniques:
  - group of women consulted on key issues so that their views are incorporated in the preparation of the questionnaires;
  - surveys undertaken to include interviews with individual women and other relevant people in communities, plus focal group discussions;
  - in-depth interviews of one or two women to form the basis of individual life histories;
○ draft case study written by the research team and discussed with all relevant members of the organization.

10

Informative discussions were held regarding appropriate analytical tools for measuring the following: economic impact; the extent to which economic empowerment has been achieved on a sustainable basis; and the extent to which economic empowerment has resulted in non-economic benefits.

To assist with the research, appropriate empowerment indicators were discussed and agreed upon. A working definition of 'economic empowerment' was formulated:

economic change/material gain plus increased bargaining power and/ or structural change which enables women to secure economic gains on an on-going and sustained basis.

In all of the above, researchers were asked, to the degree possible, to ensure that the views of women themselves were adequately recorded and prominently reflected in the case studies.

Selection of Organizations
Extensive thought was given to which organizations to include in the study. The selection process fell into two phases. First a list of organizations was drawn up which would enable the study to have adequate coverage in terms of:

○ countries;
○ forms of organizing for women's economic empowerment (village and community organizations; co-operatives; banks/credit; and unions);
○ type of organization in terms of women members only versus men plus women members;
○ type of NGO in terms of its relationship with POs/WOs, and vice versa.

Second, a list of criteria was developed which enabled a final selection to be made. These included:

○ at least 10 and preferably 15 years of experience in working with women living in poverty;
○ evidence of continuing success in terms of large and increasing numbers of women reached;
○ emphasis on economic empowerment as opposed to income-generating/micro-credit projects on the one hand, and political empowerment projects with absence of economic aspects on the other;
○ strong track record in terms of helping women to establish and run their own groups/organizations (in case of NGOs);
○ emphasis on strengthening and increasing independence of women's own organizations as opposed to strengthening the NGO itself and prolonging dependence (in case of NGOs).

11

Selection of Field Sites
Each organization was asked to come to the workshop with one or two examples of field sites and women's groups which they felt would best demonstrate their approach to organizing for women's economic empowerment. These were discussed by all participants and were helpful in thinking through the process of site selection and in ensuring that the most relevant projects were chosen for each NGO/PO.

Following discussions, each team formulated a workplan for their research in consultation with members of the steering committee. This was an essential step to ensure that the proposed research was realistic in terms of time, personnel and budgetary constraints.

Summary of the Case Studies

The eight case studies presented represent the different organizing techniques revealed in the research. In total, they include a vast quantity of new information and throw new light on many of the issues currently being debated by researchers, policy makers and development practitioners as to the relationship between poverty alleviation and women's empowerment, and the best strategies for bringing about the latter in differing circumstances.

Of the eight cases studies, two are from western India (Gujarat), two from southern India (Andhra Pradesh and Tamil Nadu), two from Bangladesh, one from northern Pakistan and one from south-eastern Sri Lanka. These give a wide range of socio-cultural, economic and political contexts for the projects, as well as giving coverage in terms of climate, environment, resource base, population density, agricultural zones and infrastructure.

Three of the case studies feature NGOs which have set up POs/WOs (BRAC, Proshika, Aga Khan Rural Support Programme (AKRSP)); four feature WOs established without a parent NGO (Women's Development Federation (WDF), Informal Sector Unions in Tamil Nadu, SEWA/Kheda, SEWA/Banaskantha), and one features an NGO set up by a network of farmers' co-operatives (Co-operative Development Foundation (CDF)) which now supports WOs.

In terms of organizing principles they cover: Village and Community Organizations (AKRSP, BRAC, Proshika); Co-operatives (CDF, SEWA/ Banaskantha); Women's Banks (WDF); and Unionization (SEWA/Kheda, Informal Sector/Tamil Nadu). While we have grouped the case studies according to the organizing principle which figures most predominantly in the organization's work, it is important to note that most of them adopt multiple approaches that draw from more than one category. For example, Proshika, while predominantly a village or community organization often uses unionization principles to help its members to protect their rights to livelihoods.

12

Some of the main characteristics of each case study are presented in the brief summaries below as a guide to the main section of the book.

Aga Khan Rural Support Programme in Pakistan
The Northern Areas of Pakistan contain some of the highest mountains in the world yet is home to close to one million people, largely subsistence farmers, who have worked to secure a living in what has been termed a 'vertical mountain desert'. The per capita income of the region is estimated at only 60 per cent of the national average. Until 1977, when the Kara-korum Highway (running from Islamabad, Pakistan to Kashi, China) was opened, the region was isolated from the rest of Pakistan.

In this rugged and arid environment, the Aga Khan Rural Support Programme has facilitated the formation of hundreds of women's organizations. The case study focuses on the experiences of women within four of these: WO Khyber; WO Hussaini; WO Aliabad-Shapissan; and WO Minapin. Through these organizations, women have gained access to production packages which provide them with the initial inputs for a productive activity, such as vegetable gardening. Some of the production packages are designed to take an activity to the commercial level. Women also take advantage of training and credit services which allow them to make effective use of the production packages.

Participation in the WOs has changed women's lives economically and socially. In a socio-cultural environment in which women were generally prohibited from participating in activities outside of the home and earned little income, they are now contributing to household income, investing money in productive activities, and saving for future expenses, including their daughters' education. These economic successes, in turn, have resulted in women's increased capacity to negotiate changes at the household level and a heightened role in village-level decision-making.

Bangladesh Rural Advancement Committee
The Bangladesh Rural Advancement Committee (BRAC), one of the world's largest NGOs, has organized over one million women into over 30 000 village-level organizations. The case study looks at two village organizations and shows how, through these, landless poor village women have received, and also helped to design and deliver, credit, enterprise, health, education, legal literacy and other services. One of the key and distinctive components of BRAC's integrated rural development programme is its subsector approach to promoting economic opportunities for women, whereby BRAC collaborates with both village women and the Government of Bangladesh to build the necessary infrastructure and provide the necessary services to promote large-scale employment opportunities in key sub-sectors of the economy. Two of these large sub-sector programmes (poultry and textiles) are featured in this case study. In the

case of poultry, village women are involved as the providers of the key services and as producers, while the Government of Bangladesh supplies necessary inputs and infrastructure. In the case of textiles, BRAC directly creates jobs for rural women in garment and embroidery production centres and sub-centres and establishes necessary backward and forward linkages to raw material sources and markets.

The two village organizations (one old, one new) featured in this case study are in Panchbarul and Shurundi villages in Manikganj, a peri-urban district of Bangladesh where BRAC, since the mid-1970s, has developed and tested most of its programmes. The case study describes, often in the women's own words, how the general members in these two village organizations (VOs) have become involved with (and benefited from) the various opportunities and services offered by BRAC, many of which are provided by specially trained fellow members. It also documents how women choose between different economic opportunities, gain awareness and confidence through social awareness and legal literacy courses, take collective actions, and begin to participate more fully in community life.

Proshika in Bangladesh
This case study looks at the work of Proshika, another integrated rural development NGO operating in Bangladesh since the 1970s. It describes the experience of the two women's groups organized by Proshika: one in a remote rural area suffering from deforestation; and the other in the overcrowded slums of Dhaka city.

In the case of Jamuna Mohila Samiti (rural), Proshika has helped members to save and benefit from loans for household and community activities. More importantly, it has enabled them to lead the fight to save their forests from local élites and to bargain for a share in the profits from forest maintenance. To undertake their forest activities the women had to overcome several social constraints, such as breaking out of *purdah* to undertake their forest activities.

The story of Lucky Mohila Samiti in Dhaka is also one of women's fight to protect their livelihoods in the face of the constant threat of eviction by government and exploitation by slumlords. Here, women have been organized to fight these threats and also to use Proshika's assistance to invest in tailoring, embroidery and other small businesses.

Thrift and Credit Groups in Andhra Pradesh/Co-operative Development Foundation
The Karimnagar and Warangal Districts of the Telengana Region of Andhra Pradesh are the setting for this case study. The area is largely agricultural with a large proportion of the population existing as small or marginal farmers or as landless agricultural workers. Other sources of livelihoods and employment are limited.

14

The Co-operative Development Foundation (CDF) is an NGO established in 1982 by the paddy farmers' co-operatives to provide services to, and undertake advocacy activities on behalf of, its members. The CDF helped local women (who were excluded from the co-operatives because they did not have title to land) to establish their own thrift and credit groups. In addition to its continued work with the farmers' co-operatives, CDF also gives assistance to the women's groups through training in co-operative principles and building up women's management and accounting skills.

The case study looks at the spectacular growth in membership of the women's groups and their federation into a women's regional association of thrift co-operatives. It also shows how women have benefited economically through access to loans to set up small enterprises, and how this economic independence combined with the self-confidence they have gained through running their own organization, has resulted in an increase in well-being for the women themselves and for their communities in general. The relationship between CDF and the groups is particularly interesting, in that CDF is increasingly able to withdraw its direct support to the groups and the regional association as they become more independent, both managerially and financially.

SEWA/Banaskantha Women's Association

The women of this desert area in northern Gujarat State are affected by persistent poverty, natural calamities, low literacy rates, high mortality and constant need for migration. The Self Employed Women's Association (SEWA) tried organizing the women here using unionization principles, but it quickly found that in an area where there are no employment opportunities, or prospects for self-employment, there is little chance of bargaining and no scope for struggle. Thus, SEWA adopted the alternative strategy of forming women's own organizations as producer groups which could eventually be formalized as producer co-operatives.

The Banaskantha Women's Association (BWA) is a federation of women's village-level producer groups which was formed with SEWA's assistance. The BWA helps its member groups to secure the means of sustainable livelihoods by building a sustained skill and asset base through linkages with the market place, with government programmes and with sources of capital, and through advocacy activities. The subsectors in which the producer groups have become involved are embroidery, leather work, garment making, salt production, plant nurseries, vegetable growing, forest produce collection and dairying.

The BWA also builds support structures through food security measures, savings and credit schemes and provision of health care. These programmes have had a dramatic impact in terms of a reduction in migration, an increase in the income and assets of women, and a change in their social status at home and in the community.

15

Thousands of poor rural women in the remote Hambantota District of Sri Lanka have turned their local societies, initially formed to deal with health and nutrition problems, into a network of rural women's development societies and rural banks which can assist them to overcome economic hardships. This network, which consists of 466 societies, 67 banks and the Federation, is run entirely by the women themselves, and now has over 25 000 members. The women working in the banks and the Federation are drawn from the membership of the societies.

The individual banks, which model their lending system on that of the Grameen Bank in Bangladesh, are giving women access to credit for the first time in their lives in an area in which few banking facilities existed, especially for women. The banks operate independently of WDF as far as approving loans is concerned, but the Federation is very much involved in giving technical support through arranging business and technical training for borrowers and through helping with access to information and markets. As the women working in WDF are all drawn from women's societies themselves, they have a good understanding of members' needs. Many of the banks are well on their way to being self-financing in terms of paying salaries, rent and other operating costs.

Hambantota is a remote district with 90 per cent of the population dependent on agriculture. Before the women started this initiative, the majority of women and men were dependent on agriculture to secure a living. Since the opening of the banks, women have been able to secure loans to lease land that is cultivated by themselves and their families (60 per cent of loans are for this purpose) and to establish small enterprises. This increased ability to contribute to family income, along with the high visibility of the institution they have created and run, has raised their esteem within family and community and led to an increase in women's self-confidence.

SEWA/Kheda
Kheda, located in western Gujarat, is one of the richest agricultural districts in India and produces 80 per cent of the country's coarse (*bidi*) tobacco. However, the wealth of the rich farmers is in striking contrast to the impoverishment of the agricultural workers and tobacco processors (of whom 60 per cent are women) who are engaged in the lowest paid, most physically exhausting work. This case study describes how SEWA, established in 1972 as a trade union of women in the unorganized sector, helped women to overcome their fear of the factory and the land owners who were exploiting their labour, and brought them together to fight for their employment rights.

While the main focus is on the unionization process, and in particular on bargaining for higher wages, the case study also shows how SEWA has

16

been able to use other organizing principles to help women to meet their needs for social security, child care, health care and insurance. It also details how SEWA has assisted women to develop alternative avenues for employment through savings and producer groups in order to help reduce the feudal nature of the relationship between the rich and the poor.

This joint strategy of struggle on the one hand, and development on the other, has resulted in a considerable increase in bargaining power, and sustained economic gains and social status for women through a strong grassroots women's organization/union.

Unions for Informal Sector Women in Tamil Nadu

There are approximately 7.8 million women labourers in the unorganized sector in Tamil Nadu, India, and the construction industry is the largest employer of unorganized labourers in the state. Employers perceive women labourers as 'unskilled', and women are invariably paid at a low level relative to their male colleagues. Most unions have failed to recognize and promote women's particular concerns as labourers.

This case study focuses on unionization in the construction and *bidi* (hand-rolled cigarette) industries. It follows the history of unionization in the construction industry from the late 1970s to the present, highlighting the struggles of women construction workers within this movement. While their struggles continue, women have achieved an increase in pay, accident compensation, and the enactment of the Tamil Nadu Workers Act which extends gains made by the construction workers to other occupational groups in the unorganized sector.

The concern of construction workers and union officials to involve other groups of unorganized labourers in their struggle for rights contributed to the formation of the Tamil Nadu Bidi Workers' Union. The case study examines the efforts of this union to secure fair wages and welfare cards for women *bidi* workers and educational stipends for their children.

CASE STUDIES

Gathering the Second Harvest: Aga Khan Rural Support Programme in Northern Pakistan

ABINTA MALIK and SANDRA KALLEDER

Before we organized ourselves in a women's organization, we used to believe everything and agreed with everything our men told us. Now we have learned to state our opinions and views – and now our men even ask us about what we think.

THE NORTHERN AREAS of Pakistan is the site of an innovative approach to rural development which has empowered women in communities where they previously had low social and economic status. The Northern Areas lies in the heart of Karakorum, Himalaya, and Hindukush mountain ranges and includes five districts: Diamer, Gilgit, Ghizer, Skardu, and Ganche. This mountainous region supports close to one million people and is characterized by a delicate balance between human and natural environments. It is in this rugged environment that the Aga Khan Rural Support Programme (AKRSP) began its work in December 1982. Since that time AKRSP has been instrumental in forming village and women's organizations, the 'engines' of rural development, throughout the Northern Areas. Four women's organizations (WOs) are the focus of this study, WO Khyber, WO Hussaini, WO Aliabad-Shapissan and WO Minapin. These organizations are located in a major geographical valley in Gilgit District which contains three distinct cultural valleys: Gojal (WOs Khyber and Hussaini), Hunza (WO Aliabad-Shapissan), and Nagar (WO Minapin). The differing cultural contexts, ages and histories of these four WOs give insight into struggles, successes and prospects of women's organizing in northern Pakistan.

Aga Khan Rural Support Programme's Approach

The Aga Khan Rural Support Programme (AKRSP) is a private, non-profit organization established by the Aga Khan Foundation to help improve the quality of life of the villagers in northern Pakistan. It based its approach on the twin objectives of improving the quality of life of the region's small farmers and developing a replicable model of participatory rural development. In working to achieve these objectives, AKRSP has

21

developed an integrated strategy of human resource development, collective capital formation through regular savings, and practical techno-economic interventions to raise local farm productivity.

These joint strategies are built upon a base of institutional development with investment in social organization as the underlying principle. The institutional model is grounded in the premiss that slow economic development has been caused primarily by the absence of effective organizations at the community level, with communities remaining structurally isolated from sources of support. Consequently, an institutional structure at the community level is a prerequisite to improve the effectiveness and efficiency of service delivery. Creating grassroots organizations is an attempt to foster such an institutional framework. Through a process of grafting modern organizational principles (for example, formalized methods of democratic decision-making and bookkeeping) on to traditional systems of social organization, village organizations (VOs) and women's organizations (WOs) have emerged as important institutions at the village level.

AKRSP's initial focus was on the Gilgit Region, and in the mid-1980s full-fledged operations were started in Chitral and Baltistan Regions. In 1993 AKRSP moved into Astore Valley in Diamer District. The programme area now comprises six districts of northern Pakistan (including Chitral District of the North West Frontier Province), with a population of more than one million living in over 1000 villages scattered across an area of nearly 75 000 square kilometers of the world's most rugged terrain.

In commencing its work, AKRSP enters into a series of dialogues with the village communities. The first part of the process is to ask small farmers to form broad-based participatory VOs, with a minimum participation of 75 per cent of the village households. The members then select their own president and manager. The VO is required to meet as a general body, at regular intervals to be agreed upon by its members. At VO meetings members contribute to the collective savings which are banked under the VO account at a scheduled bank. This equity is the anchor to which an entire savings-loan system is tied. There are no obligations for minimum savings, and each member contributes according to ability.

The VO identifies a project, termed a productive physical infrastructure project, which will benefit all village households and their members. Such projects have taken the form of irrigation channels, link roads, and microhydro installations. The VO pledges to harness village labour for the completion of the scheme, and maintain the scheme once completed. AKRSP supports the VOs by identifying and implementing profitable projects. Every stage of the planning process – identification, preparation, and appraisal – is completed in collaboration with the villagers.

AKRSP's Approach to Economic Empowerment

Organizing Women for Economic Empowerment

AKRSP recognizes that rural women are integral to any development process. Originally, AKRSP expected that women's needs could be voiced and addressed through the VO forum, particularly through the women's sections of the VOs. However, in many cases women felt that the VOs and AKRSP were not giving enough attention to women's specific needs. In late 1984 women members of a VO in Gilgit District broke off from the VO and formed their own organization. They asked AKRSP to assist them. AKRSP responded to the needs of these and other women by fostering the development of women's organizations (WOs) which are separate from, yet analogous to, the VOs. It established a Women in Development Section to support programming for women and the formation of WOs. Over time, many other women's sections have broken off from the VOs and have become WOs in their own right. Women established both WO Khyber and WO Hussaini following a growing awareness of their disadvantaged position within the VO. In other areas, such as in the cases of WO Minapin and WO Aliabad-Shapissan, women's participation in AKRSP's programmes began with their membership in the WO.

Typically, WOs are formed when a group of women approach AKRSP with the desire to organize, although in locales where religious and cultural norms constrain organization, AKRSP social organizers may approach the VO or village elders to discuss the idea of establishing a WO in the village. WOs join together individuals in a geographical location. In some cases, such as in Khyber and Hussaini, the WO unites all interested women within the village. Where the village is large and distances between neighbourhoods are long, WOs are composed of women who live in close proximity to one another, and there may be more than one WO per village. In Aliabad village, Aliabad-Shapissan is one of eight WOs functioning at a neighbourhood level. Normally, AKRSP requires that over 75 per cent of the women in an area (village or neighbourhood) be willing to form a WO. However, it has remained flexible on this point since in some communities organizing women is not culturally or religiously acceptable, and only a small number of women may be able to join the WO initially. In such areas the success of a small WO demonstrates the benefits of organizing and counters criticism at the community level, creating an environment for the growth of WOs.

As with the VOs, AKRSP enters into a contract with WOs to provide technical assistance and training for specific productive packages and training in organization and management. For their part, members agree to meet and save regularly. The WOs elect a president and a manager, each responsible for a set of tasks. The president regulates the decision-making processes and provides a guiding role to the members, keeping in mind the overall objective of the WO. The president's duties also entail checking the WO's

23

registers, supervising membership savings, as well as serving as a main contact with AKRSP field staff and other organizations. While the WO president is selected mostly on the grounds of her respected position in the village, selection criteria regarding the WO's management position centres around professionalism and capacity. This is because the WO manager is responsible for account-keeping in the WO, including depositing the savings in the bank. WO representation thus usually stretches across different generations, building on the experience of a (usually) older and respected WO president, who is representing the village elders, and the expertise of a (usually) young educated WO manager. The lack of educated female leaders who can run and manage their own organizations has constrained the growth of individual WOs. Some WOs, particularly in the earlier years of WO formation, have been under the direct influence of male managers and activists. WO Khyber is an example of a WO which does not have literate office-bearers and relies on men to handle its financial affairs.

AKRSP does not directly interfere in the evolution of sub-group structures within WOs. The roles and functions of the WO have evolved over the past decade, resulting in the evolution of a complex organizational system. In a large number of cases WOs have taken up local governance functions of legislation (setting rules and procedures), executive functions (managing activities), and judicial functions (conflict resolution). WO Hussaini, for example, has established committees on loan distribution, environmental protection, conflict-resolution and fine-collection, in addition to setting organizational regulations. WO Aliabad-Shapissan also has established committees on loan distribution and attendance.

All WOs are characterized by discussion-oriented, democratic mechanisms of membership debate. Specific regulations ensure the equal and fair distribution of rights and duties among all WO members. The WO's system of management follows a procedure of discussion, vote, and resolution. Decisions are therefore not made on a top-down basis, or rather as a woman in Minapin puts it: 'We are all equal here.' Members are not only invited, but in fact expected, to raise their voices in WO discussions. To remain silent is perceived as neglecting or not fulfilling each member's responsibilities. Topics for debate within the WO range from issues directly related to the WO's productive packages, such as input supply and marketing, to matters of general concern to the village women. The education of their children or recent issues centering around environmental protection in the villages also form a large part of discussions.

Most WO members are age 35 and above. Older women are in a senior position in the family and are able to draw on the assistance of more junior women with household tasks, thus affording themselves time to engage in WO activities. In addition, WO membership used to be a privilege reserved for the most senior women in the household. However, membership patterns reveal an increasing trend of younger women joining the WO. WOs

24

wish to reduce their dependence on male support in WO management, opening up more room for younger women to join the WO. Particularly with respect to the future role of WOs, young women – with their generally higher educational status – play a vital role in taking over responsible roles in their organizations.

Age is not the only factor which influences women's participation in the WOs. Patriarchal norms dictate that women ask their husband's permission before joining a WO. In some cases, such as with WO Minapin, religious or community leaders try to discredit the WO, leading villagers to be suspicious of its activities and thus limiting its membership. The savings requirements of the WOs can be a deterring factor for the poorest women in the village who may not feel that they can meet this requirement. In some of the older WOs, there is a 'closed shop attitude' which restricts membership to those who have been members of the WO since its inception. Furthermore, if the WO meeting place is distant from a woman's residence, she may not be able to take the time to travel to the weekly meetings.

Cultural and religious differences have inhibited the spread of WOs in the programme area equal to that of VOs. However, WO formation has shown an impressive record over time: starting with 40 WOs in 1985, there are currently 834 WOs in all six districts of the programme area, comprising over 28 200 members with collective savings of over Rs44.49 million.[1] Not only have the numbers of WOs grown, but membership within individual WOs has grown as well. In each of the four WOs under study, membership has steadily increased by an average of five women per year.

AKRSP's organization and management to support WOs has evolved over time. Beginning in 1985 with a handful of local female staff responsible for forming WOs, the WID section of AKRSP by 1990 was a full-fledged section with technical expertise to undertake separate development activities for women. By 1991, AKRSP recognized that although cultural and social practices had determined the need for autonomous WOs, the reflection of that segregation in AKRSP's organizational structure (i.e. a separate WID section) was restricting the potential expansion of the women's programme. To rectify this constraint, technical female staff were integrated into the mainstream sections in 1991, and in 1994 the remaining wing of WID, the female social organizers or extension workers, were integrated into the newly-created social organization section.

Programming for Economic Empowerment
In trying to identify an entry point for organizing rural women, AKRSP came up against the stereotype of the women's programme. In village after village, both men and women asked for handicraft centres and sewing machines. AKRSP believed that the 'sewing machine approach' to

---

[1] Rs100 = US$3.30 as at July 1995.

25

women's development lends legitimacy to the notion that women's activities in agriculture are unproductive and that agricultural activities routinely performed by women have no room for productive investment. In response, AKRSP set about identifying, through an interactive process with the WOs, a priority list of women's constraints from which emerged potential areas for productive investment.

In the initial phase of the WID programme, women's work burden was identified as a prime constraint. In response, AKRSP developed and distributed a wide range of appropriate technologies to WOs, such as butter churners, nutcrackers and fruit dehydration chambers. However, feedback from women indicated that there were several problems with these new technologies. The technologies were difficult to repair, operate and manage on a collective basis. Most importantly, AKRSP learned that women are more concerned with increased productivity and income than work-load reduction and are even prepared to increase their work-load if the monetary benefits are substantial. This recognition resulted in a policy shift leading to intensive efforts on developing productive, economic schemes rather than work-load-reducing devices.

In the Northern Areas women's only income-generating asset is their labour; they do not own land or other physical capital. Working with the WOs, AKRSP identified vegetable production, poultry production, and forest and fruit nurseries as major areas where women's productive capacity could be enhanced, and began developing a set of production packages in these areas. Training and credit services also evolved to complement the production packages.

AKRSP developed two major types of production packages, subsistence and graduated packages. The subsistence package is universal and widespread in nature, focusing on the basic, practical needs of women, such as nutritional improvements at the household level, and addressing the constraints that women face in meeting these needs. For example, subsistence vegetable packages supply women with seeds and fertilizer for home vegetable production. As social and religious norms prohibit women from travelling to the market to purchase inputs, AKRSP initially functioned as a service delivery unit with the WO operating as the disbursement mechanism. Later, AKRSP's role changed from direct supplier to that of linking WOs with local suppliers. Graduated packages take an activity to the commercial level. Women's mobility constraint combined with the isolation of the region from major commercial and trading centres of the country has remained an obstacle in the spread of marketing options for women. Recognizing this constraint, AKRSP has worked with the WOs to access markets both by developing packages which cater to village and local markets and by introducing merchants to the WOs. Gradually the WOs themselves have taken on the function of bargaining with merchants and marketing co-operatives and contracting truck drivers to haul their produce to markets.

Production packages were originally introduced as collective ventures. Collective packages, such as a WO's collective orchard (WO Khyber) or vegetable introduction package (WO Minapin), are usually applied on communal land, demanding equal participation of members and fair distribution of profit. Problems have often arisen with these collective ventures: some women have contributed more work than others, leading to difficulties in dividing profits and maintaining the plots, and in cases where land is rented some landowners have claimed their land back after the trees had matured. Due to these problems, most packages introduced to WOs are now on an individual basis, though comparative advantages in marketing still result in collective action. An individual package is introduced through the WO forum but targeted at individual members. For example, individuals adopting the vegetable introduction package use individual plots of land, or land close to the house, rather than communal land.

Training is an integral part of any production package. As women's movements are restricted, information and expertise has to be available to them in the village. AKRSP has trained village specialists to assist women with their adoption of the production packages. AKRSP has guidelines for the selection of specialists, although the WO makes the final decision. Older women tend to be preferred as they have fewer household responsibilities and are less restricted in their mobility. Also, older women are permanent residents of the village, unlike younger women who may marry into another village.

Initially training sessions for the village specialists were held by male staff at the training centre in the regional headquarters. This posed severe problems as it was not possible for women from more conservative valleys to participate. This was compounded by the difficult geography of the programme area, the fact that at least five local languages are spoken and that the vast majority of women are illiterate. These factors necessitated the development of a special training programme for women. As a result, by 1990 trainings were being held at the valley or village level to enable as many women as possible to participate. Currently there are over 4000 specialists in the programme area.

When a cadre of female village specialists began to develop, a new level of expertise also began to evolve: the master trainers. Selected vegetable and poultry specialists were given intensive training in their field of expertise. The master trainer, responsible for serving a cluster of villages (15 on average), takes on some of the functions that were previously performed by AKRSP staff, such as supply of inputs and advice on technical details. Village accountants (women trained in credit, appraisal, and accountancy) also function across a cluster of villages, providing accounting support.

For a small remuneration, specialists (and master trainers) function as 'service-contractors' to the entire village. Besides providing the WO members with crucial inputs such as drugs, medicines or agricultural seeds and

27

fertilizer, specialists assist and train members in utilizing these physical inputs. Particularly the WO's master trainers thereby function as vital multiplicators of expertise and vocational skills for a cluster of WOs (10–15). Consequently, specialists and master trainers play a role in the programme's training component, aiming at enhancing the productive skills of all WO members. The enthusiastic performance of specialists is also vital for the success of collective ventures undertaken by WOs.

Rural women also face a constraint in access to credit for the purchase of inputs and other means of increasing their productive capacity. Four credit windows are available for use: short-term loans, medium-term loans, WO Credit Programme (WOCP) and micro-enterprise credit programme (MECP). Short-term loans require no collateral and are primarily used for fertilizer and seed purchase while medium-term loans require 30 per cent collateral and are linked to poultry production. The WOCP is a one-year loan requiring 100 per cent collateral of the entire WOs' savings. The WOCP is a village banking system that is managed entirely by the WO and has had the greatest impact of all of the credit programmes in increasing female access to and uptake of credit. WOCP loans are used for a variety of purposes from consumption needs to purchasing livestock. The MECP is an individual loan aimed at providing working capital for small enterprises. It is available without collateral and is repayable from six months to one year after loan disbursement. Women have used this loan to finance shops and other village-level enterprises.

Although AKRSP has developed a range of production packages, it does not dictate which package(s) a WO should adopt. Instead, after a WO is formed, a social organizer attends a WO meeting to find out what packages WO members are interested in. Then, the social organizer brings an AKRSP technical expert to the WO to explain what is entailed in adopting a particular package. A demonstration and/or training in the use of the package follows, and the WO nominates a village specialist (who will undergo further training) for the package. For example, in the case of women who adopt the poultry-rearing package, these women take part in a training course at which some initial materials, such as feeders or drinkers, are distributed. It then is up to the individual women to set up an area to raise the chickens. A social organizer or master trainer will make the rounds to women adopting the package to determine how many chicks they need. After the chicks are distributed, the women rely on the village specialist and master trainer for any assistance with rearing the chicks. AKRSP social organizers will check on the WO members' progress with the package and provide any additional training to the village specialists and master trainers, but it is essentially up to the WO to assure the sustainability of the package.

AKRSP has also had to consider new demands made by WOs. With the development of the WO into a multi-purpose, micro-level development body, members have started articulating needs in a range of activities. The programme realized that for the sustainability of WOs it must facilitate institutional linkages between WOs and other service providers operating in the regional economy. In this regard, AKRSP has solicited support from other agencies, including the state, to access the village institutional framework. Currently, services which fall beyond the direct mandate of AKRSP, such as family planning, health, drinking water supply, and education are being channeled through the WO forum.

WO Hussaini: Creating a Village-Level Savings and Lending Institution

WO Hussaini has an interesting history in struggling to define its autonomy in the village and to emerge as a development institution for the village. The split of the women's section from the village's VO occurred as a response to the basic mismanagement and inactivity of the VO. The VO office bearers had lost the confidence of its general body, and most male members had stopped viewing the VO as a relevant village forum. For the women of Hussaini, the concept of a village-level development forum had not lost its importance, but the weakness of the VO was hampering their interests in organizing positive change for the village. The women decided to form and manage their own organization.

The split of the women from the VO was significant because, for the first time, women were going to manage their own affairs. In particular, the accounts of the organization, which until the formation of the new WO had been maintained by a VO member, were to be controlled by the women. Recognizing that the strength of development lay in access to capital, the WO manager, Bibi Safida, obtained training in accounts and bookeeping. After Safida had realized that the WO's accounts were not kept correctly, she initiated an investigation soon after becoming office bearer. 'I announced each member's savings and profit distribution, so old members questioned the quality of the previous manager, and he blamed me,' she explained. By taking advantage of her education as well as her participation in an accounts course, she successfully countered his accusation of personal enrichment. Bibi Safida also called in an AKRSP field accountant for monitoring the inquiry process.

The investigation and accusations further strengthened the WO's resolve to push for greater autonomy within the village. Hussaini village is largely dependent on potato marketing for subsistence. In this respect, the seasonal dependence leads to acute shortages of cash in the off-season. Access to credit is thus a major resource for the village households. Once the savings volume of the WO reached Rs50 000, the WO manager applied for the WO Credit Programme (WOCP).

The management structure of the WOCP loan process differs in a number of ways from that of other loan schemes. The WO is left responsible for

29

much more of the decision-making and loan procedure than with other AKRSP credit windows. Although AKRSP performs some monitoring and accounting functions, the WO itself decides who will take loans, the loan size and the loan term as well as service charges and repayment schedule. The WO is responsible for ensuring that individual loans are repaid and decides any penalty system that might be imposed on non-repayers. A 'guarantee system' demands that each member who wants to take a loan larger than her individual savings must find other members who are prepared to sign their savings over as security for the loan. In practice, however, the guarantor system is not considered binding; instead, as all large loans are discussed by the entire WO body, such loans are given 'on trust', and social pressure by all the members on the defaulter is the actual means by which loan repayment is enforced.

At first, the use of the WOCP was in traditional productive areas, such as poultry. However, the WO manager realized the profitability of the credit window if users were charged interest at the market rate. The WO decided to take maximum advantage of the WOCP by opening up the loan facility to non-WO members, in particular men. While everybody in the village may apply for a loan in order to finance private or collective ventures, the final decision-making power on granting a loan remains with the WO's general body. In this way, the WO has emerged as the local bank for the village. During this process, the WO has initiated new dialogues between men and women at the village level and has proven that the WO is a viable and dynamic force in the community. Consequently, WO members are able to influence the flow of financial resources at the village level directly. In doing so, women hold an effective instrument to influence the future development of their village and to monitor its equitable and sustainable growth.

WO Khyber: Entering the Potato Market

The introduction of WOs has also enabled women for the first time to play an active role in the market. Women's presence in the market alters market structures in the Northern Areas with respect to both demand and supply mechanisms on a local and regional level. As the case of Khyber illustrates, women prove able to enter into the market also at a national level.

With support from the Food and Agricultural Organization (FAO) of the United Nations, Dutch potato seeds were introduced to Khyber. The residents of Khyber began to intensify their traditional cultivation of potatoes as early as 1980. After their organization in a WO, women continued the financially lucrative venture and adopted potato farming on a collective and individual basis. In doing so, women are supported by the village's men, who share the work-load according to a traditional division of labour. While men prepare and water the land, women are in charge of laying fertilizer, sowing, weeding and gathering the harvest.

Potato farming results in considerable financial benefits to the WO members in Khyber, with the quality of the potato seed meeting national standards. Women are now in a position to stock potato seeds and purchase wheat for storage on an individual level (which is particularly important for the cold and long winter months in the valley). WO members sell their high yield not only to local markets but also, through Punjabi traders, to Jaffer Brothers, a national trading company. Rather than the small farmer going to the market, the market comes to Khyber in the form of Punjabi buyers. At the village level, potatoes are graded and packed in front of the traders and then loaded on to the lorries after payment is made. Potatoes from Khyber have gained a high reputation, opening up vast markets with prospects of continued expansion.

Meanwhile, the Gilgit Agricultural Marketing Association (GAMA), a small farmer co-operative supported by AKRSP, has also approached the WO. GAMA, in its function of enabling small farmers in the programme area to enter national markets, is offering the collective marketing of produce at favourable prices. Particularly for women, GAMA, with its inherent benefit of 'bringing the markets to the people', fosters women's participation in the regional and national market. The price of potato seed is also gradually rising; currently the wholesale purchasing rate is Rs3/kg, but the women in Khyber believe this is only the beginning. 'They come to us, so we tell them what we will sell at. If they don't accept, there are many more buyers', says a WO member.

Economic Impact

Impact on Women's Income
Through adoption of income-generating schemes, women are for the first time able to contribute to their household's overall income, and thus play an increasingly important role in the household subsistence economy. Women's ability to raise an income and improve the overall standard of living of their family (including better nutrition, clothing, health and education) is to them the most important benefit of participating in a WO. Women's participation in productive activities also has an impact on the future performance and range of activities undertaken by individual members of a WO.

Prior to their involvement in income-earning activities, women's input into the household economy was restricted to subsistence-level activities over the course of their involvement, women have become entrepreneurs, penetrating village as well as regional markets, while also entering off-farm services (for example, accountancy). This level of advancement seemed illusionary only 15 years ago.

Although women's actual share of the income generated varies considerably from WO to WO, as much as among the members of each individual

WO, financial benefits to a majority of women have exceeded their initial expectations. Women's contributions to the family's income has been accepted and appreciated by their husbands. 'My husband is very happy that I am a member of the WO. He says that if I wasn't in the WO we would probably be very poor today', says Bibi Zainaba Khatun, a poultry and vegetable specialist from Minapin. Following her involvement in vegetable cultivation and poultry farming, as well as her participation in two of the WO's collective packages (vegetable cultivation and apricot drying), Bibi Zainaba has raised an income of Rs19 000 in only three years. This enables her not only to hold a more respected position in the household but also increases her self-esteem in an area where debt is looked down upon: 'First we used to be in debt to the shopkeepers in the village. Now we use our own money and deposit our own savings.'

Savings are another indication of the impact of WO activities on women's income. Generally, women's savings in the case study area amount to an average of Rs3150 per member in one year, or Rs60 savings per WO member in a week. Although the cumulative savings of one member do not appear large, for women whose household never saved even one rupee, it is a huge accomplishment.

Access to credit has enabled women to enhance their income-earning opportunities. A loan from her WO in order to establish a poultry hatchery marked the entry point for Bibi Rahnuma to raise an annual income of Rs31 063. Taking advantage of her expertise as a poultry specialist and master trainer in Aliabad-Shapissan, Bibi Rahnuma was able to earn a net profit of Rs21 275 in her first year of operation. To her the chicks are like little children requiring constant care and attention. After having vacated two living rooms, followed by a series of alterations and extensions to her house at a total cost of Rs9000, the hatchery now functions as the household's main source of income. Despite certain fluctuations in annual income over the past three years, due to temporary shortages in input-supply (particularly during the winter months), Bibi Rahnuma can no longer imagine a life without her 500 'children'.

Women feel that the financial benefits of their active involvement in the WO clearly outweighs possible drawbacks such as an increase in work-load or time constraints. For Bibi Farzana from Khyber, for example, involvement in the WO resulted in an increase in her workload yet allows her to enhance her family's standard of living and, most importantly, to secure the education of her three daughters. 'Before I worked hard, but never made any money. Now I work harder, but I am able to earn an income and save regularly for my children's future. And I no longer work alone. Working together in the WO has made work more valuable for all of us.' Another WO member looks to future increases in income: 'Our WO is still very small. As it becomes bigger, our work will increase and so will our income.'

Control and Use of Extra Income Earned

Despite their vital role in the household and farm economy, women have been marginalized in the decision-making process at the household level. While women are consulted on issues relevant to the entire family, the male head of household has the final decision-making power on domestic issues. Women are only considered 'free' to decide on minor issues, such as food purchases. Control over income at the household level is furthermore determined by family ranking and seniority, limiting the influence of younger family members (particularly of daughters-in-law).

Although this situation still holds true, women are beginning to play a larger role in determining household expenditures as a result of their contributions to household income. Bibi Zainaba, WO Minapin's vegetable and poultry specialist explains: 'I am now earning money, that is why my point of view carries more weight.' A WO member from Khyber echoes her comments: 'Before we grew vegetables to eat. Now we grow potato seed and sell it every year to the Punjabi buyers. It is our work that brings income to our household so we decide how it is spent.' However, in most cases, rather than aiming for full control over their own as well as the household's overall income, women perceive themselves as 'financial control-mechanisms', who could, but choose not to, strive for a powerful position in financial matters at the household level. Bibi Lal Bano, WO manager and village accountant in Aliabad-Shapissan explains: 'Well, I could control the income myself, but instead I keep about Rs1500 with me, and give the rest to my mother-in-law, who then hands the income over to her husband'. In cases where the male head of household is absent (due to death or migration), the female head of household, often in consultation with the eldest son, holds a high degree of financial decision-making capacity, particularly if she is contributing highly to household income.

While the actual use of income earned varies according to the individual context, there is a clear trend of where women's priorities lie. First, women's income is used to meet the household's basic consumption needs. Women are traditionally in charge of deciding the family's day-to-day purchases of necessary household items. It remains the duty of the men within the household to purchase goods in the market, and thus literally to handle the family's income. Women, however, play an important role in taking decisions on what to buy. Money is usually kept in a common box monitored by the wife or the most senior female family member. For example, after the death of her husband, Bibi Hudjad Bacht became her family's 'cashier', enabling her to decide on how to spend the family's overall income. In her case, the respect her family grants her as WO president and her substantial contribution to the family's income make it easier for her to take decisions. While most of the household income is used for basic household purchases, she also uses a small amount of money to fulfil the WO savings obligations for her daughters-in-law.

33

After household consumption needs are fulfilled, women may use any additional money to pay for social services. Many women expressed the desire to educate their children, particularly their daughters, and have made this a priority for income expenditure. Women in the Northern Areas have had little access to health services, although this is gradually changing. Women use any extra money to pay for health services for themselves and their families and to pay for the purchase of medicines.

Women also save a portion of the money which they earn. Savings are used for a variety of purposes. Some younger women join WOs specifically because they can save money through the WO for future expenditures, such as weddings and their children's education. In a few cases, younger women have saved to finance their own education.

Many women use savings to invest in productive enterprises. Bibi Rahnuma from Aliabad-Shapissan has reinvested part of her savings into a cluster hatchery. Because her husband is now too old to work, Bibi Rahnuma's cluster hatchery has become the family's only income source. Particularly in the early phase of the hatchery business, costly inputs and technical equipment needed to be purchased. Without her savings the establishment of her cluster hatchery would have not been possible. 'For two years I was working hard as the poultry specialist, and saved regularly. When I had saved enough, I established the hatchery. Now, I can earn enough to provide for my entire household.'

Women tend to have more control over the use of savings than over income which is not saved. For example, Bibi Safida, WO manager in Hussaini saves all of the money which she earns from poultry production and uses money from other enterprises to pay household expenses. She has recently also taken over the WO's accounts management which entitles her to 5 per cent of the WO's total profit. In her position as the family's only income source, Bibi Safida tries not only to meet the family's immediate needs but also to plan for her family's future, including the education of children. 'I have to educate, clothe and feed my children, but we have no land and my father-in-law never educated his children. I don't want this to happen to my children', states Bibi Safida, who became her WO's first educated female manager and accounts officer. She has insisted on using part of her income to pay for her children's education. By depositing fractions of their income into the WO's savings accounts and using these savings to finance various economic and non-economic activities of their own choice, women can exercise control over the income which they earn.

Besides immediate financial benefits, women have also realized an increase in their financial security from involvement in the regular savings scheme. As the example of Bibi Safida illustrates, some WO members have exclusive responsibility for their family's welfare due to the death of the male head of household or even male migration out of the region. Savings

34

allow these women to support their families. Savings also function as a 'safety net' in times of emergency. A village woman in Khyber explains: 'My husband fell ill but I was able to avoid bankruptcy because I could use my savings. My husband was very impressed by that.'

Ability to Access Resources and Markets Independently
The combination of mobility constraints and the religious notion of *purdah* (seclusion) have denied women access to both vital physical as well as financial resources, restricting their participation in commercial activities. Women, for example, do not own land or other physical assets. With the introduction of productive packages and gender-specific credit windows, women are able to overcome their constraints in this matter, enabling them to become actors in the market. The availability of the WO Credit Programme (WOCP) at the village level, for example, has increased women's access to, and uptake of, credit by bringing the bank to their doorstep.

Enhancing women's productive and technical skills as a major pillar within AKRSP's development theme plays a crucial role for strengthening women's confidence to play a more visible role. Women feel that over the course of their involvement they have gained entrepreneurial experience and expertise, allowing them increasingly to enter markets more independently. As Bibi Lal Bano, WO manager and village accountant for Aliabad-Shapissan, explains: 'I noticed that ready-made clothes are very expensive in the market. So, I started a vocational training school. In fact, I am thinking of opening a shop soon, where we would post a woman and sell all the locally manufactured products.

With respect to the financial management of their activities, women were lacking the necessary expertise and confidence to engage in productive activities. Hence, in addition to ensuring women's access to financial resources (for example through the WO's credit programme), enhancing their skills in financial issues such as accounts-keeping or investment, is also paving the ground for women's increasing role in the market economy. 'I use all my skills now, and I will use them in the future no matter what happens', says Bibi Safida, the manager of WO Hussaini. After having passed an AKRSP-directed course on accounts-keeping, Bibi Safida has recently also taken over responsibility for the WO's financial management. Besides increasing her personal autonomy in financial issues, Bibi Safida is helping the entire WO to enhance its organizational independence from the village's VO. 'We really don't want to use men's help as long as I am around. This WO is for women, so women should work here for themselves.'

Gaining expertise and confidence in self-management has important implications for women's future activities. 'We can't think of anything that discourages us', says a member of WO Hussaini. Though women generally remain risk-averse and cautious in initiating independent income-earning activities, younger women particularly (encouraged by their comparatively

35

high educational stance), are creative in initiating new activities. Their involvement in the WO enables them to identify new areas of income-earning. 'We knew nothing about marketing, well, we knew a little,' comments a member of the WO Minapin. 'But AKRSP told us about marketing in the meetings, and now we are learning and selling more.' Many of them can even see themselves engaged in productive activities without outside support such as granted by AKRSP. As Bibi Lal Bano underlines: 'I am now well aware of what it takes to start a business. In fact, accounting is the most important thing for any business.' Hence, following their involvement in productive activities channelled through the WO, women have considerably increased their ability to access resources and markets independently.

Despite these wide-ranging achievements, women's ability to access resources and markets remains constrained. Access is dependent on the relative remoteness of the village. WOs located near a commercial centre, such as the women's organizations in Aliabad, have been able to take the opportunities available in the market place and fully utilize them to their own advantage. WO Aliabad-Shapissan decided to extend its cluster hatchery, and to embark on a profitable polyester quilt project involving six out of the village's eight WOs in order to satisfy market demand. Women carry out the marketing of their produce themselves as there is no need to travel a long distance. Aliabad is the largest market town in Hunza, with a steady increase in tourism and trade each year. WO members are thus able to identify the market niches, such as egg supply, and bargain effectively for their own financial benefit. In places where the market is located further away, such as Khyber, women have to opt for other mechanisms of market interaction.

In most cases religious norms and traditions still prevent women from becoming a dominant part of the market arena. In order to purchase, as well as to offer their produce in the market, the majority of village women are still heavily dependent on either professional middle-men or male relatives. Women, however, find ways to overcome these hurdles. WO Minapin, for example, hires a male driver on a collective basis in order to access markets, reducing member's individual costs of marketing operations. Considering women's limited mobility in Nagar, this initiative ensures market access to each individual member in a cost-efficient manner. Had members to pay service charges to the middle-man on an individual basis the women's profit margin would be considerably less.

In the economic sphere, women make use of their increased bargaining power in order to access new markets. Despite the region's expansion and rapid economic development, markets remain limited and seasonal. Collective attempts undertaken by the WO to increase women's market accessibility thus play an important role in ensuring the sustainability of women's productive activities. Given the limited demand for apricots at the local level, the women of Minapin, for example, established contacts with GAMA. Through GAMA, processed apricots, which are one of the main income sources to the women of the WO, are now marketed in the plains as well as in Gilgit bazaar. In order to access new, non-village markets for their vegetables, WO members in Minapin take advantage of their collective bargaining power in their relation to male middle-men and truck drivers by acting as a unit.

Overall Empowerment

Alterations at the Individual and Household Levels
Women have experienced impacts and benefits of participating in the WOs which go beyond increased income and economic bargaining power. At the household and individual levels, the economic benefits of organizing, and the new knowledge women possess, have been catalysts for changing gender roles.

Women recognize the norms which dominate gender-relations at the household level: 'We mostly take the decisions jointly. But even if I am upset he will go ahead with the decision. It is our tradition that what a woman decides, a man never accepts.' However, these norms are changing. Women's income-earning activities have led to a rise in women's status within the traditional family unit and an increased capacity to negotiate for changes at the household level. As a large proportion of income is deposited in the WO's savings account, women can effectively bargain for the use of that income.

Following their success in handling WO financial affairs, women increasingly show interest in participating in financial decision-making processes at the individual household level. 'In the beginning, I myself was not even interested in the issue,' says Bibi Lal Bano, the first women to become a village accountant in Hunza. 'But now I am much more aware of all the aspects involved in finance and enterprise development. Domestically, it helps me to estimate the expenses better.'

With their traditionally wide-ranging responsibilities in farm activities, upgrading women's productive skills is important for increasing farm production. Women who have undergone agricultural training find that their skills are in demand by males in the household. As Bibi Safida stresses: 'Ever since my involvement in the WO, my father-in-law especially asks and respects my opinion in all matters.' Particularly in fields traditionally in the hands of women, such as vegetable cultivation or livestock rearing and poultry farming, women now hold a strong position in household decision-making processes. After support from her husband in the initial phase of establishing a cluster hatchery, Bibi Rahnuma, for example, is now fully in charge of managing the hatchery on her own. Since her husband is too old to work, Bibi Rahnuma's hatchery is now the family's most important source of income. This economic dependence, she says, has considerably altered her family's internal structure, with particular implications for decision-making in the household. Her two sons, who are also contributing to the family's portfolio, now come to her in order to debate relevant issues and take joint decisions.

As women have gained new skills and knowledge, their feeling of self-worth has increased, and they have gained the necessary confidence to take a more vocal stand at the household level. As Bibi Hudjad Bacht explains: 'In the beginning we didn't know anything. Before we organized ourselves in a WO we used to believe everything and agreed with everything our men told us. Now we have learned to state our opinions and views – and now our men even ask us about what we think.' Women's views on marriage partners for their daughters are now seriously regarded by the male household head. Though male family members continue to choose a suitable match for the family's sons, many women report having the 'final word' in decisions on their daughters' marriage partners, a position which was previously unthinkable.

The confidence women have gained through training and through the solidarity of the WO allows them to counter criticism at the individual level. 'Even if someone opposes me, I can reply with confidence,' says Bibi Safida. She herself only recently experienced false accusations by her predecessor, a male member of the VO, in an attempt to cover his own mismanagement.

Awareness-raising on women's capabilities is beneficial also from another point of view. Finally, women's increased recognition as 'breadwinners' is substantially altering family relationships at the grassroots level. To the women, their involvement in WOs results in fewer 'problems' with their husbands. Women, as they say, are now granted more respect and authority within the family unit, reflecting positively on intra-household relationships between the sexes.

Although seclusion in the home remains a day-to-day experience for the majority of women in the Northern Areas, there have been some individual improvements in personal mobility. A few women have become more visible in the village economy by setting up 'lady' shops (small shops supplying items such as soap and other cosmetics for women) and other shops selling agricultural inputs like pesticide and fertilizer. These women serve as role models in the village, providing an example of women's mobility and visibility that challenges existing norms.

Specialists and master trainers also experience increased mobility. WO specialists, such as Bibi Azida of WO Khyber, are breaking a traditional taboo. With her husband's permission, she is now in charge of purchasing the WO's vegetable seeds in the market – a task that had previously been in the hands of AKRSP field staff. 'Now I am going everywhere, and I am no longer afraid.' With village-based specialists taking on the service delivery role, women no longer have to look far for the purchase of inputs and other resources. In her position as the WO's vegetable and poultry specialist, Bibi Zainaba Khatun of Minapin is now covering five villages. In order to provide the women with necessary inputs and to offer her vaccination services, she is regularly traveling outside her own village. 'In the beginning, it was difficult. I had to walk a lot, and people used to tell my husband that it was wrong for a woman to move around so freely. Now, people have realized the importance of my work and they have stopped talking,' she says. In this sense, WOs carry out the vital function of creating awareness of the benefits of women's increased mobility among both men and women. Building up women's confidence and, at the same time, men's trust in this matter forms a cornerstone in the long-term process aiming at fostering women's economic and overall empowerment.

Aware of the benefits deriving from outside exposure, village women are increasingly articulating their interest in broadening their knowledge through traveling outside the immediate village environment. As a WO member in Minapin makes the point: 'The master trainer understands all the trainings and now she goes everywhere. We don't understand and never go anywhere. We want to see a good WO and a bad WO so we can learn the best way to work.'

The redefinition of roles and responsibilities is also increasing women's choices and, more importantly, their expectations of life. This results in women paying attention to their daughters' education as well as in a genuine interest to enhance their skills. 'These new skills are beneficial for us because we are no longer dependent on men. We can earn an income and contribute to the household expenditure, and save,' a member of the WO Hussaini underlines. Moreover, on an individual level women are enjoying a more respected position within their family unit and are increasingly participating in decision-making processes at the household level.

Alterations at the Village Level
WOs provide a platform for women's co-operative action and solidarity at the village level. While women's traditional roles in the village community have always entailed and required the co-operation of village women in certain areas, such as at weddings or funerals, women's interaction remained unstructured, lacking a common vision. Over the course of WO performance, however, women have developed a new sense of solidarity and mutual interdependence. As a village woman in Khyber states, 'Before we used to meet at two occasions: for funerals and weddings. Now, we meet regularly and discuss many things. It is a pleasure.'

Through the WO, women have a more vocal stand in village-level decisions and more bargaining power than they did before. While women were easily marginalized in the women's sections of VOs, the independent formation of WOs is enhancing the articulation of women's needs at the

39

village level. The WO proves to be an effective instrument for fostering women's economic and overall empowerment at the grassroots level, especially in conservative areas. For example, WO members in Minapin proved their increased bargaining power in a dispute with the village's religious leaders, attempting to discredit and finally dissolve the WO. 'They started to say it was *"haram"* (sin), and there was no benefit but just a waste of time. We said no, and that we would follow the guidance of Muzzaffer Shah (the village activist). We do benefit we said, and you don't know. Now those who opposed us are silent.' By forming a united force, the WO members in Minapin were able to give their opinion more weight. In its function to synchronize women's strength and influence, the WO proves an effective mechanism to support women's issues, and to make their voices heard more clearly at the village level.

Women are increasingly ready to participate in decision-making processes on issues that affect their lives. Suffering from unhygienic and unhealthy conditions in the village, the WO members in Hussaini, for example, actively promote environmental protection in their community. For this purpose, the WO has established an 'environmental protection committee' as part of the organizational structure of the WO. A WO Minapin woman explains the WO's strategy for influencing village affairs: 'We chose the most eloquent woman to become our president. She can speak up in village meetings.'

At the village level, WO savings can mark the entry point for a new, mutual interdependence of men and women on the premiss of women's increased bargaining-power. As the example of the WO Hussaini illustrates, women can visibly influence the future development of their community through the WO's savings. Hence, despite women's limited decision-making power on financial investments on the household level, WO loan facilities initiate a dialogue between men and women at the community level. Women begin to take a role in shaping the development of their community and start to alter socio-cultural perceptions that minimize women's roles in financial issues.

Women's ultimate aim while forming a WO is to achieve independence in managing their own affairs. As the case study shows, women have been successful in accomplishing this objective to a great extent. While all WOs in this study have female leadership many others still have male managers. Following the establishment of separate women's organizations, WOs are, with the selection of female representatives, successfully completing organizational independence from the village organization. Although cooperation between the two organizational entities does exist, scale and quality of collective and individual activities differ between WOs and VOs, requiring separate management procedures.

Since WO formation is essentially built upon women's solidarity and ability to identify joint activities, women have opened up a new chapter in community-level co-operation. Following their participation in WOs, women not only shape the process of economic development of their community, but most importantly also shape its social framework. WOs illustrate women's interest and capacity to network on another level. To women WOs are an instrument for establishing linkages and co-operation with actors beyond the immediate village environment (including governmental and non-governmental development agents). Following from that, WOs help their members in developing the crucial ability to bargain and mobilize their forces in a sustainable manner.

WOs prove effective with respect to managing income-earning activities and as an instrument to increase women's bargaining power while interacting with other organizations. Furthermore, WOs function as a 'social-control mechanism' among the members themselves, tackling issues that go beyond the original mandate of the WO, such as conflict resolution among members in a broader sense. Both women's gathering in WO meetings as well as specific norms and regulations of the WO perform crucial functions in bringing women closer to each other. To conclude in the words of a village woman: 'Now we know what is happening in the village and in our neighbour's house. We have learnt to discuss and to talk about our problems.' WOs thus prove beneficial in increasing women's intra-organizational bargaining power. In doing so, women themselves are able to ensure sustainability and continuity of WO achievements and benefits.

Sustainability of Economic and Non-Economic Benefits

Women's productive activities show great prospects of providing sustainable benefits. On the demand side, market dynamics point in an encouraging direction. First, the region is emerging increasingly from its economic isolation, which is creating market opportunities for women outside of the Northern Areas. Seed potato production is a good example of how women have capitalized on this situation. Women are keen to continue diversifying their productive activities to take advantage of local, regional and national markets. The growing demand for women's produce at the village level also ensures expanding marketing opportunities for the women. Since these local markets are relatively accessible for women, they will remain as the prime arena for women's entrepreneurial activities.

Women entrepreneurs are characterized as having both a strong interest to improve their present performance and a high learning curve. As the example of the WO Hussaini and its young manager Bibi Safida shows, women continuously increase their managerial capacities through 'learning by doing'. Following an incident of hasty distribution of WO loans to non-members, the organization's loan mechanism and procedures were modified. 'We made a mistake last year. As it turned out we didn't fulfil all women's needs before giving a loan to the VO. We will not do that again.'

41

While women were not used to making decisions on finance and investment, involvement in a WO increases women's ability to take economic decisions. Gaining entrepreneurial expertise through a continuous process of involvement in the WO's collective and individual activities, women prepare themselves for the market arena.

Unfavourable market forces, however, can constrain women's entrepreneurial success and potentially can have a negative impact on women's future investments. Given the geographically unfavourable location of the programme area, women are vulnerable to scarce and/or costly resources. Although unlikely to drive women away from current activities, the lack of basic social sector services, such as access to water and electricity in many villages, may also constrain women's business success.

However, with respect to women's bargaining power in the economic sphere, sustainable changes will require more time, mirroring a long-term process of alterations in people's minds and values. Men and women's growing understanding of each partner's beneficial contribution to the overall development of the household as well as women's growing self-confidence to play a more active role in this struggle are the first steps in this direction.

Women have gained the necessary ability and confidence to play a more assertive role in their families and at the village level. Women are altering their positions and modifying traditional gender roles. 'As a specialist I am now important for many people,' explains Bibi Azida who is actively involved in WO Khyber. With the successful performance of WOs in economic terms on the one hand, and social terms on the other, women have visibly demonstrated their importance to their community. Though not always clearly visible, WOs form a major component within the mosaic of village life. In the ongoing process of village development, women are taking on roles and responsibilities that are by now widely accepted by the community.

With respect to women's increased status at the household and village levels, WO members are confident that they will sustain present achievements over the long term. In this context, women's human resource development as part of the programme's training component plays a crucial role. As Bibi Lal Bano makes the point: 'People respect my skills now, not just myself as a person.' Women feel that the respect granted to them will remain even when they are no longer involved in income-earning activities. 'My family will remember what I did for them when I am too old to work,' says Bibi Hudjad Bacht from Khyber. 'My children know, and they will tell their children, so I will be taken care of by them later on.'

WO records on external linkage development provide good insight into WOs' increasing independence and autonomy as organizations. In a majority of cases, the WOs have established a set of formal linkages with different organizational bodies within as well as outside the village. To the women themselves, WOs are an important means to establish networks at the village and regional level. Only the members of WO Hussaini genuinely reject the idea of establishing linkages with other WOs in the area. This is because they feel that the issues of concern to their WO differ considerably from those of other WOs. In Aliabad-Shapissan and Minapin, however, neighbouring WOs share input supplies and expertise (specialists/master trainers) among their members. In Minapin and Khyber, working relations were established with external development agencies other than AKRSP. These include FAO, which introduced a potato cultivation project in Khyber, the Aga Khan Health Service and the Aga Khan Education Service, both active in Minapin village.

The establishment of formal working relations with the village organization, however, remains difficult in most cases. Only in Khyber do women and men work together, sharing expertise and facilities particularly with respect to marketing issues. In other cases the relationship between the WO and its counterpart are strained, and in some cases non-existent.

Women's bargaining power and organizational autonomy has also increased with respect to women's partnership with AKRSP. One member of the WO Minapin notes: 'Over time, we have become more independent. At first AKRSP staff used to do everything for us. Now we are doing more and more on our own.' Women feel confident while interacting with AKRSP, and in prioritizing the type of assistance requested by the members. Particularly young WO members, who feel they have gained considerable experience as entrepreneurs, are looking for alternatives to expand their income-earning activities even beyond AKRSP's productive packages. To many, outside support is no longer necessary (from AKRSP or other development agencies promoting income-earning activities of women in the area, such as FAO or UNDP) since women have achieved a high degree in self-management. The WOs' dependence on male expertise is also declining. As a village woman in Khyber notes: 'Right now men still need to help us, but more and more girls are getting educated, and we will learn how to manage our own affairs.' Women's self-confidence and motivation has increased with their growing awareness of opportunities and of their abilities: 'We believe that we can expand on the work learnt. We feel more confident now and more capable.'

Transforming Women's Economies: Bangladesh Rural Advancement Committee (BRAC)

GUL RUKH SELIM

THE BANGLADESH RURAL ADVANCEMENT COMMITTEE (BRAC) was founded in 1972 soon after liberation as a relief operation for refugees returning to Sylhet district from neighbouring districts in India. Over the years BRAC has evolved from a relief operation into a comprehensive, multifaceted development organization for the rural poor, with a particular focus on the development and empowerment of poor women. Today, BRAC programmes have reached all parts of the country, making it one of the world's largest indigenous NGOs.

BRAC's Approach to Empowering Women

BRAC defines its objective as the alleviation of poverty through empowerment of the poor. In practice this is realized through the formation and development of village organizations (VOs) of the poor (both men and women) plus the provision of multiple services to them. VO membership is drawn from a target population, namely, households that own 50 decimals (0.2 hectares) or less of land and sell their labour for survival. Through the VOs, BRAC is able to deliver its various social and economic services,

Table 1 Village Organizations, Membership, Savings and Credit, 1995

	Position at 31 January 1995
1. Total VOs	25 181
2. Total VO members	1 007 584
3. Total savings (in million Tk.)[1]	624
4. Cumulative disbursement (in million Tk.)	6105
5. Disbursement for the month of January (in million Tk.)	263
6. Number of cumulative loans (in million)	2.49
7. Current outstanding loans	843 134
8. Current outstanding loans (in million Tk.)	1597
9. Current outstanding borrowers	751 961

Source: BRAC Monitoring Department

[1] Tk.100 = US$2.50 as at July 1995.

45

including primary and adult education; para-legal and preventive health education; financial services; training in craft and enterprise skills; improved technologies and marketing; and health and family planning services. Through the VOs, participants in BRAC programmes develop self-respect and mutual self-help.

Over the years BRAC has increasingly targeted landless women as a section of the rural population who are particularly burdened by poverty. By the end of 1995 almost 80 per cent of the participants in BRAC's Rural Development Programme were women and more than 75 per cent of the loans disbursed by BRAC went to women.

At the core of BRAC's work is its Rural Development Programme (RDP) which has several key components, as follows:

Village Organizations (VOs)

When BRAC staff introduce RDP to a new area of operation its staff conduct a door-to-door survey to identify the target population of the area and to encourage the target population to organize into local groups. Once a local group is formed, BRAC offers a course on social awareness to all group members: the course focuses on community problems and is geared towards the development of self-reliance among group members. These small groups, which average five members each, are federated into village organizations. On average, each VO comprises 35–40 members organized into 7–8 sub-groups. Each VO has a management committee consisting of the leaders of the small groups and an elected chairperson, a secretary, and a cashier. The management committee is responsible for the day-to-day running of the VO and serves as the link between the group members and the BRAC office. Each sub-group holds a weekly meeting to discuss its savings and credit operations and the VO holds a monthly meeting of all sub-groups to discuss common social, economic, and political problems. As they develop and strengthen, individual VOs begin to confront such local problems as domestic violence, disinheritance, dowry, divorce, and low wages. Through one of its members who is specially trained, each VO is offered para-legal training on the Muslim family, inheritance, and the land law as well as their rights as citizens. Knowledge of these laws empower the poor, and poor women in particular, by familiarizing them with the law as well as demystifying the legal process. Periodically, as needed, BRAC offers training on various issues and skills to the VOs and their members.

Credit and Savings

BRAC's credit and savings operations are carried out through the small groups which function as peer lending groups; that is, the groups serve as collateral for their members and assume collective responsibility for loan repayment by their members. A woman is eligible for a BRAC loan if she is a member of a VO and has made savings deposits with BRAC. Her application is forwarded by her sub-group to the VO. If her application is approved, she collects her loan at the BRAC office in the presence of the management committee. She then repays her loan by instalments at the weekly meeting of her sub-group. The amount collected is credited to her passbook and recorded on a collection sheet. To handle and oversee these transactions, a BRAC staff person attends each weekly sub-group meeting. By June 1995 BRAC's savings and loan portfolios had grown to over Tk.639 million and Tk.1.8 billion respectively.

Sectoral Programmes
In taking a BRAC loan, each group member decides what activity she will engage in and whether she will seek additional BRAC support. To increase the productivity and income of its borrowers, BRAC has developed an integrated package of services in several key sectors: poultry and livestock, fisheries, sericulture and textiles, agriculture and social forestry, and irrigation. In addition, BRAC's rural enterprise programme has tested and developed new lines of employment for women, such as grocery shops and restaurants, carpentry workshops, mechanical workshops, prawn hatcheries, grafting nurseries, and vegetable seed farms. In each sectoral programme a number of employment and income-earning opportunities have been created. For example, in the poultry sector, women work as key rearers, chick rearers, egg collectors, and poultry workers (paravets); and in the sericulture sector they work as mulberry tree rearers/caretakers, silk worm rearers, silk spinners and reelers, silk weavers and dyers, embroiderers, and tailors.

As at June 1995, employment in all the sectors totalled over 500 000 of which the vast majority are women: 300 000 women in the poultry sector alone.

Education
Besides the formation and operation of the VOs, BRAC has other programmes that offer social services to villagers. These services are not necessarily restricted to members of the VOs. The non-formal primary education (NFPE) programme is one such service. The NFPE schools were started by BRAC in 1986 for the benefit of those children aged 7 to 10 who are not in the state primary schools. The most common reason for children not being enrolled in primary schools is the poverty of their parents. But there are gender-based barriers as well; fewer girls than boys from the poorest households attend state primary schools. For this reason, 60 per cent of the seats in NFPE schools are reserved for girls and the children of BRAC VO members are given first preference. The NFPE schools have been very popular. They are small schools of 30 students situated within the village. After the two- or three-year course in an NFPE school, NFPE graduates continue their education in the state school system.

47

Health
BRAC's primary health care programme is designed to be low cost and to deal with common health problems. It provides a number of services at the village level beyond basic curative services, including family planning, water and sanitation, immunization, health and nutrition education. One traditional birth attendant (TBA) and one village health worker or *shastho shebika* are trained for each village. Both the immunization and family planning services complement existing government services to supplement shortfalls in service delivery. That is, where the government has not established a local health station, as in the villages of Manikganj, immunization and family planning services are provided directly by BRAC.

BRAC's programmes are developed and adapted to respond to the specific constraints, opportunities, and needs expressed by village women. Poor rural women gain access to the various economic and social interventions described above, first through becoming a member of a village organization or *samiti* and undergoing a social awareness education course. Once this is completed each individual woman can choose to be:

○ self-employed with or without the support of a BRAC loan
○ self-employed with the support of BRAC training and other services
○ self-employed in one of the BRAC-supported sector programmes
○ self-employed as a service provider (e.g. as a paramedic or poultry worker) who charges a user-fee for services rendered, and/or
○ employed as a producer in a BRAC-run production centre.

A woman's choice of which economic opportunity to pursue depends on several critical factors, including whether there are other sources of income in her household and whether she is free to work outside the home. Many women participate in more than one type of economic activity at once.

This case study illustrates BRAC's approach to women's economic empowerment by looking at the activities of women in two villages: Shurundi and Panchbarul, which are in Manikganj District, some 40 miles north west of Dhaka city, the capital of Bangladesh. In the case of Shurundi, many women are self-employed in one of the largest subsector programmes – that of poultry production – and our examples centre around this. In the case of Panchbarul, there is a thriving BRAC-run embroidery and garment production centre in which 40 women are employed. This too is our focus, although many of the women thus employed also take loans for productive investment purposes and/or engage in traditional productive activities without use of BRAC loans. Women in both villages benefit from access to other BRAC services.

The Shurundi Poultry Programme

In rural Bangladesh the vast majority of landless women are engaged in backyard chicken rearing: rearing 2 or 3 local-variety birds on average.

48

However, the mortality rate of local breeds raised under scavenging conditions is very high; and although poultry vaccines are produced in Bangladesh, poultry services in rural areas are very poor. Given these conditions, and in order to increase the earnings from poultry rearing for large numbers of women, BRAC developed a model poultry programme which is now jointly administered by the Government of Bangladesh and BRAC.

By 1983, after several years of trial and error, a 'model' for the poultry programme had evolved. The model calls for:

○ one Poultry Worker (paravet) for every 1000 birds to ensure effective vaccination and disease control
○ 10 key rearers in each village each raising 14 chickens, a mix of high-yielding and indigenous breeds
○ one model rearer in each village with three cocks and 20 hens
○ 20 chick rearing units for each RDP branch, each with a capacity to raise 250 day-old-chicks for two months
○ three hatcheries that use the 'Chinese rice-husk method', a simple, low-cost method, for each programme area and supplied by 20 breeders
○ two or three feed retail centres, owned and operated by selected VO members for every area office.

Two additional components were later added to the early model: egg collectors were recruited and trained, to protect participants from middlemen who tend to drive egg producer prices down; and poultry hatchers were trained to supply day-old-chicks.

The model in its current form provides an integrated package of support to rural women, including group formation, technical training, poultry vaccination, the supply of improved birds, credit and marketing. BRAC is responsible for group formation, motivation, training and credit support to the women who participate in the programme. The government is responsible for training and input supply. The model covers the whole process from hatching eggs to rearing birds and marketing the products, and it creates employment for 300 000 rural women.[2]

In Shurundi village, there are four women who own chick-rearing units and another ten women who raise poultry. One woman, Maliha, has a chick-rearing unit as well as a model farm, in which she had three cocks and fourteen hens when we visited. They buy feed from a feed retail outlet also operated by a VO member and receive supplies of day-old chicks from the hatchery at the BRAC Area Office or a government hatchery in Manikganj town. Chick rearers obtain loans from the VOs for working capital.

In addition to chicks and feed, chick rearing requires electricity; a clean, well ventilated shed; and time. In the first couple of weeks, the day-old

---

[2] For more details see Chen (1996).

chicks must be fed eight times per day; the shed must be cleaned out regularly for disease control; an even temperature must be maintained inside the shed; and a strict vaccination regime must be followed. This means that, at least for the early weeks, chick rearers must remain at home to provide the constant care required by young chicks.

The women who engage in poultry rearing with BRAC support are poor women who have the time but no other marketable skill with which to earn an income. The poultry rearers we spoke to were all very clear that this was the most suitable work for them. An important consideration is the preference for home-based work. In the absence of support for child care and other household chores, working away from home for small wages is clearly not worth it for most rural women. The income from poultry raising is still very small but it is an attractive way to make a small income which does not involve leaving home, violating *purdah*, or losing status (as both rich and poor women rear chickens).

Maliha joined the Shurundi VO about ten years ago. Soon after joining the VO she approached a BRAC programme organizer to say that she would like to raise chicks. The Shurundi VO had only recently decided to participate in BRAC's poultry rearing programme. She went for a three-day training session and, upon her return, spent about Tk.1500 to construct a shed with bamboo supports and walls and a tin roof. Her husband and a hired labourer built the shed. She shared the cost of accessing electricity with two of her neighbours and got her first batch of 100 day-old chicks. She lost nine chicks, but after deducting the costs for purchasing chicks, feed and vaccine services, she earned a net income of Tk.300. This was enough to encourage her to buy a second batch of 250 chicks. With the second batch, she also received a loan of Tk.4000 through her VO to cover operating costs.

Maliha's household does not have too many assets – they have two simple tin-roof huts as living quarters and a poultry shed. They have no land except the nine decimals on which their homestead stands. However, their family is poised to accumulate assets, now that her three sons are grown up and are all earning wages. The first son earns Tk.20 per day. The second son pulls the family rickshaw, bought with a loan from BRAC, and earns Tk.60-70 a day. The youngest son is apprenticed to a carpenter and earns Tk.20–25 per day. Apart from wages, these young men are likely to bring in money and assets as dowry at marriage.

Maliha's husband works away from home at a brickfield and receives Tk.250 each week. Because her husband earned a steady, though low, income, Maliha has never had to go out in search of work. She takes pride in her status as a woman who stayed home to raise her children and that her income helped to cover common household expenses. She likes poultry rearing because as she explained, 'I can stay home and also help with household expenses. I can buy my own clothes.'

The Sub-Production Centre at Panchbarul

One option VO members have is to work as a producer in a BRAC-run production centre or sub-centre. What follows is a description of an embroidery sub-centre in Panchbarul village. The embroidery sub-centre illustrates the strategies adopted by BRAC to involve village women in producing goods which, through effective design and marketing services, are sold in international markets. For example, a traditional skill in embroidered quilt-making, called *nakshi kantha*, has been revived by BRAC. BRAC provides design and logistical support to women who were already skilled or have been trained in embroidered quilt-making. Employment at the embroidery centre demonstrates the complexity of BRAC's support network for expanding women's employment opportunities. It also exposes how many women are willing to take up paid work outside their homes if opportunities are made available.

The embroidery sub-centre at Panchbarul was started in 1979. At first, about a dozen women were trained to embroider small pieces. However, the interest in embroidery soon grew and more and more women joined. Since 1983, with the establishment of a craft and textile centre in Manikganj, embroidery as well as several other craft activities have been better organized, promoted, and marketed than before.[3] As of 1991, the craft and textile centre in Manikganj town employed 1857 women, of which 1492 were engaged in embroidery and embroidered quilt-making. There are 186 sub-centres located in different villages around Manikganj of which the Panchbarul sub-centre is one.

At present, about 40 women work at the sub-centre at Panchbarul from 8 a.m. to 5 p.m.: all are either members of the BRAC VOs or relatives of VO members. Women from Panchbarul as well as from surrounding villages come to work at the sub-centre, sometimes walking several kilometres each way. Eight of the women are not yet married, one woman has been abandoned by her husband and the rest are married. The centre is housed in a large hut with a floor of beaten earth, woven bamboo walls and a tin roof. It is cool inside with light filtering in through the two windows and a door – a quiet haven away from the heat of the sun.

---

[3] BRAC has developed a network of retail stores called Aarong in several Bangladesh cities as well as London and Vancouver to market crafts, textiles, and garments produced by low-income men and women from rural Bangladesh. The main Aarong in Dhaka city also serves as a design and marketing headquarters. BRAC also established a network of craft and textile production centres at the village level run by a BRAC affiliate called the Ayesha Abed Foundation.

Although it is now a respected landmark in the village, situated next to the two village stores and the new grinding mill, the women told us of the early years, when it was difficult to convince relatives, as well as leaders of the community, of the usefulness of this work. Husbands and other household members complained that their meals were not served on time or that women were not around to serve them their meals, as is the norm. Women had great difficulty in managing the home without the support of other household members. Some women recalled that their husband or mother-in-law complained 'all the time'. Others spoke of times when they had wanted to work but could not because they did not have help in looking after children or doing household chores. Certainly, if a woman has small children it is difficult to work away from home. Some women bring their infants to the sub-centre while others who live close by may leave the child with their mother-in-law and go back at lunch break, or have the infant brought in, to nurse.

Over the years women who work at the sub-centre have developed a daily routine that helps them manage their double work-load with minimum inconvenience to family members. Early in the morning, women cook both morning and afternoon meals for the entire family, serve portions in separate containers and cover everything against cats and dogs. They also pack some rice and curry for their own lunch. They feed and help their husbands and children go off to work or to school before bathing and getting dressed themselves. In the afternoon they go back home and wash the dishes from the morning as well as the afternoon meals, and cook for the evening. It gets dark by the time all this is completed. This is all done along with the usual household chores that include: cleaning and sweeping out the sleeping hut and yard, letting out the chickens and feeding them; washing clothes for the entire family; looking after goats and cows (if any); and, seasonally, processing crops (if any are grown). Women who have grown-up daughters or a mother-in-law living with them are at an advantage since they share these and other household chores.

In the early years women had also to face the stigma attached to leaving their homes for wage work. However, embroidery work was preferred to other sources of work outside of the home – such as construction or post-harvest processing (even though it pays less money) – because it is considered more 'secure' or protected since the women work together under the auspices of BRAC. Family members do not worry about their 'safety' since they know where they are and who they are with. This is an important consideration especially for younger women – new brides or unmarried women. Increasingly in the Panchbarul sub-centre, young women are beginning to work at the embroidery sub-centre.

Khushi is 16 years old. A few months ago she was married to a young man but she has not yet been formally 'received' by her in-laws since her father, a rickshaw puller, has not completed paying for her dowry. Khushi hangs her head in shame when another woman relates this to us. She is working at the embroidery centre in order to help her parents pay for her dowry and, thereby, to save face in the village.

Over the years embroidery has gained in status in the village as a way for women to earn an income. As a result, more and more women from borderline–poor households are willing to work at the sub-centre.

Hashi lives in an extended family with her husband and three sons, two of whom are married. She has three grandchildren. Her sons are educated and two of them hold good jobs, while the third son is still in school. One son works as a laboratory assistant at a clinic and the other works at the Land Registry office as a clerk. Hashi has never done any paid work but decided that embroidery was respectable enough for her. At the same time, she was proud that none of her daughters-in-law needed to work.

Despite these gains, there is still prejudice against women who work outside their homes. When women work, they find it difficult to marry their daughters off, but embroidery is considered less demeaning in this regard than manual work done outdoors.

Kobita, a woman of about 40, has been doing embroidery work at the sub-centre since the beginning. She has had her share of problems – carrying a double work-load, convincing her husband and mother-in-law that the money she earned doing embroidery was worth the inconvenience to family members. But now her husband understands the value of her work and is willing 'to serve his own food when she is busy' and her children are old enough so that they can fend for themselves around the house. Finally, she thought, things are getting easier. But when her daughter was married to a young man in a neighbouring village, her in-laws used Kobita's embroidery work as an excuse to abuse her. Kobita seriously considered giving up her work in order to appease her in-laws, 'so that they would not hold this over my daughter whenever there was a conflict.' Fortunately, Kobita's son-in-law was supportive of her work and argued on her behalf with his family so that Kobita is able to continue working at the embroidery centre.

Although some women are reluctant to take loans in case anything goes wrong, most women in the village are eager to invest in income-generating activities such as paddy husking, paddy trade, vegetable gardening and poultry and livestock rearing. This is sometimes the case even if they are employed in a production sub-centre. For example, Jamila works as a *shebika* at Panchbarul but she also takes loans for income-generating activities through the VO.

It is about twelve years since I 'put my name with the *samiti*' [joined the VO]. I had to ask my husband for the Tk.10 admission fee. I used to save Tk.2 each week with the VO and when I had about Tk.200 or Tk.300 I would take the money and use it. Some months later I took a loan of Tk.2000 for purchasing a milch cow. Later I took a second loan of Tk.2000 for leasing a bit of cultivatable land for paddy production. The next year I took a Tk.6000 loan and mortgaged some land. We grew winter hybrid paddy. From the money I got from the sale of paddy, I was able to buy a tiny plot of land. In this way I have now bought quite a bit of land.

Economic Impact

What difference has participation in BRAC programmes and in their own organizations made in the lives of women? BRAC's Research and Evaluation Department has tried to estimate the impact of BRAC interventions using two basic methods: by carrying out surveys and by asking women to describe the changes in their lives. Using the first approach, BRAC research staff carried out a two-year research project combining large-scale surveys and in depth case studies of VOs (Mustafa and Ara, 1995). The research findings suggest that, at the household level:

o Changes in household assets, including increases in fixed and productive capital along with investments in housing structures, are related to length of membership. The data indicate greater economic security and improvements in living standards among 'older' than 'younger' members. For example, the survey found reduced seasonal fluctuation in income, expenditure, food consumption and stocks among members who joined more than two and a half years ago and have received more than Tk. 7 500 in loans.

o There is a trend toward decreased dependence on loans from both BRAC and the informal credit market for consumption or consumption-smoothing purposes, indicating an increased coping capacity during seasonal or other crises.

At the same time it was found that rural women have few opportunities to use loans by themselves without the assistance of male family members *unless* BRAC provides them with necessary support services close to the *bari*. This often means, the report concludes, that women 'cannot exercise full control over their loans and credit based resources' (Mustafa and Ara, 1995). However, the study also notes that women bear the primary responsibility for coping with everyday household subsistence as well as with seasonal and other crises; and that giving loans to women is more effective than giving it to men in increasing household assets as well as improving household consumption and expenditure levels.

When we talked to women in Panchbarul and Shurundi we found that they did not make a distinction between their own income and assets and those of the household, but they did speak of ways in which they tried to find and put away funds in order to ensure that household members are fed and clothed.

An important impact from participation in BRAC-supported economic activities is the increased ability to smooth seasonal fluctuations in household income. This is one of the factors mentioned by the women employed in embroidery. As they explained, agricultural work tends to be piecemeal, irregular and seasonal. The income from non-agricultural employment helps to mitigate the effects of season fluctuations on household consumption.

We found that women who had been involved in BRAC-supported economic activities and their local women's organization for quite some time reported investments in home construction, cows and goats, jewellery, rickshaws, and land (both homestead and agricultural). The impact survey, cited above, found that home construction is one of the first areas of investment.

Indeed, the women consistently emphasized the economic gains to their households as well as to themselves as individuals. Both Maliha and Mariam, who are engaged in poultry rearing, count their investments in poultry sheds as well as their net income as profit. They do not consider the cost of constructing a poultry shed as a production cost to be deducted from their net income. As Maliha explains: 'The poultry shed will still be here when I am no longer raising poultry. I can use it for living quarters or put my two cows in it.'

To Maliha what is important is that through the credit, extension and market linkages that are offered by BRAC, she was able to put to product-ive use the resources available within her household. In Maliha's case, these resources included her own and other family members' labour, the land on which the poultry shed was built, and her basic knowledge about chick rearing.

Women's Control Over, and Use of, Extra Income
Women's extra income is used, in the first instance, for meeting basic household consumption needs. It is only when minimum household needs have been met that women may think about buying things for themselves or about investing in productive assets such as goats, cows, agricultural implements and even land.

Dowry transactions at marriage are on the increase in rural Bangladesh. Unfortunately, as women are able to earn and access funds, they often assume the burden of saving for a dowry as well as providing for household subsistence. Khushi worked at the embroidery sub-centre to accumulate enough money for her dowry so that her in-laws would accept her in their home. At that same sub-centre, Shurma told us that she is investing her earnings in silver jewellery for her daughter, Shanti, to wear on her wedding day.

Despite the traditional burden of providing for household subsistence and the more recent burden of saving for a daughter's dowry, many women reported that they now enjoy greater personal and productive assets. Both Maliha and Mariam, who raise poultry, listed a number of items they have purchased with income from poultry rearing:

Maliha buys her own clothes with the money she earns from poultry sales and uses what money may be left over to cover household expenses. 'Before I joined the *samiti*, I never earned any money; now I can earn some money and I have some savings, too.' Maliha has Tk. 1196 saved with BRAC and her second son has Tk. 2000 saved with Proshika. Her youngest son has an additional TK. 800 saved with a village savings group. Apart from the rickshaw, they have also bought a cow with credit from Krishi Bank, a government bank set up to support agricultural development.

For women, investment in jewellery serves multiple purposes: jewellery represents a traditional form of savings (which can be pawned to obtain loans) as well as a new form of savings (to be used towards a daughter's dowry) plus a symbol of wealth and status.

Mariam has saved Tk. 1453 with BRAC and her husband has Tk. 2500 saved with a village savings group. Mariam also invests some of her savings in jewellery. Since she started earning money raising day-old chicks, she has had a heavy silver chain and a pair of gold earrings made for herself. She proudly wears these ornaments as proof of her ability to earn and save.

Several women reported that their opinions in economic decisions and other household matters are now solicited and valued by their husbands and other male relatives. This means that women are playing an increasing role in making decisions about common household funds, not just establishing control over their own income.

Malati works at the embroidery sub-centre at Panchbarul. She is one of the women who joined after embroidery production was well under way and women were earning a steady income from it. Her husband has a job as a postman and makes a reasonable income. They have a bit of land and a couple of cows. Clearly, she is not one of the desperately poor. None the less, Malati says that since she earns an income, she is able to send her daugher to school. Without her income, Malati is not sure whether her husband would have sent their daughter to school.

Women in the Capital Market

One indicator of the greater recognition of women as economic actors is their increased credit-worthiness. VO members reported that their fellow villagers – including relatives, neighbours, and money lenders – are increasingly willing to lend money directly to them. Normally women do not receive or even seek loans, except for very small amounts taken for short periods from relatives and neighbours. The men in the household are expected to take out contingency loans in times of crisis as well as loans for working capital. For low-income women who head their own households, lack of access to credit limits their ability to tide over the household during seasonal and other crises. The story of women like Ranga, below, would suggest that by taking (and successfully repaying) BRAC loans, women gain greater access to the informal credit market.

> Ranga did not take credit from BRAC until recently (in 1991), since she was not confident she would be able to repay loans regularly. She has had to scrounge around, selling chicken eggs, vegetables, and small amounts from her earnings from earthwork, and once she had to pawn a cooking pot in order to pay her loan instalments. With the first loan she bought roofing tin and with the second loan she bought a rickshaw. With a third loan she mortgaged in some cultivable land which her son cultivated. He paid back the loan in instalments from his earnings as a bricklayer.
>
> Ranga reports that after joining the VO, her sister-in-law as well as village money lenders have been more forthcoming with assistance and loans. In the past she was not able to get loans from anyone as they were convinced she would not be able to repay the loan.

There may even be a connection between women's increased economic visibility plus power and the increasing number of wheat and pulse growers contracting women labourers (as reported by the women in Panchbarul).

Not only are women gaining greater access to the informal credit market, but there is evidence to suggest a lowering of the interest rate for credit available through informal sources, primarily from money lenders. This would seem to indicate recognition of women as economic actors in their own right, but also a shift in the nature of the relationship between debtors and money lenders. The rural money lender appears to be losing his ability to exploit the poverty and lack of funds of fellow villagers to extract large profit in the form of interest. One consequence is that there are fewer reported incidents of dispossession of property, particularly of landed property, due to indebtedness.

Women in the Land Market

During discussions with Zahera's group, an interesting shift in poor women's relationships with their male kin, including husbands and sons, came to light. Women talked about a new phenomenon in the lives of women around them: namely, that more and more women are inheriting property from their husbands. Sometimes the husband leaves a legal document transferring land or homestead to his wife. At other times, there is only an oral agreement: the husband will simply call his children and announce that he is leaving property to his wife. Either way fewer women, upon losing their husband, are left totally bereft and wholly dependent on social and economic support from the extended family and kin network.

However, upon further questioning it became apparent that women cannot count on their husband to transfer property in their names:

Do husbands transfer property to wives of their own volition because they feel responsible for their wives? 'Of course not – we have to press for our own rights. Men won't leave their property without an argument. But sons are not dutiful these days, they do not take care of their elderly parents as they used to in our mother's generation, and we have to do everything we can to make sure that we have some source of livelihood and a place to stay in.'

An important factor in the transfer of property to women is the increased access of women to credit, particularly to credit for home construction. More and more women are able to claim entitlement to land and housing property since they were instrumental in accessing the funds with which these assets were purchased or built. Zahera was proud of her own house. In the context of the discussion about women's entitlement to conjugal property, she declared triumphantly:

I do not have to ask my husband to leave me a house. I own my own house. In fact, the entire homestead belongs to me. I purchased it with money I saved over the years and built our living quarters with a [BRAC] loan.

Women in the Labour Market

When considering the impact of women's organizing and BRAC interventions, it is difficult to say where the influence of other forces end and those of BRAC interventions begin. In the case of shifts in the labour market structure or in the practice/observance of *purdah*, the push of poverty has gone hand-in-hand with the pull of newly-created economic opportunities: both those created by government, such as food-for-work programmes; by the private sector such as those in the garment industries; and by NGOs such as BRAC.

Whatever the cause, the net effect has been that low-income women in Manikganj, as elsewhere in Bangladesh, have begun to break through two of the most important impediments to women's full participation in the economic life of the community: a segregated labour market that reflects the system of *purdah* (women's seclusion) which dictates that women should, ideally, work only within their homestead; and second, the devaluation of women's labour as subsistence or household work rather than productive work. The combined effect of these two forces was that, traditionally, women's work remained invisible within the homestead.

Clearly, the fact that the economic activities of women in Panchbarul and Shurundi have become 'visible' to their communities is due in some measure to their participation in local women's organizations and BRAC-supported economic activities. Most importantly, perhaps, women are seen handling cash – saving, taking loans, buying and selling, keeping accounts and, last but not least, being paid cash for work at the embroidery and block printing centres and for the purchase of chicks or silk cocoons.

Earning cash rather than being paid in kind, which was customary for women, highlights the fact that women are engaged in productive work (not just so-called subsistence and household work) and allows family and relatives as well as others in the village society to 'see' women's economic contribution to the household and the community.

There is evidence to suggest that, in Manikganj, women's wages have become increasingly monetized and that the gap between women's and men's wages has narrowed. This represents a remarkable transformation given that when BRAC first began working in Manikganj women's opportunities for paid work were highly restricted: effectively confined to post-harvest activities or domestic work in other households for payments in kind. In Manikganj, in 1976, when Saleha led a group of women from Panchbarul to a food-for-work site, a local government official refused them work stating that, 'Women in our country do not work'. It was only when BRAC staff intervened on their behalf that the women were hired in the food-for-work scheme.

As the women in Panchbarul told us, once they began earning a cash income it was easier for them to enlist the help of household members to share chores and accept a certain degree of disruption of household routine. It helps also that the women who work at the embroidery centre are no longer driven by absolute poverty. The entry of women from borderline poor households in embroidery work has in turn transformed a task associated with poor women – it is poor, elderly women who traditionally stitched *kanthas* for wages in the village – to one associated with a modest but regular income. The other ways in which BRAC members have changed over the years, through the various educational, health and economic inputs, has also helped raise the status of the embroidery work.

Further, women who have received specific service-oriented skills, such as the paramedics and paravets, are quick to point out that the employment market for these skills extends beyond BRAC programmes.

Hasina, about 40, is one of the veterans of the Panchbarul *Samiti*. Soon after she joined she was sent off for training as a *shebika*. She

59

also got an introduction to the Manikganj mother and child welfare centre. She treated minor illnesses and referred cases to the MCH centre. She also received trained birth attendant (TBA) training.

Though she no longer serves as a BRAC *shebika*, Hasina is often called upon to dispense drugs and advice to fellow villagers. They come to her for treatment of minor illnesses and advice and she has obtained accreditation as a paramedic with Ganashasthya, a health-focused NGO, and gets supplies of drugs through them. She also practises, on occasion, as a birth attendant or *dai*. 'No one can take that away from me.' she says, 'I can always earn a little money as a *daktar* or a *dai*.'

Needless to say, BRAC does not work in a social vacuum. BRAC's activities have worked to change the balance of power in the village in favour of the poor and resourceless. By making low-interest credit available to poor women, by expanding and ensuring women's access to village and government resources, by expanding employment opportunities for women, and by creating the potential for women's collective action through forming local women's organizations, BRAC has weakened the ties of patronage that bind poor women to rich households as domestic workers or post-harvest agricultural workers. Wealthy women in villages where local women's VOs exist complain that women who used to work in their homes as domestic workers no longer come when called: 'Those women used to come to work for us but now they make money [working] at the sub-centre and they laugh at the wages we can offer.'

Moreover, there is a perceived (perhaps actual) narrowing of the wealth gap between women from poor landless households and women from richer landed households, at least in terms of their respective ability to spend money on personal items. Commenting on this situation, one woman said: 'They wear more expensive saris than we do. They wear sandals and blouses . . . they never wore these things before.'

Women and Government Services
The collaborative poultry programme jointly administered by BRAC and the Government of Bangladesh has been instrumental in partially overcoming, in one area of production, the constraints on extending government services to landless poor women. This has worked at two levels. In the first place, extension services have tended to ignore the needs of women, assuming that only men are active producers. This has had the consequence that government extension services have neglected subsectors of the economy in which women are concentrated (such as backyard poultry rearing and homestead gardening) as well as selected operations in other subsectors in which women are concentrated (e.g. grain processing and seed storage).

Secondly, collaboration with BRAC has increased the capacity of the government to encompass women's small-scale poultry production in their extension plans and to reach dispersed small-scale producers with their extension services. In the process, government extension networks have not only gained valuable experience but have also learned a lesson in development. Currently, efforts are underway to train government functionaries to take over the supervision and management of the BRAC-run poultry and livestock extension programmes for vulnerable groups.

Overall Empowerment

Awareness and Solidarity
Today membership in the VO leads to a sense of belonging as well as a different world-view for women: empowering them to conceptualize themselves as members of a class of 'poor women' and to relate to people around them from a position other than as 'daughters-in-law' of the village. In real concrete terms, the VOs offer women a place to get away from their daily routine and speak to other women, even if only to commiserate. Through their participation in the weekly and bi-monthly meetings, women learn to discuss common problems and seek common solutions. For instance, VOs take decisions about which of BRAC's sector programmes should be extended to the women in their VO.

In a larger sense, women build up an alternative network through which they learn about available options, some of which are radically new, such as the opportunity to gain employment as para-professionals in their own villages or as producers for the international market; others of which build upon existing opportunities and skills, such as raising hybrid chickens. The VO is also the locus through which women learn about health and other services available to women, those offered by both the government and BRAC.

Apart from the economic interventions, the social services that are available to women through the VO are important in developing a sense of self-worth and self-confidence: these include the health, education and legal literacy services offered by BRAC. For example, having an NFPE school in a village not only enables poor families to educate their children but also highlights both the desirability and the possibility of sending girls to school.

Most importantly, through participation in the VOs, women develop a sense of solidarity as *members of poor households* and as *women* and of the potential for collective action. This is most clearly illustrated by the stories about women rallying around those among them who were abused or abandoned by their husbands. Time and again the intervention of women from the VO has been decisive in getting a better deal for poor women threatened with divorce or violence from husbands or local patrons.

Respect in the Community
Almost without exception, women VO members spoke about gaining recognition and respect within the village due to their activities within the
women's organization. Hasina put it this way,

> Powerful villagers – those who are involved in *shalish* and judgements
> (*bichaar shalish kare*) – now know us and respect us. I have also
> become acquainted with many people in the village whom I would not
> have had occasion to meet if not for our activities through the *samiti*.

The respect and status of the VO is best illustrated in the ways in which
women VO members have been incorporated in the most prestigious and
central village institution. Several of the older members of VOs, including
Saleha and Zahera, spoke of the fact that their opinions are solicited about
village affairs. Both VO leaders are now invited to go along with a few of
their fellow members to attend the village *shalish*. This is certainly a shift in
itself, since men alone are expected to attend the village *shalish*, while only
the rich and powerful have decisive power there. However, according to
Zahera, the significance of their inclusion in *shalish* is more than just the
inclusion of women: 'Our men go to the *shalish* as part of the *shalish*. We
are asked as part of the *samiti*.

In other words, when Zahera or Saleha are invited to come to attend a
village *shalish*, they are invited *to represent the samiti*. The *samiti* is thus
given recognition as an important and respected institution in the
village.

This shift in power dynamics has emerged not only out of a respect for
BRAC as a powerful institution but also out of respect for the women
who constitute the VO. These women are part of their community;
whereas in the past they were seen only as poor and pitiful, now, although
they are still poor, they are respected since they are no longer dependent
on rich patrons for a living. The very independence of women that the
village élite feared and spoke out against when the groups were first
formed has, in some cases, earned women a degree of respect from the
village élites.

The group of women who encounter the rich and powerful in their daily
work are the village women trained as para-professionals – the poultry,
livestock, and health workers. These women, like Jahanara at Shurundi,
are treated as the visible representatives of the VO. It is they who have to
face the opposition to women's mobility and visibility within the village.
During the early years these women faced opposition from the religious as
well as other leaders of the community; now they are treated with respect.
The health worker (or *shebika*) is addressed as a *daktar* (or doctor) and the
livestock and poultry worker as the 'cow doctor' and the 'chicken doctor'
respectively. Their skills are respected as well as their ability to earn an
income using those skills.

As they gain solidarity and a common voice, women in the VOs often try collectively to stop actions which are likely to harm a fellow group member or their collective interests in the village. One vehicle for the élite to exert their influence on social and religious matters is through the *samaj*. Each village comprises a number of *samaj*: groups of households which form a ceremonial and ritual unit and workshop at a common mosque. *Samaj* leaders often try to rule in social matters or create divisions within the village over social or religious matters. The members of one VO told us they had tried to protest a *samaj* ruling against the health worker in their village:

> Jahanara's in-laws tried to stop her activities as a *shebika*. They finally got a decree from her *samaj* casting her out of the village. Her father protested. We protested. The village *shalish* ruled that she be allowed to continue to live in this village. But her in-laws made her and her husband sell their house and leave. She now lives in Manikganj Town.

In other cases the VOs have been more successful in protesting injustice. One factor in their success has been the role played by BRAC's paralegal education programme and, more specifically, the role played by the BRAC-trained paralegals. Through the paralegals, VO members have learned about family laws, including marriage and divorce and maintenance payment. They have learnt that child marriage, dowry payment, and multiple marriage (without the consent of the first wife) are illegal. They learn, most importantly, that there are rules beyond the jurisdiction of the kin and *samaj* that recognize rural poor women and protect them. The language of the law may be used by women to protect themselves, and knowledge of the law allows them to invoke the law to their advantage in family conflicts as well as in village struggles.

Although individually women cannot fight or change abusive husbands, they can collectively protest and try to prevent domestic violence and other forms of marital abuse. In Panchbarul, we were told the story of Sharifa:

> Sharifa's husband wanted to marry a second time. The women in the VO knew that it was illegal to marry a second time, unless the first wife gave her consent. At first Sharifa did not give her consent. Upon advice from her fellow VO members, Sharifa threatened to bring a lawsuit against her husband if he married again. He gave up the idea of marriage.

> In the event, Sharifa's husband did eventually marry the second woman but only with Sharifa's consent. However, the VO members' intervention strengthened Sharifa's position as first wife and made her rights explicit. In this instance this meant that her husband continued to support Sharifa as well as her children after he married a second time.

There are many such examples of group-based mobilization of poor women to protect their own interests. In every village where women have been organized – where women have been mobilized to speak out against injustice – we heard stories of women whose husbands were chastised for beating them or threatening to divorce them. One such instance in a village is often sufficient to establish the VO as an organization to be reckoned with, even in what may otherwise be considered 'family' or 'private' matters.

Acquiring Identity and Voice
Women VO members are addressed by their given names in all *samiti* affairs. This establishes an identity for the women that they would not normally have as married women: in their husband's home, they are referred to as 'wife of x' or 'mother of y'. When talking about changes in their lives due to their experience in the VO, women invariably mention the fact that increasing numbers of people now recognize and acknowledge them (both in the village and outside) and that they have gained the necessary awareness and confidence to think for themselves.

> Rebecca feels she has gained in courage and the ability to speak up in public as well as to think for herself, and has gained an identity. Now people in her village know her and respect her for who she is. 'If I had stayed at home as the daughter-in-law of my husband's household, I would have been nameless and nobody would recognize me outside my home.' She has learned much through BRAC besides the embroidery and management skills involved in running the sub-centre.

Because they belong to their own local organizations and are seen to be economically active, women feel they are better able to assert their right to be heard and to have their opinions taken seriously.

Sustainability of Outcomes
Some gains will undoubtedly be reversed, others will prove resilient to reversals. Those women who have worked for a living and have got used to earning cash will be extremely reluctant to work for a meal and nothing else. There appears to be a tendency for the lowliest work, domestic labour, to be monetized. For instance, in Panchbarul we were told that women get paid money for mud-plastering work which, in rural Bangladesh, is exclusively female work and is considered household or domestic work.

Women in Panchbarul and Shurundi have developed a work ethos. They are no longer content to work only within the kinship and family structures. They want paid work for themselves and for their daughters. Indeed, one of the complaints of the veterans of the Panchbarul *samiti* was that they no longer had work. They complained: 'Now that we are older, and cannot see well enough to do embroidery, we cannot find work anymore.'

These women have a wealth of income-earning work experience under their belt and have not forgotten how they felt the first time they earned cash for work done. An entire generation of poor women have been directly engaged in wage work or have seen women out and working. This is not likely to be easily erased from the collective memory of the villages where BRAC has been active.

Further, the education women have received – whether as adult women through BRAC's social awareness classes or as girls at BRAC-run primary schools – has conditioned their lives and expanded their horizons in ways that will continue to affect their day-to-day dealings and their ability to deal with crises. The legal literacy training that we have described has helped women begin to change the power dynamics of village life. Whether or not women retain knowledge of the specific details of land and family laws – which they often now cite in discussions about marriage, divorce and land transactions – they will, in the long run, retain the knowledge that laws exist which give women a legal leg to stand on in fighting for or defending their rights and interests.

Demanding Accountability: Proshika in Bangladesh

LAMIA RASHID and Md. SHAHABUDDIN

FROM FOREST PROTECTION to countering actions by slum racketeers, women in Bangladesh have found collective strength through organizing. This case study focuses on two women's groups, Jamuna Mohila Samiti and Lucky Mohila Samiti, organized by Proshika Manobik Unnayan Kendra (popularly known as 'Proshika'), a Bangladeshi non-governmental organization begun in 1976. Jamuna Mohila Samiti is located in Paikpara, a village 60km from Dhaka. Its members are involved in protecting 40 hectares of government forest land. Members of the Lucky Mohila Samiti have worked to improve living conditions in the Dhaka slum where they live and work. These groups provide insight into the variety of activities taken by Proshika women's groups and the impact of these activities on individual women and their communities.

Proshika's Approach to Organizing

Proshika was one of the first organizations in Bangladesh to build organizations of the poor. It began by facilitating the formation of primary groups (PGs), often called 'samities', among landless and marginally-landless women and men in rural areas. PG formation proved to be an effective approach for the rural poor to achieve active co-operation amongst themselves; undertake economic and social actions; receive support from NGOs and other institutions; and begin the process of changing exploitative social relationships. Based on the experience of organizing poor women and men in rural areas, Proshika began the urban poor development programme in 1990 to build up PGs among the urban poor. During nearly two decades working with PGs, Proshika has found that poor women and men who join these groups become part of a process in which they can make conscious and responsible choices – they become empowered. By doing so, they become examples for those who are not yet organized, and inspire them to join the PGs. As of December 1995, there were 47 758 PGs in Proshika's programme area with a total of 841 733 members.

Through its development education programme, Proshika provides PGs with human development and practical skills development training. Human development training courses involve a systematic process of consciousness-raising. They give group members the necessary skills for identifying and analysing their problems, developing effective problem-solving strategies, improving their personal motivation and communication, and developing management and leadership capacities. Practical skills development training focuses on providing groups and individuals with the basic knowledge and skills to implement employment and income-generating activities in areas such as livestock management and sericulture.

Associated with practical skills development is Proshika's employment and income generation programme, which works toward poverty alleviation by creating employment and income-generating opportunities. By providing credit and technical assistance, this programme increases the capacity of poor women and men to access, acquire and utilize resources and services.

As they mature, primary groups tend to take on large socio-economic issues, such as the oppression of women, corruption, and property rights. In order to deal effectively with these and other issues, broad-based co-operation and co-ordination is necessary. Federations at three levels (village, union[1] and thana[2]) have been formed to facilitate networking and solidarity among Proshika groups. Village co-ordination committees are composed of six or seven PGs in the same vicinity. Union co-ordination committees bring together approximately ten village co-ordination committees, and the thana co-ordination committees unite all of the union co-ordination committees (and hence all of the PGs) within a thana.

These federations have taken on functions previously performed by Proshika staff, such as organizing PGs, conducting non-formal training for PGs, organizing adult literacy and non-formal primary education classes, managing conflicts among PG members and non-members, and mobilizing group members for seminars and protests. Following its strategy to create sustainable organizations by delegating management responsibilities to the federations and PGs, Proshika has incoporated participation from these groups into the annual planning process. Proshika is now able to stretch its staff and financial resources further.

Over the last 18 years, loan disbursements to primary groups have been increasing each year, keeping pace with Proshika's capacity to manage the fund efficiently and the growing capacities of groups to utilize credit. A number of Proshika groups have now graduated to self-reliance and no longer need financial and managerial support from Proshika. They contribute to, and participate in, the various federations and are able to implement employment and income-generating projects without Proshika staff support and with their own savings.

---

[1] Union is an administrative unit composed of villages.
[2] Thana is the sub-unit of a district.

Proshika's Approach to Empowering Women Economically

Proshika views the empowerment of women as crucial to the development process in Bangladesh. National problems of poverty, illiteracy, malnutrition, low productivity and unemployment are directly linked with the denial of rights and opportunities to women. In working with women, Proshika takes an integrated approach that addresses women's practical and strategic needs and aims to empower women to be active participants in their own development through accumulating savings; acquiring management, leadership and practical skills; implementing employment and income-generating programmes; and engaging in environmental protection and regeneration activities. Organization building is key to achieving this aim, and Proshika has fostered the growth of women's groups, the foci of women's activities. In December 1995 there were 25 940 women's groups with a total of 425 581 members.

Women group members benefit from Proshika's training courses. Human development training courses are designed to enable women to understand and identify the problems they face as poor women and to develop strategies for tackling these problems. One objective of these courses is to empower women to raise their collective voices against practices such as dowry, wife battering, divorce under false grounds, and unequal wages. Since poor women typically have had little opportunity to take leadership or management positions, the courses also enable women to acquire the skills necessary to take these positions in women's groups, and in their communities.

Poor women in Bangladesh have few practical training opportunities because their gender and levels of education and income exclude them from most formal training institutes. Recognizing these constraints, Proshika provides practical skills development training for women in numerous fields, including those that traditionally are not considered 'women's work', such as apiculture, sericulture, social forestry, animal vaccination, and irrigation. The main objectives of practical skills development training courses is to help women make better and more efficient use of the resources that they already have; to identify and tap unused or under-used local resources (for example, denuded public forest land, open water bodies, and *khas* land[3]); and to improve women's technical ability to implement income-generating activities.

Women need credit to finance economic activities yet have little access to credit except from local money lenders who charge high interest rates and use coercive means to ensure loan repayment. Therefore Proshika provides women with credit from the revolving loan fund. As at December 1995, women received 54 per cent of total loan financing available from

---

[3] *Khas* land is land owned by the government.

69

Proshika under this fund. Group savings are used in combination with this credit to finance income-generating activities.

Women have undertaken a variety of income-generating activities with Proshika's assistance. They are engaged in traditional activities such as handicraft production, sewing, and vegetable gardening, in addition to many 'non-traditional' activities. For example, during the period 1989–94, women made up 71 per cent of the participants in Proshika's livestock development programme, and women's groups ran 4336 livestock projects. Women have also been active in the fisheries, sericulture and apiculture programmes. In undertaking these and other programmes they have greatly benefited from Proshika's innovations in the fields of irrigation, apiculture, sericulture, social forestry, open water fisheries, sanitary latrine construction, cattle and poultry vaccination, and tubewell sinking. While the activities are run by the women themselves, Proshika staff provide on-the-ground technical advice and marketing assistance when needed.

Proshika views women's income-generation as a starting point for women's empowerment. By making a contribution to family income, women begin to gain the power to make decisions within the family. With the ability to earn income, women gain the means for survival and self-reliance. Proshika encourages women to undertake productive activities outside of the home which help alter the gender division of labour and creates opportunities for women to acquire new skills as well as to use new and higher technologies.

Proshika's approach to economic empowerment is well illustrated by the growth and development of the Jamuna and Lucky Mohila Samities. Jamuna Mohila Samiti began in 1989 after five women went to meet with a Proshika group in another village. The women expressed an interest in starting a similar group in their village and together with nine other women began saving Tk. 0.50 per member per week.[4] After four months of regular meetings and savings, Jamuna Mohila Samiti met with Proshika field staff at a meeting of two already active women's groups. Since then Jamuna Mohila Samiti and Proshika staff have been working together, and the group has grown to 20 members. Group members have participated in Proshika's practical skills training courses on livestock and environmental sustainability, among others. They have also used their savings and taken advantage of credit from Proshika to finance a cattle fattening project and a large-scale vegetable farming project. Through these and other actions, the group has become strong and has now attained a high level of self-reliance.

In 1990 Proshika encouraged Shahanara, now a member of Lucky Mohila Samiti, and Aleya, another woman from Dhaka's Mirpur E-Block slum, to take a human development training course to raise their awareness

---

[4] Tk.100 = US$2.50 as at July 1995.

about the problems that have caused their exploitation. Afterwards, Shaha-nara and Aleya organized ten other women and began to meet regularly at the Proshika urban poor development programme office in Mirpur. They had to do this secretly because the local *mastans*[5] tried to prevent the women from organizing. Some time later, other women also organized themselves to form three distinct Proshika women's groups in the slum. The three women's groups together used their first savings to make a Tk.1200 contribution towards the purchase of a tubewell in their slum, with the assistance of credit from Proshika. Due to the extreme scarcity of water, the tubewell made a great difference in women's lives. However, it was ruined in 1993 during their slum eviction. The Lucky Mohila Samiti has taken two other loans from Proshika, the most recent for sewing machines, embroidery workshops, small shops, and a rickshaw.

Both women's groups have been involved in major struggles which have brought women to the forefront of their communities. As the following sections detail, one of the Jamuna Mohila Samiti's major efforts has been to protect nearby forests while women in Lucky Mohila Samiti have worked with other Proshika groups to counter the *mastans* in their slum.

Protecting the Forests

In Paikpara, forest depletion is a serious problem which has been perpetu-ated by the local élite who have been engaged in cutting and uprooting trees for profit. Most land in Paikpara is government reserved forest land administered by the local Forest Department, and the actions of the élite have been unofficially sanctioned by some corrupt Forest Department staff.

From their personal experience, and through Proshika training on environmental sustainability and regeneration, members of the Jamuna Mohila Samiti realized that depletion of the forest was not only a serious threat to the environment but also to their livelihoods. In their parents' lifetimes, many types of fruit-bearing trees, vegetables and wildfowl were found in the forest. There was no longer such an abundance of wildlife, trees, and plants, and the forest mostly contained 'sal' trees. Women used the fallen branches and leaves of these trees for fuel and mulching[6] but recognized that even this use of the forest was threatened by illegal tree felling. Not long after forming their group, the women decided to take action to protect the forests from further destruction.

In 1990, women members of Jamuna Mohila Samiti began guarding the forest in shifts, despite the dishonour that inevitably follows women who challenge *purdah* and are publicly mobile and visible. Religious leaders,

---

[5] Hired thugs or racketeers paid for by powerful local patrons.
[6] Mulching is the process of protecting newly-planted saplings with leaves or other organic matter to preserve moisture.

village elders, and local government officials all opposed the women's presence in the forests, and their open disregard for *purdah*, and used means of intimidation to inhibit the women from continuing their actions. To some degree the grounds for this opposition were a pretext: the élite realized that they could no longer cut and uproot trees as easily and heedlessly as they had done before. They also recognized that the dependency of poor women on their wealthier neighbours had been eroded by the group's activities. Once the women began their group work, they less frequently needed to work as domestic labourers in the rich households because they had other income-generating activities. Women group members no longer needed high-interest loans from the rich money lenders (which often resulted in the borrowers losing whatever land or other assets they had if they failed to repay) because they could get low-interest credit from Proshika.

However, in the early period of women's forest protection activities, the village élite took the opportunity to strike back. They cut the trees that had grown quite tall under the women's protection and battered some Paikpara women who confronted them. After this incident, Paikpara women and men alike, with residents from nearby villages, mobilized a signature campaign followed by a rally of about 2000 people, including journalists, to protest the forests' destruction. They made it clear that they would rather die than stop protecting the forests.

Although the élite convinced some local forest officials to register false cases against some Paikpara women and men, these cases were eventually withdrawn. The rally drove the women's point home, and they have faced fewer problems from the élite, as well as other interest groups, since then. The women continue to maintain and protect the forest. They pruned the forest (cut dead branches from the trees) in February 1995 without permission from the Forest Department. Although the Forest Department knew about this work, they made no trouble for them this time.

With the assistance of Proshika, women are in the process of negotiating benefit-sharing with the government. They have proposed a scheme under which they (and other groups) would receive 40 per cent of the profits from wood cut during forest maintenance. Since groups in the community will assist the Forest Department with this maintenance, they will have a further incentive to protect the forest. Although it has been a long and drawnout process, Proshika staff feel an agreement may be forthcoming. The women are also negotiating with the government for *khas* land on which to build houses, since many Paikpara residents are landless.

Struggling for Slum Dwellers' Rights
Residents of the Mirpir E-Block slum in Dhaka confront threats of eviction, violence and extortion on a daily basis. They are struggling for the right to remain on the government land where they are now squatting and

72

to rid their slum of the menacing *mastans* who prey on the slum dwellers' vulnerable position.

In 1990, 18 women and men's groups banded together to take action against the *mastans'* daily harassment. One *mastan* had erected illegal power lines for electricity in the slums and was charging the residents for this service. The slum dwellers calculated how much he was earning from the illegal electricity supply and decided to stop paying him. With Proshika's assistance, the community successfully negotiated for a legal electricity line from the Dhaka municipality, paying for it with their own savings and loans from Proshika. However, several months later their slum was razed, and the electricity line was destroyed.

After the slum dwellers stopped buying electricity from the *mastan*, Shahanara, a member of Lucky Mohila Samiti, was beaten in retaliation for these actions. The *mastans* have always seen women joining Proshika groups as a threat to their activities. Before the slum dwellers organized, the *mastans* used the slum as a place for drinking and gambling. They also tortured and raped slum women, blaming other slum dwellers for this violence. Once the women became a united force against the *mastans*, they no longer feared these thugs and could confront them. Without inciting fear, the *mastans* could no longer 'control' the slum. For example, eight women's groups prevented Monir, a powerful *mastan*, from constructing a rickshaw repair garage in the slum. They argued that the slum dwellers needed the space for latrines, which were eventually constructed there.

The slum dwellers continued to struggle against the *mastans'* coercion. Through Proshika's human development training, they learned that the *mastans* had no right to collect rent in the slum because the government owns this land. In 1991 the slum community joined together to protest against the *mastans* and refused to pay them any more 'rent'. They also instituted cases against the *mastans* on numerous charges and succeeded in banning them from the slum.

In 1993 the slum dwellers faced another threat – eviction – when the government began to develop the land on which they were squatting. The squatters took action against the government in court, and a stay order on development was issued. For several weeks while the case was being heard, there was no land development. Ultimately, however, the court ruled against the slum dwellers, and land development continued. The squatters continue to live in the slum and have rebuilt their homes. Lucky Mohila Samiti members have also set up workplaces in the slum. They live in the hope that one day they will gain legal rights to the land on which they live, just as they have gained legal bans on *mastans* in their slum. One recent gain is the government's decision to give voting rights to slum dwellers and recording their slums as their places of residence on the voters' rolls.

ANWARA: A COMMUNITY LEADER

Anwara, a strong leader in Jamuna Mohila Samiti, is a unique individual in her community. Her husband died five years ago after a long illness, leaving her with two sons to raise. She knew that she had to work in order to educate her sons to graduate level. However, her husband's family was very religious and expected her to maintain *purdah*. In order to have the freedom to work, she has lived alternately in two of her brothers' houses in Paikpara since her husband died, instead of with her in-laws. Anwara is now living with one brother who is the president of the village co-ordination committee of which she is joint secretary.

Anwara's life has changed a great deal since joining the Proshika group. Before, she earned about Tk.100–200 per month from hand sewing clothing and quilts and making hand-held fans. Now, her monthly income is Tk.1000 per month as a tailor. Every three months she and fellow member, Adorjan, also rear silk worms with a Tk.700 Proshika loan. She does apiculture work, which she learned through Proshika skills training, once a week. With this money, she has educated her sons; one is taking his pre-college exams and the other had to leave school after Class 8 due to a lack of funds and is now working in his paternal uncle's store. This situation is of great concern for Anwara, and she is saving as much as she can to send her second son back to school.

At present Anwara has more leisure time than she did before she joined the group. She used to do domestic work all day when she first lived with, and was financially dependent on, her brothers. Now Anwara spends only three to four hours doing domestic work, assisted by her husband's sister, and tending livestock. She spends her other time doing tailoring, group work, and forest protection. Anwara feels that the most important work she does now is tailoring (for her economic development) and group work (for human development in the community). This is in contrast to her two priorities before joining the group: traditional hand sewing for economic survival and household work in her brother's house for domestic survival.

Since she is a widow, Anwara has full control over the money she earns. Before she joined the group and began earning an income she could only afford to buy one sari every three years, but now she buys four saris every year. Her mobility has also changed due to participation in the group. When she was dependent on her brothers she was not allowed to go to the market. When she goes to the market now to buy cloth, or for other reasons, she is not afraid because she gets respect from passers-by and the people from whom she buys. When her husband was alive and she lived in Dhaka, she worked at a tailoring shop in the marketplace. She hopes one day to set up a tailoring shop in the market itself so that she will get better rates and more orders. However, the market is too far from where she lives, so this is not possible at the present time.

74

Anwara has emerged as a leader in her group (she is the secretary) and in the community. Since she excels at reading and writing she helps Proshika groups in her village write all of their weekly meeting resolutions. She also periodically conducts adult literacy courses for Proshika group members and earns Tk.250 per month from this activity. She stands up to the Forest Department in support of the forest protection activities in her area. Because of her dedication to this community work, women and men treat Anwara with much respect. Anwara feels that the social benefit she has gained from her work in the community outweighs the economic benefit of her work.

NAJMA: STRIVING FOR INDEPENDENT INCOME

Najma is 24 years old and has a 6-year-old son. Her husband died one year ago, and she still lives with her in-laws, but boards separately with her son.

Najma's husband was the eldest son in the joint family of several brothers and their wives. When he was alive, Najma was in a position of respect as the wife of the eldest son. At that time, Najma worked alongside her husband making *bidis* (cigarettes). Now her financial sources are from egg production, growing vegetables, and domestic labour. Her father-in-law sells the eggs and vegetables at the market for her and gives her the earnings. As her income work is seasonal and unsteady she is only able to save temporarily, as the savings must be spent at times of no work. She occasionally must borrow money from her father-in-law or father.

After her husband's death Najma embarked upon a new stage of life, moving from a position of respect within her husband's family to a position of dependency. Her fellow group members understand her vulnerable position and have taken action to ensure that she will be able to fend for herself and her son if her in-laws stop supporting them – a situation which often occurs in these cases. They have successfully persuaded Najma's father-in-law to allow her to learn tailoring, usually a man's profession, so that Najma can have more independent income. Her in-laws now realize that Najma's work is her means of survival. Moreover, her in-laws do not object when it is necessary for Najma to do domestic labour in wealthy households – work which normally carries the risk of harassment from male members of these households. Since Najma has the support of her group, they see to it that she is treated fairly in any activity she undertakes.

Najma has been apprenticed to a tailor for more than a month now. Without the prospects of becoming a tailor in the future and earning her own income, Najma knows that she and her son would be entirely dependent on her in-laws. With tailoring skills, however, Najma will have the opportunity to be independent, and her in-laws and parents will be freed from providing her with financial support.

SHAHANARA: WORKING FOR SLUM DWELLERS' RIGHTS

Shahanara is a member of Lucky Mohila Samity and also the joint secretary in her slum federation's 17-member co-ordination committee (eight women and nine men). She is married and has two daughters and two sons.

Before Shahanara began doing group work, she spent about seven hours each day getting water because there was only one water source in the vicinity. The remainder of her day was spent on cooking, cleaning, and other household tasks. For a couple of hours each evening, however, she had some time to rest while she oversaw her children's studies. She had to be up by 6 a.m. went to sleep after 11 p.m.

Shahanara still rises at 6 a.m. but does not get to sleep until around 1a.m. Since there are now tubewells and wells within the slum, Shahanara spends only two hours getting water each day. She also spends only one hour cooking as she uses an electric cooker instead of firewood because there is electricity in the slum now. The time it takes for her to go marketing for food has also gone down four-fold as there is now a bazaar much closer to the slum. However, this saving in time has been replaced with the three to four hours she spends on group work and income generation – her total workload has actually increased. Early on, she had spent much time organizing women and persuading them to form a group, and now as a leader she provides assistance and advice to her own group, and other groups in the slum, as well as the slum federation and arbitrations.

Shahanara spends six to eight hours per day doing or overseeing embroidery work with her two sons. Before she began her embroidery work, Shahanara took a loan of Tk.30 000 from Proshika to start a shop selling pots, pans, and other metal goods. Several months later the slum was razed, and the entire shop was destroyed. Shahanara spent more than two years repaying the loan. Now, she does embroidery for ten months of the year, and during off-months she does whatever work she can find, such as selling vegetables at the market or hand-sewing designs on clothing.

Through her participation in the Lucky Mohila Samity, Shahanara has become a convincing speaker and a leader in the community. For example, a few years ago she was directly responsible for registering a court case and legally banning Monir, a powerful *mastan* in the E-Block slum, from entering the slum. This action resulted in the slum dwellers no longer having to pay him extortionate 'rent' and other 'fines', and quelled the other *mastans* who now make less trouble for the women. Shahanara also was one of the main arbitrators three years ago in a case in which a group member was battered by her husband because she went to her mother's house without telling him. Shahanara and the other community arbitrators had to confront the actions of a religious elder who had ruled in the husband's favour and had granted him a divorce.

Shahanara, her husband, and sons typically manage to earn about Tk.4230 per month which they use to pay expenses (food, Proshika loan repayments, electricity, group savings, clothing, medicine, and other items), sometimes saving a small amount for months when household income is less. Shahanara hopes to take another loan from Proshika to open a small shop or buy a rickshaw which she will rent. She would like to save her earnings to pay for training her children in tailoring and driving so that they are able to find jobs in the future.

SHORUFA'S STORY

Shorufa, the secretary of Lucky Mohila Samiti, is now a tailor and embroiderer – trades that she learned from friends and relatives. She and her husband moved to Dhaka soon after marriage, more than eleven years ago. At that time she worked in a garment factory and earned Tk.300–1000 per month. She spent much of her earnings on rent (Tk.600 per month), and she had little savings. When Shorufa and her husband managed to save some money to buy materials for a shelter, they were encouraged by Shahanara to move to the E-Block slum and squat there rent-free. That was over ten years ago.

Now Shorufa manages her household work around her tailoring and embroidering and is able to earn as well as save. Along with her 9-year-old son, she earns Tk.300–1400 per month, depending on the season. For tailoring, the peak months in 1995 were January and February and for embroidery the peak months were October through February. These peaks occur because there is a great demand for new clothing in the months leading up to Eid-ul-Fitr[7] which took place in March 1995. Shorufa's husband is a mosaic labourer who earns Tk.600–2000 per month, depending on the number of days he can find work. Shorufa's household expenses are similar to Shahanara's although her family spends about Tk.1500 for food because it is smaller. She also pays for doctors, medicine, clothes, group savings, electricity, school, and other necessities.

When Shorufa joined the group, she received human development training. She feels that the work she does now is not as exploitative as her job in the garment factory was. She also has less fear of being harassed when she ventures out of the slum. Since the slum dwellers have united against the *mastans*, Shorufa can now move freely around the slum and access markets independently.

---

[7] The Muslim festival following the month of Ramadan.

Economic Impact

By participating in the groups and accessing credit from Proshika, women have gained new opportunities for earning income. For example, members of Jamuna Mohila Samiti obtained a loan of Tk.37 000 from Proshika to purchase cattle. They then fattened the cattle and sold them. The group's forest protection activities have also afforded the women new income-generating opportunities as they now gather dry leaves and firewood for sale as fuel. Members of the Lucky Mohila Samiti have realized similar opportunities. Eight women took a loan of Tk.60 000 to purchase three sewing machines, two embroidery workshops, two small shops, and a tri-cycle rickshaw.

As a result of these projects and other Proshika interventions, many of the women say their incomes have increased. With their earnings, the women are now able to make loan repayments and contribute to household income. In some cases married women have been able to contribute half of the household's total income from their activities. Previous to joining a group, women typically had few income-earning activities and some of these activities, such as domestic work, were low-paying jobs based on exploitative relationships with local élites.

The experience of earning income through group activities has encouraged women to think of new ways to earn money. Although many of the women are engaged in activities that they have always performed in some way (such as raising cows, goats, chickens, fruits and vegetables), they are now concerned with ensuring that the output of eggs, milk, vegetables and fruits are enough for sale and not just consumption. Through experience and Proshika's training courses, women have become more aware of how to manage their time and finances than before, and they consciously fit their daily household work around income-generating work.

There are differences in control over earned income between the two groups. Three-quarters of Jamuna Mohila Samiti members said that they control the income they earn, whereas almost all of the Lucky Mohila Samity members reported having control over the income they earn. This difference relates in part to women's access to the market which in turn is related to income levels. Less than one third of Jamuna Mohila Samiti members go independently to the market. In the case of the cattle fattening project, a few women group members went with male relatives to buy the cows from the market and later to sell them. Those women who did not participate directly in the buying and selling had to receive their profit from their male relatives. Most women did not feel that their husbands or other male relatives cheated them out of any profit, but one woman said she would go to the market herself if she thought she had been cheated. All except one of the Lucky Mohila Samiti members travel to the market to buy food or to purchase goods, such as thread, for their income-generating work. While women in both groups are poor, women living in the slums are at the lower end of the poverty scale. Their extreme poverty ultimately makes it necessary for them to be mobile.

Women use the money they earn for consumption and production purposes. For example, many women in Jamuna Mohila Samiti have purchased metal roofs for their houses, beds and medicine, particularly for their children. The women also buy more saris of better quality, and some have been able to buy jewellery. They note that they would not have been able to make these purchases if they had not earned the money themselves. Many women use their earnings to reinvest in productive activities, such as poultry rearing. For Lucky Mohila Samiti women, increased income has resulted in more and better food, better clothing, and the ability to send their children to school. Women have also financed the building of homes in the slum. The assets of half of the group members have increased since they joined the group. Women, who previously had no assets, will become the owners of sewing machines, embroidery workshops, small shops, and a rickshaw when all their loan repayments have been made.

Increases in income have been accompanied by increases in savings. While women have always acknowledged the need to save money, few had the resources to put into savings. With the money they have earned from various activities, women have been able to save for their children's education and house construction, among other purposes. Savings also serve as a 'safety net' for women during times of slow business or illness. Many women work in occupations which are seasonal, and savings assist these families through times of low income.

Group savings have also increased over time and are often used to enhance women's productive capacities. Until recently, Jamuna Mohila Samiti's savings stood at Tk.11 000. Now, the women have invested Tk.2600 in a block plantation of commercial trees, given loans and emergency funds to members and have bought school material for Paikpara students and signboards for their forest protection effort. With their savings, and a loan from Proshika, the women have decided to reclaim land lost by one of the group members and use it for a large-scale group vegetable farming project. Lucky Mohila Samiti's savings stand at Tk.10 000. Recently the group used Tk.2000 of these funds for emergency loans to members. Money borrowed, however, is put back in the group savings fund as soon as possible.

Solidarity among the women has increased some women's bargaining power in the marketplace. In the E-Block slum, embroidery is a very common occupation for women. Women in all of the Proshika groups have set a fixed rate for their work. They charge Tk.60–190 per piece, depending on the amount of embroidery required. The women are well aware that there are women in other slums who are willing to work at lower rates, therefore the rate they set cannot be too much higher than the other rates as orders would simply be distributed elsewhere. Nevertheless, this strategy is effective in establishing a solidarity amongst the embroidery workers within the slum, who agree at the very least not to undercut each other.

Women in the group support the entrepreneurial efforts of group members, such as the tailors and the small shopkeepers, by becoming their regular clients. In turn, some of these entrepreneurs give fellow group members preferential rates. For example, among the tailors of Lucky Mohila Samiti there is an agreement to give fair rates to fellow group members in order to maintain their steady business.

Women are working to ensure that the economic gains they have made are sustainable over the long term. Although the women of Jamuna Mohila Samiti still struggle for social services, they feel their income earning work is sustainable at its current level. For instance, recognizing the pitfalls in depending on one type of animal rearing for income, women members of Jamuna Mohila Samiti have diversified from rearing only poultry to rearing goats, cattle and poultry and have taken on other income-generating activities. The women shopkeepers in Lucky Mohila Samiti feel that their businesses are sustainable and can expand. One of the small shop owners has already been able to increase the variety of items in her store as a result of the volume of business she receives. On the other hand, embroiderers and tailors are uncertain as to whether their work will expand and bring higher remuneration. It is critical to note that the sustainability of all work done in the E-Block slum depends to a large extent on how long the women can live in their slum.

From Economic to Overall Empowerment

Proshika's integrated approach of organization building, human development and skills training, credit, and income generation have brought economic, social, and political changes to the lives of Jamuna and Lucky Mohila Samiti members. One of the most important changes is that women now recognize that they can effect change in their households and communities. As the women have gained awareness and self-confidence, they have realized that they have choices and need no longer to be victimized. They are taking stands against exploitation, abuse, and unfair treatment from the élite, employers, *mastans*, husbands, and family members. In doing so, they are challenging norms about women's behaviour.

The work of the Jamuna and Lucky Mohila Samities provide excellent examples of how women have used their collective strength to struggle against oppressive and destructive practices. In both groups, poor women found that powerful groups of people (village élites in the case of Jamuna Mohila Samiti and *mastans* in the case of Lucky Mohila Samity) were impeding their ability to achieve sustainable livelihoods. Although neither of the two groups' efforts have come to a legal conclusion yet, they are well on their way. They have altered the long-standing notion that women cannot be actors in the public arena, much less forces for change. This breakthrough and the successes the women have had in bringing change have, in turn, made the women more self-confident than before and have given them a feeling of self-worth. Five Jamuna Mohila Samiti group members, who felt scared and whose families objected to them engaging in the controversial forest protection, left the group several months back. Now, however, they have returned to the group because they have seen the group's strength and resilience in the face of continuous threat and opposition from those who try to destroy the natural forests.

Group solidarity in these two groups extends beyond these major struggles. Group members help each other with child care and house building. Anwara, a tailor, gives her fellow Jamuna Mohila Samiti members good rates, and they use her services whenever possible. The women's groups have been instrumental in assuring that members' rights are recognized. When the former husband of a Jamuna Mohila Samiti group member, Ayorjan, abandoned her and illegally took a second wife, the group, in collaboration with the village federation, saw to it that he was jailed and then forced to take Ayorjan back. Ayorjan, however, decided not to go back to him and was compensated with Tk.5000. Not only do women help fellow group members, they also take up the causes of other women in the village and work with other women's and men's groups through the village and higher-level federations to make their voices heard. They have become arbitrators and now sit at arbitrations for the broader community.

The women's groups have become decreasingly dependent on Proshika and are taking on issues and activities in their own right. While Proshika is available to give them advice and support in taking on these issues, it is the women's organization that identifies important issues and seeks assistance from Proshika when it is required. For example, Jamuna Mohila Samiti has attained a high level of managerial capability, needing little assistance with its affairs. Anwara, the group's secretary, asks Proshika staff members to come only when the group needs assistance on particular matters. As the women's groups have become less dependent on Proshika, they have found strength through their participation in the federations. Lucky Mohila Samiti has taken on a number of issues with the slum federation and participates with various federations in collaborative activities, such as stage performances on International Women's Day and national holidays.

The empowerment that women have achieved at a group level is also felt at an individual level. Increases in women's contribution to the household income have eased the financial burden on other family members. Due to this increase in income some women report that their relationships with their husbands and other family members have improved and there is now less conflict and violence in the household. 'Where there is want, there is conflict,' noted one woman. The reduction in violence in some households

81

is also due to a change in women's response to violence; they stand up to their husbands now and no longer tolerate violence from them. Some women said that husbands even 'fear' their wives a bit now.

Increased income has reduced women's dependence on their husbands and other family members. For the majority of women in Lucky Mohila Samiti, this has translated into greater mobility than they had before. They can go marketing for food and other items themselves and do not have to wait until their husbands can go or have the money to go marketing. These women all move freely about the slum, while more than half also go to various parts of Dhaka city, including markets. They realize their worth and feel equal with men because they are able to work and earn money just as well as their husbands. Women embroiderers travel quite far from the slum to pick up orders and deposit them, as well as going to the market to buy the necessary threads and other materials. They do this without any assistance from male relatives. The tailors also work independently of their husbands, as do women shopkeepers.

Jamuna Mohila Samiti members have not realized the same increase in mobility. Less than one-third of Jamuna Mohila Samiti members go independently to the market. Although all the women agree that being poor forces them to be mobile, traditional thinking dictates that there is no need for women to go to the market if they have male relatives to go for them. As such, it is usually those women who are already outside of the restrictions of traditional culture – older women, widows, and those who are separated, abandoned or divorced from husbands – who access the market independently, largely because they have no alternative. All women, except one whose husband objects, travel to places other than the market such as the hospital, relatives' homes or the Proshika office. Yet Anwara and Najma's cases demonstrate that even widows have had to struggle against family members for the right to work outside of the home. Furthermore, these cases and Jamuna Mohila Samiti's forest protection activities illustrate that women have been able to overcome some restrictions on their mobility.

In pursing income-generating and group activities, women are challenging ideas about gender-typed occupations and gender roles. A few women in Jamuna and Lucky Mohila Samities have become tailors, a non-traditional occupation for women. Although hand-sewing is regarded as a women's occupation, tailoring is usually the domain of men as it generally involves interaction with both male and female customers and keeping a public shop. Women shopkeepers are also challenging existing norms about women's public visibility. In both women's groups there are strong women leaders who have become active and prominent at the community level. Such roles were uncommon for women before Proshika began ac-tivities in their areas. These women leaders and women business people are paving the way for future generations of women who will be active, visible and influential in their communities.

A recent study on Proshika reveals additional ways in which women have become empowered which are consistent with the findings from this case study. Women's literacy, a basic step towards empowerment, has increased as a result of Proshika's interventions. Twice as many Proshika women group members can write their names as compared to women who are not Proshika group members. They are also more often able to count to 100 and more often able to read and write.

Over the past two years Proshika members have had almost four times more marriages without dowry than those who are not Proshika members. The incidence of violence against women in Proshika members' households is also less than in other households. Women organized in Proshika groups are much more often involved in income generation and have decision-making power regarding the spending of money. Proshika women group members have decision-making power regarding investment twice as often as women who are not Proshika group members. They also make decisions on children's education, marriages, and family planning more often than their counterparts.

Towards Sustainability

Like many NGOs, Proshika works with its primary groups and federations to ensure that these organizations and their endeavours are sustainable over the long term. As long as women group members maintain the unity and potential for mobilization in their organizations, the changes they have brought about are unlikely to be reversed. It is those changes that have not yet occurred, for example in legislation, that threaten the sustainability of present gains. The more women are successful in bringing about favourable change, the more their confidence will grow to take on further challenges. For example, now that the women of the E-Block slum have challenged the *mastans* on some issues, they do not fear confronting them on other issues. Similarly, the women of Paikpara no longer fear confronting local élite and the local-level forest officials any time their forest protection work is threatened.

In addition, Proshika has recently begun to engage systematically in policy advocacy through its recently-established Institute for Development Policy Analysis and Advocacy (IDPAA). The organization views policy advocacy as the strategy through which all of the achievements and goals of Proshika organizations can be firmly established in the economy and society of Bangladesh. Therefore, Proshika is using its many years of experience at the micro (grassroots) level to advocate change at the macro (policy) level. For example, with the support of Proshika and IDPAA, policy changes may be made to enable Jamuna Mohila Samiti members to gain legal entitlement to profit from forest maintenance. Lucky Mohila Samity members may gain legal rights to, or be able to purchase, the land on which they have lived for so long.

CO-OPERATIVES

'Like my Mother's House':
Women's Thrift and Credit Co-operatives
in South India

NANDITA RAY and D.P. VASUNDHARA

This sangham[1] *is like my mother's house . . . I have the confidence that financial help is at hand in the hour of need.*

WHEN THE CO-OPERATIVE DEVELOPMENT FOUNDATION (CDF) began to promote women's thrift and credit groups, it saw this move as a first step towards the establishment of alternative financial institutions for women. Today, with a membership of just under 12 500 in Warangal and Karimnagar Districts, Andhra Pradesh, the process is well under way in the form of informal co-operatives. Alternative institutions such as these have become imperative due to the near-total failure of existing banking structures to cater to women's needs, or to reach them at all. This applies to women in all strata of society, although poor, rural women find it particularly difficult to access financial institutions. While the CDF's target groups live in the rural and generally dry regions of Andhra Pradesh, the popularity of thrift and credit groups in the state and elsewhere in India, South Asia and beyond proves that they fulfil a very basic need. They also have a fairly rapid multiplier effect both in terms of membership and the amount of funds saved and borrowed. While some critics may argue that this type of economic intervention achieves little more than an improvement in women's incomes and leaves basic gender inequalities intact, the impact actually goes much further. Without economic empowerment, women simply feel helpless against gender inequalities and usually do not even have the time to think about them in the course of their daily struggle for subsistence. The following case study assesses the CDF's efforts to empower women economically, and at the same time socially and politically. It focuses on the Mulukanoor and Narsampet Co-operatives in Karimnagar and Warangal Districts, respectively.

The Co-operative Development Foundation

CDF (which also bears the local name of Sahavikas) is a voluntary social action group established in 1982. Its primary objective is to promote

---

[1] *Sangham* literally means association and refers in this case study to the thrift and credit groups.

an environment where co-operatives may flourish as decentralized, democratic, self-help and mutual aid organizations, effectively harnessing and fostering local resources in consonance with the principles of co-operation, as enunciated by the International Co-operative Alliance. The co-operatives may be registered and formal, or unregistered and informal. The promotional activities of CDF are largely confined to paddy farmers' co-operatives and women's thrift and credit groups in Andhra Pradesh. It networks with thrift co-operatives of all kinds through its sister organization, the Federation of Thrift and Credit Associations (FTCA), which covers four states in South India.

When CDF started its promotional work, it had no specific emphasis on women. The CDF assumed that women would participate automatically in its various activities. However, few women could become members of the agricultural co-operatives as they did not own any land. Nor was CDF able to interest the largely urban, employee-based thrift and credit groups of the FTCA to increase the number of women members. Thus, CDF started the women's thrift and credit groups with the objective of helping women who so far had been excluded from co-operatives. Groups were, and continue to be, informal. In 1986 CDF initiated its first groups in Raipole, a village in Ranga Reddy District, adjoining Hyderabad. Subsequently, at the request of the state government and UNICEF, CDF helped form thrift and credit groups in association with government's DWCRA programme (Development of Women and Children in Rural Areas), in Cuddapah and Adilabad districts. These groups, with around 6000 members, have been federated into the Regional Association of Thrift Co-operatives under the FTCA umbrella. Subsequently, CDF decided to focus only on Warangal and Karimnagar Districts, where CDF was already doing promotional work with paddy farmers.

It has been CDF's policy to carry the menfolk with them in its women's activities, realizing that little could be gained from non-cooperation or confrontation between men and women For the most part it has been rewarded by men's active co-operation in supporting the women's thrift and credit groups, even though men had been unwilling to integrate women's issues into their paddy farmers' co-operatives. Today, the membership is growing steadily and neither CDF nor the women have looked back since they started working together in this area five years ago.

Women's Thrift and Credit Groups

In February 1990 CDF began promoting the women's thrift and credit groups in Warangal District, and six months later in Karimnagar District. By 31 October, 1994 there were altogether six co-operatives whose profiles are detailed in Table 1.

The rate of co-operative growth has been spectacular, particularly given that most of it has taken place since 1993. The total members' savings,

Table 1 Profiles of Co-operatives, March 1995

Co-operative name [1]	No. of thrift and credit groups	Age of co-op (months)	No. of co-op members	Total savings (Rs.) [2]
Makhdumpuram	37	46	1710	1 049 000
Machapur	52	26	2692	1 430 000
Narsampet[3]	21	35	1117	561 000
Mulukanoor	100	43	5657	2 879 000
Porandia	11	37	582	341 000
Gattundudenapalli	14	39	670	562 000
Totals	235[4]	–	12 428	6 822 000

[1] Makhdumpuran, Machapur and Narsampet Co-operatives are in Warangal District and Mulukanoor, Porandia and Gattundudenapalli Co-operatives are in Karimnagar District.
[2] Includes interest on savings.
[3] Narsampet Co-operative was earlier part of Makhdumpuram Co-operative.
[4] The total number of villages involved in the co-operatives is 90.

including interest, in 1995 was Rs6 822 000.[2] The total number of loans disbursed since inception is 39 825, amounting to Rs2.32 *crores*.[3] This is all the more impressive if one compares these figures with those from the Regional Association of Thrift Co-operatives (which is spread over four states and includes 300 primary thrift co-operatives) whose total funds amount to Rs2.50 *crores.*

The women's thrift and credit groups were originally organized on the basis of individual villages or hamlets with each village having its own president, secretary and accountant. A group of villages in a single geographically convenient area forms a single co-operative, of which there are six. However, in 1995 after a change in co-operative law (as detailed below), CDF decided to alter this structure partially in order to facilitate compliance with legal requirements, such as audits. Every village, or a village and its surrounding hamlets, which has a membership of 500 women will register as a co-operative. As this study was conducted while the new co-operative law was being enacted, the study mostly refers to the co-operative structures before the new law.

To facilitate the collection of savings and loan disbursement, the village organizations are being modelled on the basis of groups of 50 members each. Each group is divided into five sub-groups of ten members each and has a leader who is responsible for savings collection, preparing and scrutinizing loan applications and following up on repayments. The group leader also holds a group meeting every month for the transaction of all business, primarily the disbursement of loans. Women also discuss problems and other co-operative matters at the group meetings. The sub-group

[2] Rs100 = US$3.30 as at July 1995.
[3] One crore equals ten million.

leaders within each six co-operatives' area together form a Representative General Body, which in turn elects directors to a committee, meeting once a month. Generally, there is one director to represent each village, but if there are more than 200 members in a village, there are two directors. The committee is the main executive body for the co-operative and the sub-group leaders are the link between members and the co-operative. It is the committee which appoints, for every 2000 members, a bookkeeper and a facilitator. It also appoints an auditor for the co-operative and an office assistant. The committee elects a president and a secretary from among its own numbers. All members together form the General Body. At the end of 1993, the six co-operatives formed a Women's Regional Association of Thrift Co-operatives (WRATC). This currently has a secretary, who is also the president of the Mulukanoor Co-operative, Mrs Kotte Lakshmi, one of the oldest and most respected *sangham* members. It has not yet elected a president. WRATC has applied for registration under the Societies' Registration Act along with the Mulukanoor Co-operative.

The present system in virtually all the co-operatives is that members save Rs10 per month. The rate of interest is now uniformly 24 per cent on loans and 12 per cent on savings. Earlier, some village groups used to charge as much as 36 per cent. The loan entitlement is three times a member's savings, with an upper limit of Rs2000. New members now have to save for six months before they can take a loan, although in the beginning this was not the case. Group members are supposed to meet every month, but some attend meetings only when they need a loan. If there are more members requiring loans than there are funds, a decision on lending priorities is made at the meeting. Every borrower signs a contract and has to have a guarantor. Certain articles are used as collateral against a loan. Every member has a passbook in which transactions, interest and bonuses are entered.

Previously, surplus funds were kept in the custody of the president or at the local post office. Now they are transferred to a central account at the Mulukanoor Co-operative Rural Bank in the name of WRATC. This surplus may be loaned to individual co-operatives if they are short of funds for loaning purposes. Apart from pooling surplus funds, WRATC also administers a death relief insurance scheme, whereby all loans outstanding against a member at the time of death are written off. Members subscribing to it have agreed not to withdraw their bonus, the interest on which is used to finance the scheme.

The CDF decided to form thrift and credit groups because women lacked access to credit, a basic requirement for engaging in mainstream economic activity. Poor rural women work hard all their lives and have little to show for it in terms of savings or assets. Bankers are not interested in lending to women because they lack collateral in the form of land and property and because their requirements are very small, which makes processing expensive. Poor women, in particular, require small, timely loans, often for what are termed 'consumption' – meeting basic family needs. Their savings also are too small to interest the banks. Women's lack of mobility outside the village, illiteracy and inability to speak to male officials are further handicaps. As far as informal finance from moneylenders is concerned, loans are available at very high rates of interest, usually with jewellery or future produce to be sold at fixed rates as collateral. For the poorest even this may be inaccessible. Repayments usually have to be made in a lump sum, which is extremely difficult. Alternative financial institutions are thus an urgent need for women.

CDF feels that it is imperative to help women to build their assets. It helps them to do this through making their savings work for them from the beginning. Women save between Rs10 and Rs20 per month, depending on the group. The size of the loans grows with savings, as does women's capacity to use larger sums of money. There are no restrictions on consumption loans as poor women cannot function if basic needs such as food, health and shelter are not met. However, there is great emphasis on timely repayment, which is ensured through group pressure. Two internal studies by CDF have revealed that over time the proportion of productive loans increases along with women's ability to absorb money productively. Starting with loans for household expenses and health, women take loans for house repairs and children's education, then for agriculture and their families' existing economic activities, and finally for new businesses or economic activities.

CDF believes that organization-building should accompany savings and credit activities so that women learn to run their own groups and can move towards managing their own financial institutions. They further believe that democratic functioning develops women's capabilities and leads to greater independence, both economically and otherwise. Most of CDF's input after group formation is in the form of enhancing women's management skills. CDF has trained women in co-operative principles, preparation of by-laws, running of meetings (including minute-taking), accounting, and monitoring. Today, most of these tasks are done by the co-operatives themselves. The co-operatives have appointed their own bookkeepers, facilitators and auditors. In 1995, for the first time, the co-operatives were responsible for the preparation of their own accounts. The objective of this training is to ensure women's control over their institutions in a manner that best serves their needs. CDF feels that whatever the legal form these organizations may eventually take, the co-operative principles of democratic self-help based on local resources form the surest basis for long-term sustainability and autonomy. This is one of the major premisses of CDF's approach to women's economic empowerment, and it is fundamentally no different from the general principles under which it operates.

Membership is open to all women who wish to save and are in need of loans. The assumption is that those women who are well off (not a large number in these rural areas where agriculture is uncertain) generally will not be interested in small savings and loans. Such women prefer to keep a social distance from their poorer neighbours. However, there are some members who cannot be categorized as poor or needy, and there are others who have fallen on bad times even though they belong to normally better-off castes. They, too, savour the independence and solidarity with other women which the groups have brought them. As such, there is no justification for barring them, provided they work for the good of the organization and their fellow women. In practice a few have made important contributions to the thrift and credit groups, since they usually have a slightly higher level of education than other women in the group, useful management skills (acquired in the course of managing their agricultural lands), and the ability to contribute more time to the organization than their poorer neighbours. CDF believes that it is necessary to draw upon the resources of as many women as possible because all women suffer various degrees of financial and social disability. In general this policy has worked well, and women from all strata of society have participated in making the thrift and credit groups a success, while feeling a sense of solidarity with each other as women.

Another distinctive feature of CDF's approach is that at the thrift and credit groups' stage of development, it does not believe in the introduction of external funds to expand the lending base. This policy makes the women far more independent, and they take pride in their self-sufficiency. It also makes control over default much easier because women seem to have far less patience with the erring member when 'their own money' is involved. Although offers of funds to enhance savings have been made as a result of the success of the Warangal and Karimnagar thrift and credit groups, so far the women themselves have turned down these offers. CDF feels that although there may be a case for larger loans and the input of external funds at a later stage, the women are not yet ready for this and an influx of money from outside may undermine discipline and adversely affect the organization. Even at a later date extra funds could be accessed from within the thrift/co-op structure, thus making external financing unnecessary.

Recently CDF has started a literacy drive among the women so that they may at least be able to read their passbooks. The low levels of literacy, even among the leaders, has become a constraint as it prevents the leaders from maintaining proper control. In spite of women's poor response to this initiative, CDF is persisting in the task because of its importance. Skills training is needed also, but CDF believes that this is better provided by other organizations in the area with which it has created linkages.

The ultimate goal of CDF's work is the self-sufficiency of the co-operatives. For this to occur, financial independence is necessary. CDF has actively encouraged this process and substantial progress has been made in this direction. The co-operatives pay most of their own expenses, such as the salaries of the bookkeepers, facilitators, auditors and half of that of the secretary. The computer was financed through a soft loan from CDF, but maintenance costs will be paid by the Mulukanoor Co-operative, which in turn will charge for services to the others. The cost of arrangements for the General Body meetings (e.g. microphone, snacks, photographs, printing of annual reports and invitations) are all borne by the co-operatives. Travel costs are usually paid by the members themselves, but the enthusiasm for these meetings is such that this is no deterrent. In 1994 more than 2300 women attended the 5th Mulukanoor General Body meeting. At the Narsampet General Body meeting, the first since it separated from the Makhdumpuram Co-operative, 350 women were present. Some women even attend the General Body meetings of their sister co-operatives.

Co-operative Advocacy: Creating a Better Environment for Co-ops in Andhra Pradesh
CDF is involved in co-operative advocacy both within and beyond Andhra Pradesh. Recently, it was engaged in a major effort for a change in the co-operative law both at the central and state government levels. The primary purpose was to free the co-operative sector from excessive government control and interference and to make the laws relating to co-operatives enabling, rather than controlling, instruments.

The Andhra Pradesh Mutually Aided Co-operative Societies Act of 1995 was enacted on 4 May, 1995. The effect of this act has been to restore member control of all co-operatives which do not hold government share capital and to allow informal organizations, such as CDF's women's thrift and credit groups, to register as formal co-operatives. The women's thrift and credit groups have begun to register as co-operatives under the new act, and CDF hopes that other groups outside of the CDF umbrella will follow their example. It is proposed that many of the old, informal co-operatives, such as Mulukanoor Co-operative, register as a co-operative federation. Makhdumpuram and Narsampet Co-operatives may join forces and register as a co-operative federation. The CDF ultimately hopes to register a state-level federation of women's thrift co-operatives.

Economic Impact

Table 2 shows the growth of women's co-operative membership in the Warangal and Karimnagar Districts and the growth in funds. Membership size and financial growth are no longer problems as the co-operatives continue to grow in all respects. Due to this success the women's thrift and credit co-operatives have attracted considerable notice. Recently the World Bank conducted a study of the Mulukanoor Co-operative. The

Kotte Lakshmi: Leading the Co-operatives Forward

Kotte Lakshmi lives in Kothapalli, a village adjacent to Mulukanoor. She is neither poor nor well-off, and when the representatives of the CDF came to her village to promote the savings and credit groups, she was interested. Women like Kotte typically have no assets, no access to credit, and no savings to fall back upon in their old age. Also there are many times when they need small amounts of credit for consumption or production purposes.

The idea of women organizing to address problems of credit and savings caught Kotte's attention, and she decided to join the group. Kotte worked as a cultivator, but her husband paid the first instalment of her savings. In July 1990 the group began with 116 women, and another 160 joined during the second month. Kotte participated in group decision-making and by the third meeting, she was chosen to be the group's president. She recalls that she was initially afraid to sit on a chair and had to ask her husband what it meant to be 'president'.

Other *sanghams* were formed around Mulukanoor, and membership grew by leaps and bounds. Kotte was so successful in running her *sangham* and in advising other groups that she was elected in December 1991 to be president of the Mulukanoor Co-operative. Her leadership skills and knowledge were such that she made appearances on television and radio. Her radio programme was repeated every two months as the whole concept of thrift and credit groups grew in popularity.

Kotte is a soft-spoken and unassuming woman who found her voice and her calling when she started working with women. She attributes her strength to the strength of the women behind her. Kotte regards her rise as a public figure as not extraordinary: 'When people ask for that sort of help, you have to get out of the house and help them'. A friend and colleague notes that Kotte is a successful leader because of her patience which moves the co-operative forward. Kotte's leadership was further recognized in 1995 when she assumed the post of secretary of the Women's Regional Association of Thrift Co-operatives, the first paid position she has held.

Reflecting on the success of the co-operatives, Kotte notes: 'Initially, we just saved Rs10; we never thought we would bring the "cart" so far.' She is happy in her position of pulling the 'cart' and envisions a prosperous future for the co-operatives. Her vision for the co-operatives includes 'bigger loans, as with a bank. Helping women acquire larger capital assets, promoting larger businesses.' She clearly is not afraid to think big.

Table 2 Growth of Co-operatives in Warangal and Karimnager Districts

Year	No. of members	Savings (Rs.)	Total funds (Rs.)	Loans disbursed (culmulative) (Rs.)
1990–91	2 307	168 822	183 337	416 330
1991–92	6 021	740 756	834 061	2 135 208
1992–93	10 221	1 838 257	2 069 612	4 109 027
1993–94	11 536	3 390 625	4 099 938	9 353 402
1994–95	12 428	5 344 924	6 822 957	23 248 151

purpose of the present study is to assess the extent to which savings and credit activities promoted by CDF has led to the empowerment of women as a whole.

The primary reason why women join the *sangham* is ready access to loans at reasonable rates of interest. These rates – set at 24 per cent by the women themselves – may seem very high to outsiders but the women are used to even higher rates. Among the 24 women interviewed (12 each from the Mulukanoor and Narsampet Co-operatives), the Mulukanoor members had taken 60 loans since they joined the co-operative and the Narsampet members had taken 42 loans. Taking into account the number of years each woman had belonged to the co-operative, Narsampet and Mulukanoor members took on average one loan per year. Women's loan amounts ranged from Rs200 for new members to around Rs2000 for older members.

Women remember very clearly the number of their loans. Of the women interviewed, two women (one from each co-operative) had taken seven loans each, the most taken by any women in the sample. Two others in Mulukanoor have taken six loans each. The large number of loans taken by these women is evidence of the high rates of repayment within the co-operatives, the terms of which are usually fixed at the monthly meetings. These terms generally do not allow loans to remain outstanding for more than a year.

The number of loans women take for productive purposes tends to increase over time. Table 3 shows that in Mulukanoor, the proportion of business loans is substantially higher than in Narsampet where the membership is newer. Women's involvement in economic activities has increased substantially as they have accessed loans. Women have been able to start new businesses and expand old ones. The businesses, both old and new, consist of small grocery stores, tea/coffee and *paan*[4] shops, spice grinding units, vegetable vending, home-based cut piece cloth businesses and tailoring, bangle selling and a desilting crane. Of the 24 women interviewed, 14 believe that they now have more choice in the selection of

---

[4] Leaves containing a sweet paste, betel leaves and a mixture of spices.

Table 3 Purposes of Loans in Mulukanoor and Narsampet Co-operatives.

Purpose of loan	Mulukanoor Co-operative		Narsampet Co-operative	
	No. of loans	Percentage of total loans	No. of loans	Percentage of total loans
Business	13	22	8	19
Agriculture (business ventures: e.g. water buffalo, poultry)	10	17	0	0
Agriculture (e.g. agricultural inputs, wells)	17	28	6	14
Children's education	5	8	2	5
Household expenses	6	10	12	29
Health	3	5	5	12
Jewellery (gold and silver)	2	3	4	9
Other	4	7	5	12
Total	60	100	42	100

Based on a sample of 12 women from each co-operative.

economic activities, while two others said that they have more opportunities but have not taken advantage of these so far. Four women from Mulukanoor noted that as a result of their membership of the *sangham*, their credit-worthiness with other financial institutions and money providers had improved, thus giving them greater access to funds.

Greater access to loans and the ability to save has made women feel economically independent, although women defined this independence in a variety of ways. A few women stated that it was good now not to have to depend on others for loans – 'earlier I had to beg others for money, now I'm independent.' Others noted that 'instead of knocking on several doors for a loan, we can borrow from our *sangham* whenever necessary and prosper' and 'today if 10 of us get together, we can raise Rs10 000.'

The ability to borrow without collateral and in a timely manner figures in some women's definitions of 'economic independence.' In the past women did not have access to loans without pledging or pawning articles of value. Alternatively they had to pledge their produce to merchants at lower than market rates. One woman noted: 'Earlier we did not know where to get money. With the *sangham* it's very convenient and we can get money at convenient times also.' The increase in the ability to repay is also important, as it is the normal practice among money lenders to expect repayment in a lump sum and not in easier instalments. Surprisingly the rate of interest does not figure as large as might have been expected and only a couple of women mentioned it – 'previously we used to borrow at high rates of interest and face a lot of difficulties but now we are able to meet our needs easily.'

Many women from Narsampet expressed 'economic independence' in terms of independence from their husbands. They felt it was good not always to have to ask their husbands for money, although women who work as agricultural labourers or who run their own businesses may always have had some control over money. Most women talked about their role in family decision-making. Whether or not the women spend any of the loans on themselves personally was considered a good indicator of independence. Over half of the respondents spend money on their own needs, which include health care, clothing, and jewellery. It should be remembered that jewellery is considered a personal asset by most women. Also, the fact that some women are actually spending money on their own health speaks of a change in attitude, as this is usually the last priority in the family. Some women are simply savouring having some spending money of their own – 'if I want to buy a sari or something else,' said one woman, 'I now do it straightaway.'

Women have a greater sense of financial security now than before joining their co-operative. The most frequent reason given for this security was that their money was within their own organization and therefore secure. Poor women, and sometimes others, often have nowhere to keep their money safely. At home, it may at any time be taken away by their husbands. Many were originally suspicious of the CDF's activities. A comment by one woman illustrates this point well: 'Previously, we thought the "madams" would run away with our money. Today we look forward to their visits to share our problems and experiences.' In general CDF and the leadership of the co-operatives have won the women's trust. Although problems with group leaders surface from time to time, on the whole it is not an obstacle to the success of the co-operatives. The CDF places great emphasis on proper training and systems and emphasizes the safety of money as an ingredient of security.

There were other reasons why women felt that their financial security had increased since joining the co-operative. For some women, the ability to save and to increase their savings was a sign of security. Others noted the improvement of their financial situation and having 'money at hand' as their reasons for feeling secure. One woman said quite movingly: 'This *sangham* is like my mother's house. I have the confidence that financial help is at hand in the hour of need.' A few women made general statements that they felt secure because the *sangham* was behind them. Other reasons that women gave were the ability to repay loans, ability to manage their finances better, timely availability of loans and that 'husbands now come to us for money.'

Women's confidence has also increased as a result of joining the *sanghams*. As one woman expressed: 'I feel now that I can take up any work and do it.' Since it is CDF policy to ensure that growth in savings and credit go hand in hand with ability to organize and manage the same, the women have developed considerable financial and managerial skills through their involvement with the co-operatives. Women's ability to manage their personal and organizational finances has made them confident in their economic ventures. At present, the routine operation of the *sanghams* is being managed by the women themselves, who less than five years ago knew nothing about these things. The organizations' bookkeepers and auditors, with the help of some literate leaders, ensure that proper accounts are maintained, rules and regulations followed and members kept suitably informed. In 1995 for the first time all co-operatives were given the task of finalizing their own annual accounts for the general body without CDF's assistance. The bulk of the organization for the general body was done by the women themselves, with CDF only as an observer.

As women within the *sanghams* have gained experience in running these organizations, they find that they need CDF's assistance less and less. Women noted that the *sanghams* can now manage without CDF, for the most part. One member stated, 'They [CDF staff] are the ones who taught us everything. Now we don't have to listen to them.' Today CDF's role is more of a friend, philosopher and guide, and it is mostly involved in strategic planning for the next stage of co-operative development rather than conducting routine operations (for example, dealing with loan defaults and attending to other administrative details) which the women are well able to do themselves. CDF is currently helping Kasi Viswanath Mahila Podupu *sangham* at Mulukanoor computerize its accounts. For this purpose, CDF selected five possible computer accounting systems, the features of which were explained to the leaders. However, the women made the final system selection, demonstrating the level of sophistication which many have reached. It is expected that this group, in turn, will provide computer services to the smaller co-operatives.

Most women's skills in money management have improved since they joined the *sangham*. One woman said that she had learned 'the value of money', another stated that she had become 'more thrifty', and another noted that she was now 'able to invest wisely'. 'Before, we used to spend irresponsibly,' said one woman, 'now we save and use money whenever necessary'. Oral counting and handling capacity was mentioned as having improved.

Although still overawed by large numbers, women's ability and confidence to handle money is increasing. Of those women who were asked about the balance in their thrift account (including interest), 66 per cent could recall this amount, another 20 per cent knew approximately how much was in their accounts, while 13 per cent did not know at all. However, few women knew how much money was in their village cluster or group fund. Generally the leaders also have only an approximate idea. The low level of literacy is the main factor which explains this situation. Furthermore, most women find it difficult to think in large sums since, until now, they have had little or no opportunity to deal with this much money. While most women understand the lending practices of the *sangham*, and there are few disputes regarding outstanding balances and interest charged, the financial position of the *sangham* is understood by very few. Unfortunately, this is one factor which causes suspicion towards the leaders. Originally, when amounts were not banked, there were one or two instances where amounts not lent out were misused. However, now all surpluses have to be banked with WRATC after the monthly meetings. The women have reached a sufficient degree of financial sophistication to understand and accept this.

Women have been particularly successful in the management of loan defaults. Even the rank and file of members jealously guard what they consider to be 'our own money'. 'Previously,' said one woman, 'we had little money. Now we have money in thousands and *lakhs*,[5] and we are constantly thinking of how to safeguard and disburse it.' One leader claimed that she spent sleepless nights worrying about how to secure the groups' funds. One of the ways in which women said they helped their *sangham* was by making sure that women repaid loans on time. There have been times when women have acted in a group to discipline an erring member. For example, a leader in one of the villages selected for this study had taken several loans in various members' names and failed to repay them on time. The women sorted out this and other default problems themselves, and the matter was duly reported at the Narsampet representative general body meeting.

The overall loan default rate fell for all the co-operatives from 5.4 per cent of total loans to 2.2 per cent during 1993–94 and from 2.2 per cent to 1.13 per cent in 1994–95. It may fall even further with the closer monitoring introduced with computerization. Currently, much depends on the individual sub-group leaders.

The economic impact of the thrift and credit-co-operatives goes beyond the individual woman and her family to the larger community she lives in. Women feel that if a substantial number of women in a village benefit economically, then the entire village benefits. 'Previously,' one woman commented, 'we lived in isolation. After watching others improving financially as a result of the co-operative, one after another everybody joined. In this way the *sangham* is helping everybody prosper in the village'. These and other similar remarks show the cumulative effect of thrift and credit activity, specially in those villages where the bulk of households are members. For example, during the long drought period in Mulukanoor, the *sangham* made loans available for deepening wells and other uses, thus preventing migration. These loans were particularly important because interest rates from other lenders during this period were around 5 per cent per month. Also in Mulukanoor all members in one village took a special

---

[5] One lakh equals one hundred thousand.

loan to get a piped connection to their house from an overhead tank provided by Andhra Pradesh Council of Science and Technology. Furthermore, the co-operatives' interest rate of 24 per cent per annum has forced other lenders to lower their rates. Women in a village in Narasampet reported that the interest rate outside the *sangham* dropped from 36 per cent to 30 per cent per annum.

Beyond Economic Empowerment

The economic impact of the thrift and credit co-operatives on women has been considerable, although women consider other impacts of participation in the co-operatives to be as important as, or even more important than, the financial benefits. As a result of co-operative membership, women have realized greater confidence, security and independence and have gained respect inside and outside of the household as well as a greater awareness of issues affecting them and their communities.

Women have gained confidence from an increase in their relative financial independence and security. One way in which this confidence has been manifested is in women's increased confidence in dealing with a range of problems, including those outside the family sphere and in the community. One woman noted: 'I used to be scared even to discuss financial or other matters with others. Today, I'm able to handle any situation.' The majority of women interviewed now feel confident to handle problems outside the family, which they were unable to do earlier.

Women's involvement with the co-operatives has also increased their ability to speak in meetings and to authority figures. All women felt that they had become more articulate, at least on a one-to-one basis, and most believed that they had become more confident in speaking to strangers (such as the women who interviewed them for this study) and authority figures. Women have also become more comfortable speaking in public fora and group meetings. 'Before', said one woman, 'I never spoke to anyone on any subject. Now the strength of the members gives me the strength to speak to anybody.'

Women have become more mobile as a result of their *sangham* activities. However, it must be remembered that those working outside the home already had some degree of mobility. Most members agreed that mobility outside the village has increased with travelling between villages for *sangham* meetings. Some women have travelled for the first time outside of their district to attend *sangham* activities.

Women view the co-operative as their window to the outside world and as a place where women can discuss their problems with each other, indicating that the co-operatives have had a profound impact on many women. The members consider the unity and solidarity among the women in the *sangham* to be one of the most important benefits of membership. Women

98

of different castes and classes meet for a common purpose in the *sangham*, a situation which is new for many who are used to a hierarchical and divided society. Women in Narsampet Co-operative noted that the absence of caste desegregation in the *sangham* was an important change in their villages. The solidarity in the co-operative gives women, used to the isolation of their homes, somewhere to go to share their problems and seek help. For widows and single women who face particular pressures in society, the co-operative is a refuge.

There are a few members who do not appear to be in great financial need but who are members for the sake of companionship and the sense of solidarity with other women. Such a woman is Jayapradha, president of the Narsampet Co-operative, who joined because as a literate woman she was persuaded to contribute to the co-operative. Although a cultivator, her talents were obviously not sufficiently stretched. Other women asked her: 'What is a woman like you doing spending so much time watching television and reading novels?' Not many women would dispute that Jayapradha has contributed greatly to the co-operative. She has spend long hours working to revive an organization plagued by default and a flagging membership.

Membership involvement is key to the success of any co-operative, and most women take this responsibility very seriously. The level of participation was high among the women interviewed, and the majority attend meetings on a regular basis. A committee director in the Narsampet Co-operative noted that she had only missed one meeting in five years. Membership participation goes beyond simply attending meetings, and most women actively engage in decision-making during the meetings. Also they take the responsibility to ensure that others repay loans regularly, and occasionally make the thrift contribution on behalf of other members who may be away. In one instance where the village *sangham* was malfunctioning one member decided to intervene. Ketamma (who recently stood for the local *mandal*-level elections) explains: 'When one of the leaders was not performing and it affected the *sangham* affairs, I took over the responsibility as leader and coped with the situation.' Today confidence in the group is restored, and the membership is increasing again. In another instance a leader lent Rs5000 to a member without informing the other members, which was against the rules. When the membership learned what had transpired they took her to task, threatening to take possession of her house and electric pumpset. She was made to repay the loan with a penalty.

Families who have taken a hostile stance against women's participation in the *sanghams*, seem to have been the exception rather than the rule. Two-thirds of the husbands of the respondents were described as 'supportive'. Others were indifferent, sceptical about the advantages of co-operative membership, or initially hostile. One woman describes the transformation of her husband's attitude about the co-operative: 'In the

99

beginning he asked, "Why do women need a co-op? Why should they go out? The work is getting delayed. Complete your job at home." Now he says "you must go to learn about various things that are happening. You are a free citizen." He recognizes us [co-operative members] in this way.' Another woman noted a similar change: 'Would they [the men] have let us sit like this before? Now they urge us to attend even if it means missing work.' Some women have been quite successful at negotiating more independence within and outside of the household. For example, Edla Bharati, a former co-operative president and committee member seems to go her own way, apparently without protest from her family. She allowed herself to be interviewed late at night while her family waited for their dinner. 'We are minimizing housework,' she said, 'and spending most of our time with the *sangham*.'

There are two main reasons why husbands have not been against women's involvement with thrift and credit groups. The first is that CDF was careful at the outset to take the men along with them and that the organization's credibility was already established with the men. The second is that men realized that the co-operatives' activity was to their own economic advantage. 'No matter how much men borrow for agricultural purposes,' said one member at a group meeting, 'it's never enough.' Women have helped support many family economic activities and have added to family incomes. However, the rise in women's status has aroused the hostility of the 'elders' or male leaders in at least one of the villages studied. Also, although most women said that their mothers-in-law were supportive or indifferent to their involvement with the co-operatives, there was at least one mother-in-law in the study area who felt that her daughter-in-law was going beyond the bounds of decorum. 'What is happening,' this mother-in-law is reported to have said, '[is that] she [the daughter-in-law] is actually going out with her brother-in-law to solve village problems!' Another mother-in-law who had been initially critical of her daughter-in-law's involvement with the *sangham* has now joined herself.

With a few exceptions, all women said that they participated in family decisions. One woman stated that she advises her husband on which crop to grow, an unusual role since men typically take decisions regarding agriculture with little consultation with their wives. Another woman had the opposite experience: 'No I don't take any decisions. I can only do things with his guidance.' Still another woman noted: 'Usually I follow my husband's advice but when necessary I take my own decisions.' While women said that decision-making was a joint process, it was not clear to what extent it had changed as a result of the women's membership in the co-operative. There were, however, some indications that change has taken place. One woman said that she had gained greater recognition in the family because she could now meet her own needs, while another explained that earlier her opinions had little value in the household, implying that they were now solicited and valued. A few women stated explicitly that family members now seek their advice, and others noted that due to their co-operative activity, they made decisions regarding themselves (purchases and movement outside of the household, for example) independently. As one of the co-operative leaders remarked: 'Men never heard what we said earlier. Now that our value has increased, it is not like that.'

As a result of their participation in the co-operatives and their financial success, women have earned the respect of those in the community. Referring to women's status in the community, one woman noted; 'It has changed and will go on changing. I feel awareness, freedom, knowledge, courage.' Widows and single women have particularly benefited from an increase in status in their communities. The neighbours of a very poor widow noted that although she is 'alone in all the world' because of her involvement in the co-operative 'she can live'. Furthermore, through her participation in the *sangham*, the widow has become empowered to participate in the political process in her area. She refused to vote for a local politician, telling him that he had not even got her a ration card[6] – in short, he had done nothing for her. As women's opinions become respected and recognized in the community, politicians have started coming to the *sanghams* to find out how their members will vote. This respect and recognition is very important to the women. 'Respect at home and outside has increased,' said one woman, 'I feel freedom.'

Women are becoming involved in the community as a result of their experience with the co-operative and consider such work to be important. 'My whole outlook has changed,' said one woman confidently. Another commented: 'Previously we only used to think about the family. Now we think of all of us.' In more than one village the active intervention or advice of the *sangham* is sought on community matters. One *sangham* arbitrated in a divorce case, taking a stand against a People's War Group (local leftist guerrillas) member, one of the parties concerned. In another case, *sangham* leaders were consulted about the installation of sanitary latrines in their village. In 1995 in the local government *mandal* elections, four women members stood for election from women's reserved constituencies. One of these women was interviewed for this study. If elected, she hopes to be able to represent women's interests.

Toward the Future

Women generally see a bright future for their co-operatives and believe that they are sustainable. While the co-operatives must deal with a variety of problems (such as the safety of increasing funds; members quitting

---

[6] A card which allows people below the poverty line to buy essential commodities at subsidized prices.

because they want to enjoy their thrift before they die; the need to increase membership in some areas; and the necessity to increase efficiency), these are problems which the co-operatives will solve in due time. Regarding interference from outside, political or otherwise, most women felt that the organizations have demonstrated that they are strong enough to deal with such issues.

Women have suggested future activities for the *sanghams*. Some women want a rural bank for women on the lines of the Mulukanoor Co-operative Rural Bank, while others would like a superbazaar or co-operative store. Several women suggested that the *sangham* provide training for income generation activities, such as sericulture, basket weaving and tailoring and for setting up shops dealing in women's accessories. Providing such training is against CDF policy on thrift co-operative activity, but the women who desire this activity are free to organize training for themselves. It is CDF's objective to enable women to organize their own economic activities, not to do it for them. A few women simply wanted their organization to grow and become more efficient – 'everybody should be inspired to join' – and one particularly poor woman wanted financial counselling for the members. The latter is not done in any formal way though members do advise each other informally. Kotte Lakshmi, the secretary of the WRATC, believes that the co-operative will strengthen and evolve over time. Using a rural metaphor, she said: 'Ideas will grow with the experience; "as you go down the well, you will understand the depth." '

Rural Women Manage their own Producer Co-operatives: Self Employed Women's Association (SEWA)/Banaskantha Women's Association in Western India

SHARIT BHOWMIK and RENANA JHABVALA

WOMEN HAVE INITIATED a new wave of economic development in the arid environment of Banaskantha District, Gujarat State, India. Persistent drought, interrupted occasionally by heavy floods, is common in this district, forcing much of the population to migrate seasonally. Until the Self Employed Women's Association (SEWA) began its activities, little had been done to improve the lives of the women in the district who had the lowest literacy rate and per capita income in Gujarat.

The Self Employed Women's Association

The Self Employed Women's Association (SEWA) is a trade union founded in 1972 to organize the weakest, most exploited section of workers – self-employed women. Self-employed women are extremely vulnerable both economically and socially. They earn less than a minimum wage and have no assets of their own. Their employment is insecure and often there is no work at all. They have limited access to social services such as health and child care. They belong to the weakest social groups and, as women, they have few rights within the family.

Self-employed workers in India comprise about 93 per cent of the labour force. SEWA's membership falls into three broad categories of self-employed workers. First, there are the small-scale traders and hawkers who sell various goods (for example, vegetables, fruits, fish and household wares) from baskets, carts or small shops. Home-based workers, such as weavers, potters, and garment-makers, constitute a second category. The third membership category consists of manual labourers and service providers, including agricultural labourers, construction workers, head loaders and domestic workers. All together, SEWA's membership totalled 220 000 in 1995.

In its work over the last two decades, SEWA has developed a joint strategy of struggle and development. Struggle strategies relate to SEWA's role as a trade union to protect its members. Such strategies include securing minimum wages for self-employed women, obtaining licences for street vendors and striving for laws that protect home-based workers from exploitation and legal rights for street vendors. However, SEWA recognizes that for self-employed women, struggle strategies are often not enough. There may be no one employer to struggle against and, in rural areas, work is often only available on a temporary or seasonal basis, forcing workers to migrate from place to place in search of work. Given these conditions, a developmental approach is necessary to assure secure employment for women. To address women's employment needs, SEWA has helped its members to organize co-operatives. These co-operatives promote employment and allow women to become the owners of the products of their labour. SEWA has promoted over 70 different types of co-operatives, including dairy, gum collection, patchwork and block printing co-operatives. In addition, access to social security is required as a support to their lives. SEWA has helped the women to organize co-operatives providing health care, child care, insurance and housing.

How SEWA Entered Banaskantha

Because of SEWA's reputation of representing the interests of poor women, the Gujarat government and the Centre for Women's Development Studies (a Delhi-based women's research organization) asked SEWA to evaluate a piped water scheme from the poor rural women's point of view. Finding that the scheme was not reaching these women, SEWA made several recommendations to improve the scheme, including making it more participatory. Impressed by this work, in 1988 the Gujarat government requested SEWA to participate in the socio-economic component of the scheme.

The SEWA Executive Committee readily agreed to participate in the scheme but realized that its union strategy of direct struggle would not work in this case. Since most of the families in the district were poor, there was no one and no institution to struggle against. It also was unclear how a struggle would benefit them. A new strategy would have to be developed, and SEWA intended to do this through a combination of action and research.

A New Strategy

SEWA initiated an action research programme in collaboration with the Foundation for Public Interest, an action research organization. They found that women's most acute problem was the lack of regular employment. Farming was the major occupation in the area, and although most families had land, a combination of water shortages, desertification and soil salinity had forced many families to migrate out of the district in search of work. This was also true for families involved in dairying and cattle breeding. Due to an acute shortage of fodder in the summer months, families had to migrate with their cattle to other districts where fodder was available.

106

The action research programme had identified women's basic need, their skills and available local resources. It was clear that a major employment programme was needed in this area.

However, a question that arose was: is it the role of a trade union to promote employment and economic enterprise? SEWA's executive committee felt that SEWA should certainly take on that role. They said that the major objective of any trade union is to increase the bargaining power of the workers through collective action. In a situation of no employment, the only way to increase bargaining power was by bringing employment into the area. Furthermore, actions to bring about full employment are very much part of a trade union's mandate.

However, a trade union by its very structure is not suited to run enterprises and employment schemes. So the strategy SEWA adopted was to promote local employment and develop local economic organizations that would be run by the women producers. Building women's capacity for self-management was an inherent part of the strategy.

SEWA continued to work with local women to identify local resources and skills for employment development. Although SEWA intended to initiate any employment programmes, it felt that women's own locally-managed economic organizations should soon take over the programmes. Since the government had launched many local employment schemes, SEWA decided to work closely with government employment programmes so these programmes could reach women in Banaskantha.

SEWA identified the government-run Development of Women and Children in Rural Areas (DWCRA) programme as a suitable partner for economic development in the district and worked closely with the programme to help women form their own DWCRA or producer groups. In the initial stages SEWA helped the producer groups[1] with group formation and management, needs identification, and linkages. In addition, SEWA assisted the women through advocacy work and struggle strategies when necessary.

The producer groups have now federated into a district-level federation, the Banaskantha DWCRA Women's Association (BDWA), registered in 1993. The BDWA is gradually assuming SEWA's former functions with the producer groups. It is actively promoting the producer groups and linking them with markets, banks, government agencies and other institutions at the state, national and even international levels. BDWA office bearers work with the producer groups to solve any problems they are having. The BDWA procures the food for the Shakti Packet programme, a food programme administered through the DWCRA producer groups. It provides inputs to the groups, such as seeds for the nurseries and plantations, and

---

[1] Village-level organizations are referred to as 'producer groups' in this study, although in some cases these groups may not physically be producing anything.

gives interest-free loans to members for house repairs and mortgage payments.

The BDWA maintains a close relationship with SEWA. The union continues to play a role in building the capacity of BDWA members, executive committee and organizers. The BDWA relies on SEWA to take up struggle issues that hamper the progress of the federation, the producer groups or the women themselves, and to play an advocacy role. The women are simultaneously members of SEWA and the BDWA with the membership of SEWA in Banaskantha growing from 1500 members in 1991 to 43 500 members in 1995 and the BDWA membership growing from 1500 to 15 300 in the same period. As members of SEWA, the women are linked with the entire SEWA membership, 220 000 strong. At the same time, they manage their own employment through the BDWA which also gains credibility through its relationship with SEWA.

Evolution of Programmes for Economic Empowerment in Banaskantha

When SEWA began its action research in the district it sought to identify local resources and skills that could be developed into employment opportunities for women. Neither government agencies or academic institutions gave SEWA much encouragement for this endeavour. 'What kind of resources or employment can you find in the desert,' they said. 'A desert is by its very nature barren.'

However, SEWA identified many opportunities in this arid environment, including a wide variety of natural resources, local skills and government programmes that SEWA could draw on to develop the area. Further proof of the district's economic potential came after the programmes developed and became linked to the market. As resources and capital were attracted to the producer groups and the BDWA, the women's development programme grew into a regional development programme, involving not only women but men, village leaders and the local government.

SEWA used the DWCRA programme as the nucleus for organizing women in the district. The programme, a component of the Integrated Rural Development Programme (IRDP) sponsored by the Indian Government, targets rural, poor women. Women identified under IRDP can form DWCRA groups of 20 members or less and collectively can start income-generating activities at the village level. Each group elects a leader who acts as a liaison between the group and other agencies. The District Rural Development Agency gives each group a revolving fund of Rs25 000[2] to fund activities. Through the DWCRA programme, women have become

---

[2] 100 rupees = US$3.30 as at July 1995.

involved in the following remunerative activities: tree nurseries, plantation cultivation, embroidery work, gum collection and salt farming. In addition, DWCRA members benefit from support programmes for food, savings, and medical care.

SEWA's work in the district is not limited to assisting the formation of DWCRA groups. It has also promoted women's milk co-operatives at the village level which are linked to the existing district dairy federation. Within these structures, SEWA has assisted women with securing adequate supplies of fodder. SEWA has not neglected its original purpose – the equitable provision of drinking water – and has sought to find suitable village-level administrative and physical structures to ensure such provision. These programmes and the DWCRA programmes are detailed in the following pages.

Eco-Regeneration Programmes: Nurseries and Plantations
When SEWA asked women about possible employment opportunities in Banaskantha District, a common reply was: 'Could we not undertake something to push back the desert or at least stop it from advancing?' After discussions with local leaders and government agencies, SEWA found two feasible activities which would encourage eco-regeneration. The first was to establish plant nurseries to supply saplings for afforestation schemes. The other involved women cultivating food or fodder crops on previously barren, uncultivated lands. Both activities, SEWA believed, would contribute to arresting desertification.

Gokhanter is one village where women have a nursery and a plantation. The village poor are mainly Muslims and Thakurs. There is little agricultural work available in the area. Prior to forming a DWCRA group, women were able to get agricultural work during the monsoon season, but this amounted to only 20 days a year. In order to supplement their low income, many households cut trees to sell for firewood or for charcoal production. Both of these activities are illegal, but a lack of any other source of livelihood has driven people to these means of subsistence.

In the village 15 women began a plant nursery. Under this scheme, each woman has 5000 saplings at a time to her credit. Saplings are grown at least three times in a year. Because the work is familiar and the returns high, women adopted the scheme enthusiastically. The cost of seeds is low, which ensures a reasonable return from sale. However, nurseries are difficult to maintain. Seeds are planted in long plastic bags filled with soil which are placed in rows for ease of tending. The seedlings are delicate and need great care in their early stages of growth. They must be watered regularly and protected from the harsh desert sun. Watering is a problem as sweet water is scarce. In some cases women pay fees to use water from deep tube wells constructed by the *panchayat*. In other cases women must purchase water from the private owners of tube wells. To protect the seedlings from the sun, women construct shades made of dried grass, supported by sticks.

The Forestry Department purchases the saplings for use in its eco-regeneration programme. Since there is only one buyer for the saplings, prices are fairly arbitrary. The Forest Department pays a very low price, 45 paise,[3] per sapling. The DWCRA groups in Kheda District[4] (also supported by SEWA) earn between Rs2.50 and Rs3.00 per sapling. Plants must meet certain height specifications before the Forestry Department will buy them. The minimum height is difficult to achieve in a limited time under desert conditions. During their first year the DWCRA groups in Banaskantha grew one million plants. The Forestry Department officials found that only 100 000 of these saplings met the specified height, and they rejected the rest. The women were shocked; they had invested a great deal of resources and back-breaking labour in nurturing the saplings, and it appeared that this had come to nought. SEWA organizers ran from 'pillar to post' in the Forest Department to seek redress. Finally, after SEWA's efforts, the Forestry Department agreed to modify its rules and accepted the plants.

The *panchayat* granted women in Gokhanter a few acres of waste land in the village. SEWA organizers approached five women from the poorest households in the village and encouraged them to start a plantation on this land. Although these women had plans to grow many different crops, they had little idea how to proceed with such a venture and lacked the necessary technical expertise. The BDWA (then within SEWA) solicited help from the Gujarat Agricultural University. The university readily agreed to provide advice and training to the project free of charge. Since that time the BDWA has developed close links with the university, which continues to provide training and advice on plantation development.

Women are now growing a variety of crops, mainly vegetables and cereals, on the plantation land. They earn about Rs300 per month from this activity and are able to work all year round. The BDWA has asked the *panchayat* for 25 acres of waste land for cereal cultivation. This increase in land would provide work for more women and the plant stalks could be used as fodder which, in turn, would help the dairy co-operative.

The DWCRA groups in Gokhanter village, and others in Banaskantha District, have gained more than employment and income from their nursery and plantation activities. They have also gained bargaining power at the village and governmental levels. They now can bargain with the Forestry Department on the strength of their membership and solidarity at the producer group and federation levels. It is possible for women to sustain their struggles because they have economic security. But even today the amount the Forestry Department pays for saplings is too low. SEWA is

---

[3] One hundred paise equals one rupee.
[4] See the case study on SEWA interventions in Kheda District (page 143).

lobbying the Forest Department to raise its rates and to allow the producer groups to sell saplings on the open market where the rates are higher.

Earning Through Embroidery
On SEWA's first visit to villages in Banaskantha District, women brought out pieces of exquisite embroidery. Women did the embroidery work themselves over long periods of time as they could embroider only during their spare time. This skill was handed down from mother to daughter over generations, and mothers worked on garments that they would give to their daughters after marriage. Since the women were already skilled in embroidery they asked SEWA for assistance in turning this traditional craft into an income-generating activity. SEWA realized there was a demand for embroidered garments in the urban markets. If women were able to enter the urban market, it would be possible for them to gain regular income from embroidery. DWCRA associations could assist in the efforts to develop embroidery as a viable economic activity.

In Datrana village, 150 women are now engaged in embroidery and patchwork through DWCRA groups. Women from the Aahir caste (other backward classes) are typically engaged in embroidery since they have a long tradition in this craft, while women from scheduled castes are employed in patchwork. These groups use the capital provided under the DWCRA scheme to buy raw materials and, in the initial stages, to support themselves. Women embroider clothes (dresses, skirts, and caps) and furnishings (cushion covers and wall hangings). The BDWA markets these items in its shop in Ahmedabad, Banas Craft, keeping only a small margin for its administrative costs. On average, women earn Rs500 per month from embroidery and patchwork.

Before the establishment of DWCRA groups in Datrana, women and men were engaged in agricultural work. They had little or no land and mainly looked for work as agricultural labourers. When farm work was not available they worked in government relief programmes. However, there never was sufficient work during the year to support their families. So, it was normal for entire families to migrate during the lean periods to seek work in the neighbouring districts. Women in Datrana said they would migrate to the Kathiawad area of Junagadh District during the cold season as there was agricultural work available there and wages were slightly higher than in their home district. They would return to their village only after they were able to save enough money to prevent further impoverishment for a few months.

During long drought periods (which are not infrequent), families would spend one or two years away from their homes. Women found this long-term migration traumatic. 'Though migrating out of our village was a regular practice for us, we could not accept this reality', recounted the village *agevan* (SEWA village leader). 'We dreaded the time when we would be

111

forced to leave our homes. There would be tearful scenes in the village at that time. We were all very sad. Those of our sisters who did not need to migrate out would plead with us to stay. We felt as if we were in a funeral.'

Despite the evident need for economic development in Datrana, building DWCRA groups here was not easy for the SEWA organizers. All sections of the village, including the women, were cynical about the scheme. The SEWA co-ordinator for Banaskantha, Reema Nanavaty, recalled that when she first approached the *panchayat* with the scheme almost all members were suspicious of SEWA's motives. The government sponsored the DWCRA programme, and people in Datrana had lost faith in the government's sincerity to help the poor. In the past they had been enthused by promises of better payment for their crafts by the government-sponsored handicrafts organizations. However, these promises did not materialize. Villagers did not get fair prices because these bureaucratic organizations were not interested in selling the goods, and payment was not regular. Such instances made the villages people suspicious of government bodies since they did not seem to help the poor. In fact, some of these organizations procured their goods through middlemen who underpaid the craftsperson in order to increase their commission.

The SEWA organizers had to make several visits to the village to convince the women that SEWA had not come as a government organization. The organizers explained that although the DWCRA programme was supported by the government, the women could use it to further their own interests. SEWA would merely assist them in the initial stage, and ultimately the women would take charge of their own producer groups. Impressed by this notion, the women became interested in the proposition.

SEWA guaranteed the women that their products would be marketed, no woman would be denied work, and immediate payment would be made for the work done. After this reassurance, a dozen women of the Aahir community joined the DWCRA scheme. Within a couple of years, many more women belonging to other communities, such as Harijan and Parmar (scheduled castes), joined to form DWCRA groups.

In the beginning the organizers gave the producer groups much guidance and assistance. Women group members were not used to making decisions without their husbands or other male household members. SEWA's objective was to increase women's self-sufficiency, including their autonomy in decision-making. As a first step toward this objective, SEWA organizers took groups of women to the market to familiarize them with purchasing raw materials, such as thread and mirrors, which they used in their work. They were encouraged to make these purchases on their own. Secondly, the women went to shops in the local towns to negotiate the sale of their goods. Both of these measures presented new possibilities to the women. They gained confidence in their abilities to negotiate business deals and procure raw materials at reasonable cost.

The most important impact of the DWCRA groups is that women have regular work and steady incomes from embroidery and patchwork. Most women engaged in these traditional crafts pursue them as a full-time activity. They no longer have to migrate out of their villages in search of work. The men, however, continued to migrate during the dry season for work or cattle fodder.

Many women have earned income over and above their immediate basic needs and have used this extra income for purchasing assets. Cattle are a major asset in these communities, and several women purchased cattle after they started work in the DWCRA groups. The women noted: 'Earlier we had hardly any assets. We had only our broken-down huts. After we started this work, we are much better off. Now all of us have at least two cows or buffaloes. We want to start a milk co-operative to improve our conditions further.' Women are investing in housing improvements. The village *agevan* related the housing changes which have taken place: 'Earlier our houses had thatch roofs and were dilapidated. Now many of our sisters can afford tiled roofs. Their houses also have wooden beams to support the roofs. These were out of our reach earlier, but now many of us can afford them.'

Gum Collection

During the action research, SEWA organizers found that women's main activity in remote, desert villages was gum collection. These villages were isolated, had little access to drinking water, and were not connected to the water supply scheme due to logistical difficulties. There is little arable land in these villages, and what arable land existed was low-yielding. However, villagers owned cattle, and dairy products provided the sole source of income for many. For these reasons, inhabitants of these villages had lower incomes and less access to services and resources than their counterparts elsewhere in the district.

The Forest Department planted large-scale plantations of *Proscopis juliflora* (locally known as Ganda Baval) trees in the desert region. These trees can survive under the extreme desert climate and are used to form a green belt which checks soil erosion from the strong wind blasts during summer. During the dry season gum oozes out of the branches. This gum has several uses and a commercial value. The Forest Department collects this gum through licensed contractors who then employ workers to collect the gum. However, in almost all cases, instead of hiring workers, contractors buy the gum from the women in these desert villages. This is a cheap method of gum collection since the women collect the gum illegally without licenses from the Forest Department. Therefore they are willing to sell gum cheaply to the contractors.

Gum is available for around eight months in the year, but its quality varies over this time period. Soon after the monsoons the trees ooze white gum which is regarded as the best quality and is edible. After a few months, with the onset of the cold season, the gum turns red. This is not edible but is used for glue making and screen printing. The price for this variety is lower than that of the white gum. With the approach of summer, the gum turns black and is of the lowest quality. This gum is used in making fire crackers and in producing colour chemicals.

Women gum collectors leave early in the morning, just before sunrise, to begin their long trek to the forests. They collect gum until late in the afternoon. This is not an easy task. The trees have poisonous thorns, and gum is typically found on branches surrounded by these thorns. The women have to be very careful in their work. Deep thorn pricks can make them ill and keep them off work for several days. Their clothes also get torn during the process. They usually tie a tin can around their waist to collect the gum, or use cloth bags. Normally a person can collect no more than two kilos of gum in a day.

To address women's exploitation at the hands of gum contractors and their difficult working conditions, SEWA organized the women gum collectors into DWCRA groups. The BDWA obtained licences from the Forest Department for gum collection on behalf of these groups. As a result, women have been able to get better prices for the gum they collect. They sell the gum to the Forest Development Corporation and are paid at least three times more than they had received from the contractors. The Forest Development Corporation supplies them with protective clothing, such as boots, gloves and aprons.

Anternesh is one of the desert villages where SEWA has a strong membership. There are 125 households in the village; 35 of these are Muslims and the rest are Thakurs, Bhawads (both belonging to backward classes) and Harijans (scheduled castes). When SEWA activists first visited this village the women mistook them for officials of the Forest Department and refused to talk to them. On subsequent visits the activists found that the women would run into the fields as their vehicle approached. It took them quite some time to convince the local women that SEWA was interested in their well-being and wanted to work with them. After gaining the women's confidence, SEWA began to organize a DWCRA producer group in the village.

The group leader in Anternesh is Rannbai Malek, a 50-year-old Muslim woman. When SEWA initially came to the village she was the main opponent to its work because she thought that SEWA was representing the Forest Department. Now Rannbai is very involved in SEWA's activities. Her duties involve collecting gum from the members, keeping records of gum collection, and receiving payment from the Forest Development Corporation.

Rannbai completed elementary education in her childhood but long ago forgot what she learned. After becoming the group leader, she decided to

114

'revive' her education. She explains: 'I practised reading and writing in Gujarati until late in the night and I was able to relearn what I had forgotten.' She can now maintain accounts and write reports with ease, and has motivated a group of women in the village to attend literacy classes. Working with SEWA has brought many changes in her life and, she claims, in the lives of the other women. 'Earlier all women in the village had rarely ventured out of its boundaries. They were also shy to speak out in public. This has now changed. Many of the women have been to other villages and to Santalpur and Radhanpur in connection with SEWA's activities and they are no longer hesitant of speaking out in public.' Rannbai frequently goes to the depot of the Forest Development Corporation to negotiate with officials. Sometimes she takes other women with her to familiarize them with these activities. She has also gained confidence to speak before large audiences at public meetings.

The increased income stability from gum collection under the DWCRA scheme is welcomed by the women, but gum collection involves hard and often hazardous work compared to embroidery, nursery and plantation work. The average income from gum collection is Rs15 per day during eight months in a year. Hence, the income levels in this village are lower than those of the other villages in this case study. Infant mortality in the village is high, and almost all the women interviewed for this study had lost one or two babies. Since their income is low, women cannot afford to lose work after childbirth. Many of them return to work within four or five days after childbirth.

The gum collectors' problems are compounded by the Forest Development Corporation's actions. In 1992 the corporation lowered the price of gum from Rs12 per kilogram to Rs6 per kilogram. The women were surprised at this sudden fall in their earnings. After making enquiries they were told that the government was now allowing imports of lower-priced gum from African countries. The group leaders went to the headquarters of the Forest Development Corporation in Baroda where they met the Commissioner. The rates were raised to Rs8, but this was still very low. Meanwhile, the rates in the open market have risen to Rs16, but the Forest Department will not allow the BDWA to sell gum in the open market. SEWA has been supporting the BDWA in its struggles to raise the rates and to allow the BDWA to sell in the open market.

Salt Farming
In Banaskantha District the soil's high saline content is conducive for producing salt. This district and the neighbouring Kutch District constitute the major salt-producing region in the country.

SEWA undertook a study in Banaskantha on the salt workers' working and living conditions. The study found that employment in salt production is available from September to April. Women and men are engaged as

115

workers in the salt pans. They come either from nearby villages or are brought to the site by the salt pan owners and then live near the salt pan. The pay is very low, only about Rs20 per day. The salt workers borrow money from the salt pan owners in the off-season which they have to repay through work. Therefore, they are tied to the owners as long as they can work. The working conditions are extremely harsh; salt workers labour under the desert sun, often physically immersed in brine. Their children are left at the edge of the salt pan. Drinking-water has to be brought to the salt pans but is often not available. Some women labour during the nights as head loaders. These women described their work: 'It is very hard work. It takes us all night to load a truck. We work in groups of four and we are paid Rs60 for loading a truck. Each of us makes Rs15 a night. We get tired and sleepy but we cannot be lax. If we slip while carrying a sack we can get hurt.'

For women living in areas where soil salinity prohibits much agricultural activity, salt production is one of the few income-generating opportunities. SEWA suggested that DWCRA groups in these areas could form salt co-operatives and lease their own salt pan land from the government. Women enthusiastically supported this venture since it would allow them to share in the overall profits of salt production and they would have control over the working conditions in the salt pans.

It took a year to register the first salt production co-operative. During the 1991–92 season (from October 1991 to April 1992), the co-operative produced 2200 tonnes of salt, worth Rs4 *lakhs*.[5] Unfortunately, the co-operative could not get land of its own, as there is a legal 'stay' on allotment of land because of the dispute between the Forest Department and the Revenue Department. Since the co-operative was not allotted railway wagons, it had to sell its salt to the local traders. The women supervised the loading and transportation of the salt and transacted the sale. In the end, the co-operative had a net surplus of Rs75 000 from its activities during 1991–92. If they had had their 'own' land and railway wagons, the surplus would have been many times higher. Presently, seven co-operatives have been registered.

Support Programmes: Food, Savings and Medical Care
In addition to the productive activities detailed above, DWCRA groups support schemes for food, savings and medical care. The food scheme, the Shakti Packet, is available to DWCRA members. Essential food items, such as cereals, pulses, cooking oil, jaggery, sugar, and tea, are purchased at wholesale rates by the BDWA and are sold to DWCRA members at cost plus the price of transport. The village-level SEWA leader is responsible for selling these items.

---

[5] One *lakh* equals one hundred thousand.

The Shakti Packet Programme has eased women's food problems considerably. Previously they depended on the ration shop for their basic provisions, but this was not sufficient. Although village shopkeepers charged high prices, women had to buy from them as there was no alternative. After the Shakti Packet was introduced, they could get additional food at prices which are less than those in the village shops. Also, during the monsoons, the village is marooned and the shops, including the ration shop, are closed. Women now can depend on Shakti Packet for food during the monsoon season.

Before DWCRA producer groups were formed, women saved little money because their earnings were directed toward immediate subsistence needs. When women's incomes increased as a result of DWCRA activities, initially women used this income to meet consumption needs. Some women began to save small amounts of money, first as individuals, then informally as groups. Building on this experience, SEWA introduced the producer groups to the idea of savings and credit groups. The women articulated that they were interested in savings but less so in credit since they were already in debt to local money lenders after repeated natural disasters in the district.

Now there are 50 savings groups in the desert areas of Radhanput and Santalpur in Banaskantha District, with a total membership of 3000 women. The average monthly rate of savings is Rs10 per member. Women involved in the savings groups have similar characteristics: low but secure levels of income; the need to own a productive asset, such as a cow or a sewing machine; and indebtedness to a local money lender. Therefore, most women save to purchase seeds, repair their houses, purchase new tools, improve their wells, buy cattle and pay off debts. Savings also assists women to pay expenses during the frequent droughts in the area. The savings groups provide savings-related services which provide information on ways of repaying debt; how to buy new assets, such as houses or cattle; how to expand an existing economic activity; and how to mitigate the economic impact of natural disasters.

The group leaders and local organizers attend training programmes conducted by the SEWA Co-operative Bank. At these training courses they learn bookkeeping, fund management, and how to expand the membership of the savings groups. The women learn group management techniques through visiting similar groups in other districts.

While women are reluctant to extend the savings groups' activities to cover credit, some credit is available through the BDWA. The federation grants interest-free loans to members for house repair and mortgage payments, among other things. A guarantor (either another group member or the group leader) is required to access these loans. The BDWA receives the funding for these loans from the Council for Advancement of People's Action and Rural Technology, a government-sponsored agency that provides assistance to self-help organizations.

117

Women have also benefited from the mobile medical relief programme. Previous to this intervention many people had died from minor illnesses, and infant mortality was high. The medical relief programme has helped ease some of these problems. The medical team visits the village once a week. Pregnant women are monitored by the health workers, and special care is given to newborn babies. Medicines are also available from the mobile clinic.

Reviving Dairy Co-operatives
For most families in Banaskantha District living below the poverty line with little or no land, cattle are the only source of subsistence. Women are responsible for most of the activities related to animal husbandry, yet they get little credit for this work. In most cases men own the cattle and conduct the commercial transactions. The milk co-operatives are invariably dominated by males since cattle ownership is a requisite for membership.

Before SEWA began its work in Banaskantha, the district had village-level milk co-operatives and a district-level apex body, the Banas Dairy. However, the latter was not as successful as its counterparts in the state. Given the importance of cattle in the local economy, dairy co-operatives should have served as important instruments of economic empowerment for the poor. However, when the SEWA team conducted its action research programme in the district, it found that 100 village-level milk co-operatives were defunct. Most had stopped functioning during the drought in the preceding years.

SEWA organizers explored several possibilities of reviving the defunct co-operatives. They first negotiated with Banas Dairy to recommence its milk procurement programme. Then, they visited the villages which had dairy co-operatives and convinced the members to reactivate them. By 1990 SEWA was able to revive 75 of these societies.

Merely reviving the co-operatives was not SEWA's objective. SEWA also sought to increase the number of women co-operatives members and to involve women in co-operative management. It encouraged women to become joint owners of cattle with their husbands and to purchase cattle. Both of these moves would make it possible for women to become members of the existing co-operatives. Once women were members of the co-operatives they could get elected to managing committees. Furthermore, SEWA has promoted co-operatives with exclusively women members.

SEWA worked with farmers in Antarnesh to revive the dairy co-operative. The first women became members of the co-operative in 1993 when many women took loans from their savings group to buy cattle. In other cases women became joint owners of cattle along with their husbands; now half of the co-operative members are women. At the present time only men sit on the managing committee, but during the next election period women are going to stake their claim for membership in this body. In this

118

manner they will gradually make inroads into an exclusively male domain. The women's interest in controlling the milk co-operative stems from their active involvement in the DWCRA producer groups. This activity has increased their confidence and ability to manage many enterprises.

Dairy co-operatives do not entirely solve the problems of the poor in this area. Fodder for cattle remains a serious problem. Usually fodder is available until April or May, but after this time the cattle owners have to migrate out of the district in search of fodder. In most cases the males of the household migrate, leaving women to provide for their families alone. This form of forced migration, though temporary, disrupts family life.

To address the fodder shortage, SEWA began a scheme to develop village fodder banks which would provide fodder to the members of the milk co-operatives during the dry season. This scheme has been successful in reducing out-migration in these villages.

When the fodder bank was introduced, fodder was totally subsidized. After a year the subsidy was reduced to 50 per cent, and at present fodder is subsidized by 25 per cent. SEWA's objective is to make the scheme sustainable by reducing the dependence on external aid. As of late 1994, co-operative members are required to give deposits of Rs500 to their co-operative. This will serve as capital for buying dry fodder which will be stored for future use. When they draw fodder from the bank, this amount will be credited against their account. The interest on the deposit will be transferred to the members and will be their share in the scheme. Initially, the scheme was not totally successful because most members could not pay the deposit amount in one lump sum. The scheme was modified later to allow members to pay the deposit in instalments, a change which most women found preferable to the original scheme.

Resolving Drinking Water Problems through Participation
SEWA's activities in Banaskantha District began with its evaluation of a drinking water scheme in the district. While SEWA initiated the DWCRA producer groups and dairy co-operatives to address women's pressing economic problems, it did not forget that drinking water remained an issue in the district. While conducting a survey on water use, SEWA organizers found that the *pani panchayats* or village water councils were defunct bodies that existed largely on paper. These committees had been established in consultation with the local *sarpanch* (village leader) and the Gujarat Water Supply and Sewerage Board (GWSSB). In several cases those individuals who were selected as *pani panchayat* members were not even aware of their membership on these councils. Often, *pani panchayat* members did not meet because the convenor (the *sarpanch*) did not know what the water council's functions were.

SEWA stressed the need to revive the *pani panchayats* so that the local people could be involved in managing the villages' water resources.

119

Furthermore, SEWA emphasized that women were primarily involved in household water provision; therefore women should be adequately represented on the *pani panchayats* since they are often the best judges of water use or misuse in the village. As a result of SEWA's advocacy, women are members of *pani panchayats* in many villages. In several cases all members, except the ex-officio *sarpanch*, are women.

Some villages have no access to the water supply system, either because they cannot receive water due to low water pressure or they are too remote to be reached by the scheme. SEWA has tried to make alternative arrangements for a drinking water supply in villages not reached by the scheme. In one village residents built a large pond for capturing and storing rain water. However, water collected from the rains turns into salt water a few months after the monsoons due to the salinity of the soil.

To combat the salinity problem in water catchment ponds, SEWA and the BDWA, with the assistance of other organizations, undertook an experiment in Gokhantar village which, if successful, could be replicated elsewhere in the district. Indian Petro-Chemicals Limited (IPCL) had developed sheets of vinyl known as agrifilm. IPCL was willing to supply these sheets free as a part of its rural development endeavours. Water experts in the Foundation for Public Interest felt that these sheets would be useful for lining ponds in Banaskantha because they would prevent the saline soil from contaminating the water. The pond in Gokhantar was selected as the experimental site. The project was discussed with the *panchayat*, and since this was a common project for the village, it was felt that all of the villagers should be involved. IPCL, the Gujarat Jalseva Training Institute and the Foundation for Public Interest provided technical assistance for the project.

The village committee determined how the work would proceed, and began the work in December 1993. The first task was pumping water out of the pond. It took around a month to empty the pond with volunteers working around the clock. Once the water had been pumped out of the pond, the villagers discovered a thick layer of salt brine at the bottom. While attempting to scrape out this brine, it became apparent the brine was oozing from the soil and could not be stemmed easily. The IPCL experts said if the agrifilm was placed over the brine, it would be damaged in no time. Therefore the experiment at the pond site was abandoned and an alternative site was found.

An area near the pond was selected as the next site and digging (by tractor and by hand) began immediately. The work had to be completed before the monsoons in order to store the rainwater. Once the digging was completed, the bed and sides had to be lined with evenly-cut stones over which the agrifilm sheet would be placed. These stones had to be purchased from a quarry, and this process took time. By the time the stones were set in the new pond, the first monsoon showers were over. A lot of water was lost, but the pond was able to capture the onset of the second flush of the monsoons, which unfortunately were not as heavy as the first. Although the pond was only partially filled during the first season, the villagers recognized that the experiment had succeeded and that they would benefit more greatly from the pond in the years to come.

The pond is presently managed by a committee of women who represent all communities in the village. This committee ensures that water is used only for drinking and for watering the animals. It also looks after the pond's maintenance and levies fees for this purpose.

Economic Impacts

SEWA and the BDWA's interventions have resulted in several economic impacts: year-round employment, new employment opportunities, greater financial support for enterprise development, increased income and assets, gains in bargaining power, and increased resource allocation to the district. Of these, women feel the most important contribution of the DWCRA programme has been the provision of employment throughout the year. Previously, women could work for only part of the year, a situation that contributed to periodic out-migration for work. For example, women in Gokhanter worked before as agricultural labourers for 20 days a year. Now they work for the entire year in their village and no longer need to migrate in search of work. The DWCRA programme has also created new employment opportunities for women. In the case of Datrana, women were able to turn a traditional craft, embroidery, into an income-generating venture with the assistance of the DWCRA programme.

The financing, credit and at cost inputs available through the DWCRA programme and the BDWA have made it possible for women to pursue new economic activities and expand existing activities. In the past, women borrowed money from money lenders to pay for agricultural inputs. The interest rates on these loans are quite high, a situation that prohibits many women from taking these loans. In many cases, women who take loans for seeds are expected to pay back the loan in kind (including 'interest') with a portion of their harvest. Under the DWCRA programme, women no longer need to turn to local money lenders for credit. Instead these women can take advantage of the initial start-up grant from the programme, interest-free loans from the BDWA, and inputs at cost from the BDWA. These forms of support have allowed women's enterprises to grow and flourish.

For women who earned little in the past, the DWCRA programme and dairy co-operatives have increased women's incomes. Most women have used a portion of this increased income to satisfy basic needs, but many have also been able to purchase assets. Women embroiderers in Datrana, for instance, have been able to make improvements to their houses with their earnings. Some women have used their extra income to purchase cattle and with this asset have been able to enter another income-generating venture. Also, women have begun saving any income over and above household expenditure for future investment or to avert the risk of future calamities.

Women's bargaining power has also increased as a result of their participation in the producer groups. As individuals, women had little recourse if they were given unfair prices for their products. Now the producer group, backed by the BDWA and SEWA, has leverage in financial negotiations with buyers. Women involved in nursery work have bargained with the Forestry Department for changes in specifications for saplings. Women embroiderers can now bargain more effectively than before with traders for raw materials and for fair payment from the sale of their articles. While women gum collectors were successful in getting the Forest Development Corporation to increase its rates, they continue to struggle for fair remuneration.

Governmental and non-governmental resource allocation to the district has increased as initial perceptions about the 'barren desert' have changed. The success of the DWCRA producer groups and the dairy co-operatives has demonstrated that economic opportunities exist in Banaskantha District, and programmes to tap local resources can encourage economic growth. Previous to SEWA's organizing, human, physical and monetary resources were flowing out of the district as drought and desertification forced individuals to look elsewhere for economic opportunities. Currently the government is launching many development programmes in the district. The BDWA is drawing funding from a number of governmental and non-governmental sources for its programming. Economic development in the district is also evidenced by the success of the Banas Dairy. This district dairy, once the poorest dairy in Gujarat, is now paying the highest prices in the state to milk producers.

Overall Empowerment

Changes at the individual, household, community and public policy levels have accompanied the economic impacts. Participation in the producer groups has provided women with new opportunities and experiences. Most women had little experience of speaking in public. As Rannbai, the group leader in Anternesh noted, some women in her group were initially too shy to speak at meetings, but now they speak out with confidence. Women have also become more confident in dealing with public officials and authority figures. Furthermore, producer group activities have taken some women beyond the boundaries of their villages, a new experience for many.

The most perceptible change for women at the household level is men's attitudes towards housework. As one woman explained, in the past women had few income-earning opportunities and were mainly engaged in housework. Their husbands gave them little or no assistance with this work.

'Before we took up embroidery work for the market, we had to do all the household work which included cooking, fetching water and fuel-wood, cleaning etc. This was in addition to our work in agriculture.' Their present work through the producer groups gives them full-time employment. This remunerative work often requires a considerable time commitment each day so that women can earn an adequate living. Housework and food preparation cut into the time that women can devote to paid labour.

According to many women, the tension between remunerative and housework has been resolved by men taking on some housework. For example, the daily work schedule among women embroiderers is as follows: Women wake at 4 a.m., wash the utensils, tend the cattle and make *rotla* (unleavened bread) for the family's meals. They then begin their embroidery at 8 a.m. and work throughout the day. In the late afternoon and evening, their husbands assist them with cleaning the house and the cattle shed and cooking vegetables for the evening meal. 'Our husbands never helped with the housework earlier but now they volunteer on their own,' noted one woman. Her fellow group member added: 'It is only after we sisters got together, started this work and got involved in SEWA's activities that they have changed.' Women credit this change in the gender division of labour in the household to men's recognition that women are contributing to the household's financial stability. Any disruption in women's remunerative work could result in less income for the household.

Through their participation in the producer groups, women are effecting change at the community level. Previously, women rarely held leadership positions within their communities and were largely excluded from decision-making bodies. Now in some communities the producer groups themselves are recognized as important institutions. Women are also beginning to take on leadership positions as members of the *pani panchayat*.

The BDWA and SEWA have been able to effect policy changes which have, in turn, created a better policy environment for the producer groups' activities. Women gum collectors can now obtain licences which allow them to sell gum directly to the Forest Development Corporation, reducing their exploitation at the hands of gum contractors. Women continue to push for more policy changes; they recognize that such changes may be possible only if they become members of the boards or management committees of government agencies and other organizations. Women dairy producers want to gain positions on the managing committees of the dairy co-operatives so that they may influence the co-operatives' policies.

Resistance to Change: A Hardening Attitude of the Community

An increase in women's employment opportunities has not reduced gender inequalities in every community. Aahir women form the majority of the craftswomen working with SEWA. These women have experienced a

123

backlash against their participation in SEWA's activities. The caste council of the Aahir, known as *Nath*, has imposed and enforced restrictions on women's free movement and on girls' education.

The *Nath* is a large body which meets once a year in one of the Aahir-dominated villages in Banaskantha. Its membership is composed of two to five representatives from each village in its jurisdiction. Most of the *Nath's* members are village elders, and women are prohibited from membership. Given the strong traditional views of its members, the *Nath* usually has a conservative attitude towards women's issues.

Men whose wives are involved in these programmes appreciate the social and economic changes which have accompanied SEWA's employment generation programmes. These relatively young men are typically not members of the *Nath* and when they are members, they find themselves outnumbered by the more traditional elders. The *Nath* holds two rigid views on female members of the caste: no Aahir woman should be allowed to leave her village unaccompanied by a male relative (husband, father or father-in-law) and girls should not be educated. Both of these views reinforce women's and girls' dependent status in the household and extended family.

Aahir women related that these restrictions were prevalent for a long time, but they were not rigidly applied. It is only since 1992 that the *Nath* has hardened its attitude and has begun enforcing these restrictions. This was, the women said, mainly due to the women's involvement in SEWA's activities. Aahir women were actively involved in the employment-generation activities and in organizations such as the *pani panchayat*. As a result of these activities, they wanted to have representation on the *Nath* as well. The members of the *Nath* opposed women's membership, arguing that the *Nath* is traditionally an all-male assembly. Women showed their displeasure with this decision by refusing to cook for the *Nath* during one of its meetings. This angered the members and they retaliated by resolving to enforce the two restrictions severely.

Both restrictions have affected the status of women and their work. If the ban on women's movement is enforced rigidly, women will not be able to procure raw materials or market their products on their own. Moreover, they will not be able to attend the monthly meetings of the group leaders organised by SEWA at Radhanpur or the annual meetings of the DWCRA Association. These meetings are important for the women because they provide them with opportunities to raise important issues, discuss their problems and find solutions through consultation with each other.

Similarly, restrictions on girls' education ensure that the next generation of women will be equally as illiterate as the present generation. The women in the DWCRA groups regard illiteracy as their greatest handicap. They are aware that their disability prevents them from maintaining accounts, recording the stock of goods and raw materials and participating in several activities where reading and writing are necessary. They therefore do not want their daughters to suffer the same fate. Women recognized the importance of girls' education after they achieved some stability in their lives. Since women no longer migrate periodically, it is possible for their daughters to attend the village school regularly. Once educated, their daughters could help them with activities which require literacy and numeracy.

Women in Datrana are determined to fight the restrictions with the support of their husbands. The men have argued to the *Nath* that since these restrictions decrease the family income, all household members suffer. The women would like the SEWA organizers to attend the next meeting of the *Nath*. They are convinced that the elders will listen to SEWA and will lift the restrictions.

Resistance to the *Nath's* decisions is not restricted to Datrana. In other villages where SEWA has its activities, Aahir women have united to show their displeasure at the autocratic stand of this body. In 1994 the *Nath* reluctantly consented to be flexible in enforcing the restrictions. Women are allowed to leave their villages but only to go to SEWA's office at Radhanpur. The women regard this small concession as an achievement of their resistance. They are convinced that if they continue to show their displeasure, the *Nath* will rescind its decision. Unfortunately, the decision regarding girls' education stands, even though many of the younger men on the *Nath* bitterly oppose it. The women intend to continue pressuring the *Nath* on this point. If the *Nath* does not relent they intend to defy the ban and send their girls to school.

Organizing for Change

In Banaskantha District, women have formed organizations which are effecting economic and social change. Through producer group activities, women have realized increased income, economic stability and greater bargaining power and decreased dependence on employers, middlemen and money lenders. In sum, they have become economically empowered. As women have become economically empowered there have been changes in gender roles at the household and community levels. In some cases, men have begun taking responsibility for household tasks. Women have become visible as agents of change at the community level through their participation in the DWCRA producer groups and the *pani panchayat*. These economic and social changes have been challenged at times by members of communities, such as the *Nath*, who feel threatened by change and women's new status in the home and village. Yet, the producer groups, the BDWA and SEWA are mobilized to meet these challenges. These organizations and their achievements indicate that the desert is no longer barren in Banaskantha District.

WOMEN'S BANKS

Women Banking for Success: Women's Development Federation (WDF) in Sri Lanka

W.M. LEELASENA and CHITRANI DHAMMIKA

Before the samiti[1], *we had nothing like the banking societies. I am amazed now at how we lived.*

AN ECONOMIC TRANSFORMATION has occurred among women in Hambantota District in south eastern Sri Lanka. Since the advent of the Rural Women's Development Societies and the Janashakthi Banking Societies, both united under the Women's Development Federation, women have had unprecedented access to savings and credit services as well as other support for women entrepreneurs. With a population of 518 366, Hambantota District is one of the most economically disadvantaged districts in the country. In this economic context, women's needs for banking services are great. The organizations established in the region have successfully met these needs. This case study is based on research undertaken in Hambantota town and the rural area served by the Pallemalala Banking Society. This choice of areas reveals a range of experiences with the women's organizations and the banking societies.

Women's Development Federation

The Women's Development Federation (WDF) was founded in December 1989 as a federation of the Rural Women's Development Societies (RWDS) in Hambantota District. These societies had been formed earlier in 1989 under the Sri Lankan government's Janasaviya programme, which targeted the rural poor. Initially the societies were fora for education on nutrition and primary health care. Women were also given training on leadership and how to run a meeting. Gradually, they began to realize that while they ran their societies independently, there were some overarching policy and management issues which all of the societies shared. There was also a need for a central body to handle liaising with governmental agencies and potential donors. The WDF was formed to perform the functions of policy-making, co-ordination and guidance for the RWDS. The WDF staff

---

[1] *Samiti* literally means association and refers to the Rural Women's Development Society in this case.

are members of women's societies who generally have had experience in RWDS leadership positions and who have been trained in programme and organizational management. A 17-member elected executive committee is responsible for most policy decisions. Annual meetings, which convene the 466 RWDS presidents, are also opportunities for policy development and debate.

The WDF presently co-ordinates a set of programmes which are delivered at the individual member and RWDS levels. The nutrition programme focuses on improving the nutritional standards of children, pregnant women and women who are breast-feeding. Volunteers from the RWDS are trained in health monitoring and education and make the rounds in select areas, identifying individuals at risk and providing advice on improved nutrition to women. Related to the nutrition programme is the home garden programme which aims to increase family nutrition and generate income for women. The 'barefoot library' programme circulates books and newspaper articles during RWDS meetings through a system of 'barefoot librarians', who also provide basic literacy training to women. The HelpAge programme was developed to assist elderly people in accessing social services and to generate community support for the elderly. The WDF also has a broad-based environmental education programme which promotes soil conservation, safe drinking water, composting and family planning, among other objectives.

To support the delivery of these programmes, the WDF conducts training for the volunteers working at the RWDS levels, such as the 'barefoot librarians'. The organization has also offered training programmes on financial management, administration, leadership and accounting. The WDF acts as a link between the RWDS and other service providers, for example the Department of Agriculture, which provide training in specialized areas.

Women's Development Federation's Programme for Economic Empowerment

When the Janasaviya programme began in Hambantota District, a survey revealed that approximately one-third of the population was living under adverse health conditions with no access to potable water or sanitation. Furthermore, most of the population was indebted to local money lenders and pawnbrokers who often charged in excess of 200 per cent interest per annum. The Janasaviya programme sought to improve local conditions through a two-year programme of food assistance and compulsory savings targeted at 'the poorest of the poor,' after which it was expected that the recipients would be self-reliant.

The Rural Women's Development Societies (or *Kantha Samitis* as they were originally called) stemmed from the Janasaviya programme. Women, who were already organized for primary health care education, wanted to ensure that they could sustain themselves after the Janasaviya programme ceased. The women's societies began organizing common funds to which each woman would contribute a few rupees a week. The funds were intended for emergency loans, and for loans to women who wanted to start income-generating activities. While the loans were small, they were often the first time a woman had ever accessed credit herself, since social norms in the district prevented many women from approaching money lenders for money. Over time, thousands of rupees accumulated in these informal funds, and the women realized that they needed a more systematic and structured approach to managing the funds if they were to be successful. They contacted government officials in Hambantota for assistance.

During the course of deliberations about the future of these small common funds, it was determined that neither the women's society nor the village were economically viable units for a banking scheme because the gross savings at these levels are too low. Instead, approximately seven women's societies were grouped together to form one Janashakthi Banking Society (JBS), a new credit and savings institution inaugurated in October 1990. The JBS offices were established in donated space, often in the front room of an RWDS officer's house. The number and location of the banks has made them accessible to a large group of women who cannot take the time to travel to one of the towns in Hambantota to deposit savings or to take a loan. The JBS offices are staffed by a financial secretary and an administrative secretary, both members of the women's society. These staff typically have completed high school (A-level or O-level) and have been trained by the WDF in keeping accounts and administration. Each JBS is managed by an administrative board, composed of the 'financial and administrative secretaries and the seven RWDS presidents, and is 'owned' by its women members, since they contribute share capital to the JBS.

There was still one stumbling block to the JBS's success: women's lack of collateral for borrowing money. Taking its cue from Grameen Bank in Bangladesh, the JBS organized the approximately 55 members of each RWDS into groups of five and instituted a procedure which made the group collectively responsible for ensuring that a group member has paid her loan instalments. If one woman in the group defaults on a loan, none of the other members of the group may take out a loan. In effect, 'peer pressure' is used as a substitute for collateral. Also it is the group which first reviews a group member's loan application before it is sent on to the RWDS and JBS.

A further consideration was how poor women, who on the surface seem to have no money to spare, can save money through the JBS. The WDF addressed this concern through training social mobilizers to work with the groups of five to develop group and individual strategies for the constraints which they face. Three social mobilizers work for each JBS who periodically meet with the groups of five. Through the work of the social mobilizers,

129

many of the groups now purchase essential consumer items, such as laundry detergent, in bulk. The money which they save from this bulk purchase is placed in an account under the group's name in the JBS which is used for small, 'soft' loans since they require only the group's consent and not a formal application to the JBS. Social mobilizers have also assisted individual women to find ways to earn money for deposit in their own JBS savings accounts, such as producing charcoal from coconut shells or setting aside a handful of rice from every meal for eventual sale.

Labour is another key constraint that women face, and some women initially felt that they could not afford the time to take part in the activities of the groups of five (which meet once a week) and the RWDS (which meets twice a month). Social mobilizers have been successful in organizing the groups of five to exchange labour and have counselled women on time management. For example, when one woman's husband was absent during the peak field preparation period, her group assisted her with constructing bunds around the paddy fields. Not only do the social mobilizers follow the progress of the groups of five, but the groups themselves prepare and present reports on their activities and savings at the RWDS meetings.

Through the groups of five, women can access a variety of loans. The JBS classifies loans according to the type of investment or purpose for the loan: cultivation, self-employment, small business, fisheries, housing, consumption and distress. In terms of total rupees lent, cultivation loans make up the bulk (61 per cent) of the loans taken from the JBSs in Hambantota District and are used for buying or renting land and purchasing agricultural inputs. Self-employment loans have comprised approximately 20 per cent of the JBSs' lending to date. These are loans for beginning a business, whereas small business loans are financing for already existing business. Fisheries loans are specifically targeted for use in purchasing fishing equipment, such as nets, or financing the purchase of a boat. As women do not engage in fishing, these are loans that they take out for their husbands. Housing loans are granted to women who wish to make improvements to their homes or to construct new homes. The JBS instituted consumption loans to address women's need for small, short-term loans (up to Rs1000[3] for three months) to purchase goods such as food or fertilizer. While interest on other loans is 3 per cent per month, interest on consumption loans is 1.5 per cent over three months. Distress loans of 500 rupees are available to women who have an emergency need for money and can be obtained without preparing a formal loan application. These loans are typically used to meet unexpected health expenses and are on 'soft' terms of 3 per cent over three months.

To qualify for a loan a woman must first save Rs500, her share capital in the JBS. Women obtain a loan application form at the JBS office. Since

---

[3] Rs100 = US$2.00 as at July 1995.

approximately 75 per cent of women in Hambantota District are literate, illiterate women can usually turn to a group member for assistance in completing the application, or can seek the assistance of JBS staff. After filling out the application, they discuss it with their fellow group of five members who must guarantee the loan. The group has the prerogative to turn down the loan application if it feels that the applicant has not properly planned for the use of the money. The loan application is then reviewed by the RWDS president, and in some cases by the membership of the RWDS at an RWDS meeting. The financial and administrative secretaries of the JBS also assess the application and indicate how it could be improved. Once the application has been approved by the financial and administrative secretaries, it goes forward to the administrative board of the JBS, which is composed of the RWDS presidents in the JBS's operating area, the financial secretary and the administrative secretary of the JBS. The entire procedure takes about two weeks since the administrative board meets only fortnightly.

The individual Janashakthi banks are to a large degree independent of the WDF and make their own decisions on granting loans. The WDF facilitates the exchange of information and expertise among the banks, as well as offering training to the financial and administrative secretaries of the JBS. It develops the overall policies for the JBS and sends zoner secretaries to each JBS every two weeks to review the books and assist the financial and administrative secretaries with any problems. The WDF has instituted a set of insurance schemes to insure the banks and their clients against loan defaults and other risks. Since it is in a position to co-ordinate the activities of all of the banks, the WDF may move money from one bank to another, should the need arise for more capital at one bank.

Since their inception the number of JBSs in Hambantota District has grown to 67 with a membership of 25 950 women. Over Rs11 million are invested in the banks as members' shares, and the members have saved Rs5 million in savings accounts. The banks also accept savings from non-members and have a special programme for children's savings, although only members are allowed to take loans from the JBS. Loan recovery rates across all JBSs are an average of 97 per cent, with rates of 100 per cent in many banks.

The WDF is beginning to develop new training programmes to support women entrepreneurs and to assist them in using their savings and credit more effectively. It has conducted four programmes for small-scale entrepreneurs, focusing on how to make food products (for example, chutney, yoghurt, ice-cream and sweets), maintain quality control, and market the products. The WDF is planning to introduce another training programme on medium-scale entrepreneurship to assist successful small-scale entrepreneurs with scaling up, and to help women launch new medium-sized businesses. It also has been sending women to various training institutes in Sri

Lanka for more advanced training and has facilitated linkages between the RWDS and other service providers.

From Wage Labourers to Tenant Farmers

The realized and potential benefits of the JBS are well illustrated by the following case from Tissamaharama Division in Hambantota District. In Tissamaharama, money lenders' interest rates average around 20 per cent per month. There are many landless poor families in this district who work as wage labourers on irrigated commercial paddy fields. Male labourers earn around 150 rupees per day while female labourers are paid Rs100 per day. The seasonal nature of the work means that men and women are employed periodically during the rice-growing season (September to January) and face unemployment the rest of the year. Many families would like to lease paddy land so that they can increase their incomes and better feed their families. However, these families typically have no savings, have no collateral to finance a loan from a commercial bank, and cannot afford to borrow money from the local money lenders to lease land and buy agricultural inputs. Often the families are already in debt to money lenders for moneys borrowed in times of emergency.

In 1992 the first Janashakthi Banking Societies were established in Tissamaharama Division. Once women had fulfilled their share requirements for the JBS, they began taking cultivation loans from the banks. With these loans, women were able to lease paddy land for their families' cultivation. The result has been that many families have been released from the uncertainty and low returns of wage labour and now cultivate paddy fields on their own account. While the impact on individual families has been great, the JBS has also had an effect on the wage-labour system in the area. Women report that wages for both male and female labourers have risen as the number of individuals engaged in wage-labour has declined. Since women can now access the JBS consumption and distress loans for small amounts of money, dependence on money lenders in times of emergency has declined sharply as well.

Economic Impacts

By far the most significant economic impact from women's participation in the RWDS has been increased access to credit. One woman explains: 'Before the *samiti* [RWDS] we had nothing like the banking societies. I am amazed now at how we lived. If we needed money, we had to go to pawnbrokers or money lenders. Even they demanded some collateral.'

As women have accessed credit from the JBS, their reliance on money lenders and pawnbrokers has decreased. A survey of 48 women members of the Pallemalala JBS found that while 32 of the women and their families

132

had borrowed money from money lenders in the past, now only three have continued to borrow from the money lenders. The lower reliance on money lenders translates into monetary savings for women and their families, who no longer have to pay the money lenders' high interest rates.

The interest rate charged for the majority of JBS loans, 3 per cent per month, or 39 per cent per annum, is higher than the rates charged by other banks in the region which vary from 16 per cent to 24 per cent per annum. However, women continue to access credit from the JBS for many reasons. First, most women have no assets they can use for obtaining loans from other financial institutions. While the JBS's interest rates may seem high, they are calculated on a diminishing basis on the outstanding principal. Finally, women trust the JBS because it is their bank; it is run for and by its women members.

Women take the majority of JBS loans for cultivation purposes, principally for cultivating paddy land. Access to irrigated paddy land is important in this region since rice is a major part of the local diet and the risk of crop failure is lower on irrigated land than on the rain-fed *chena* lands (high lands) where other crops are grown. Rice also has commercial value and access to paddy land provides an opportunity for families to earn some income from the sale of paddy. However, many poor families have had difficulty in gaining access to paddy land because of a lack of credit. Women have taken loans to buy and lease paddy land, to pay for agricultural inputs and, in a few cases, to pay for labour. In the case of Sunitha, she and her husband had never been able to afford to lease any paddy land. Through using her savings and borrowing some money from the JBS, Sunitha now leases paddy land from a local government officer which she and her husband cultivate.

In the coastal areas of Hambantota District, such as in Hambantota town, women have taken loans to finance the purchase of fishing equipment and boats for their male relatives. Fishing is the main income-generating activity in these families, yet it has become more and more difficult for fishermen to earn a living from the sea. Fishermen who do not own their own boats or nets must give part of their catch (up to 50 per cent) to the boat and net owners. While fish and shellfish are very expensive at the present time for the Sri Lankan consumer (and out of the reach of most consumers), the fisherman sees none of this profit. Instead he sells his catch to one of several middlemen through whom the fish will pass before it reaches the market. Declining fish stocks due to overfishing by foreign trawlers has reduced the amount of fish caught, and fishing incomes. According to Seetha, a RWDS president and the wife of a fisherman, many women do not know how they can alter this situation. She is trying to attack part of the problem by encouraging women to purchase fishing equipment with their savings and loans, thus eliminating some of the middlemen in the fishing industry.

Few women engaged in any income-generating activities before the inception of the JBS, but access to credit has now enabled some women to purchase productive assets to enhance their income opportunities. Fatima, a Malay Muslim woman living on the outskirts of Hambantota town, has used loans from the JBS to build up a large poultry business with 390 laying hens. She notes that without money from the JBS she could not have succeeded at her business. She has been trying to get credit from commercial banks since the credit demands of expanding her poultry business exceed the amounts she can borrow from the JBS. Other businesswomen in the RWDS have been successful at getting loans from commercial banks since their participation in the JBS has made them 'credit-worthy' in the eyes of these financial institutions.

Credit has also allowed women to scale up and diversify their businesses. Babanona was a widowed casual labourer who began a business selling roasted peanuts in the local market with a small loan of Rs150 from her group of five. Using this marketing experience, she decided to borrow 500 rupees from her JBS to buy and market vegetables. With the profit from this successful business and additional loans from her JBS, Babanona eventually built her own house and shop and bought a parcel of paddy land.

While there are women in every RWDS who have had extraordinary successes due to their ability to save and access credit, for the majority of women participation in the RWDS and JBS has afforded them economic security and an enhanced coping capacity. In times of illness or food shortages women can use their savings or the JBS consumption and distress loans. As in the case of wage labourers in Tissamaharama District, access to savings and credit has reduced the seasonal vulnerability of rural families to fluctuations in food availability and work.

Savings and credit have created a 'safety net' for women in times of family breakdown, if the male head of household loses employment or when a woman is widowed. This 'safety net' is particularly important because alcoholism among adult males in the region has been estimated to be as high as 30 per cent. The case of Somawathie is illustrative of the difficulties that some women face. Somawathie's husband was an alcoholic and owned a small shop in the village. He was abusive to Somawathie and forbade her from joining the RWDS. In spite of this, Somawathie secretly joined the women's society and began saving money. Due to her husband's drinking problem, the shop began to lose money and eventually it had to be sold. Somawathie then informed her husband that she had some savings and could access a loan to begin a new business. She used the money as leverage to get her husband to stop drinking. In Somawathie's case, she and her husband remained together, and he continued as the main income earner in the family. In other cases, women have had to take on the burden of providing for their families if the male head of household leaves, is incapacitated or dies.

Women have also realized an increased ability to pay for household assets, such as improved housing and household goods. Over 600 women in

134

Hambantota District have taken housing loans for improvements to their existing homes or for building a new home. For example, Gunaseeli obtained housing loans of Rs10 000 to build a new house with a tin roof. Using their savings, small loans from the group of five or consumption loans, women have also purchased glassware, kitchen utensils and furniture. Since many RWDS members had no source of independent income before joining the RWDS, even these small purchases signify economic change.

In a small way, the bulk purchasing activities of the groups of five have increased women's bargaining power in the marketplace. Before, poor women could only afford to purchase small amounts of goods, such as a handful of chillies, from shopkeepers who inevitably would inflate the price of these small purchases. Purchasing in bulk not only saves the group members money, but it also places them in a better position when bargaining with local merchants. Bulk purchases also save women's time as one member of the group takes her turn at purchasing bulk goods for the entire group.

The WDF and RWDS have assisted women with aspects of enterprise development other than credit. The WDF has conducted training programmes for women entrepreneurs and has assisted them with accessing larger markets outside of Hambantota District. The WDF linked Fatima with a large poultry and egg concern in Sri Lanka that supplies her with inputs and markets her eggs. Similarly, a group of RWDS members are engaged in weaving baskets for a tea export company which had initially approached the WDF, looking for women home-based workers. For small entrepreneurs, the RWDS and its network of women assist with the marketing of products. Daisy uses fabric scraps from the nearby free trade zone's garment factories to sew sheets, pillowcases and children's clothing. While a few non-RWDS members are also engaged in this activity, she notes that she finds it much easier to market her products than they do because fellow RWDS members find buyers for her.

The WDF and JBS have created formal employment opportunities for women in the district. The WDF hires social mobilizers and maintains a small office staff. Each JBS has two employees, the financial and administrative secretaries. Few positions like these were available for women in the district before the inception of the WDF and JBS. These jobs are particularly important for women who have attained O- or A-level qualifications in school as otherwise they have few opportunities to use their skills.

The overriding economic impact of participation in the RWDS and JBS is that women are now able to contribute to family income and assets in a substantial way. Before these organizations began, women earned and saved very little. Now, a 'savings culture' has been established in Hambantota district, enabling women to save for future expenses. Since

135

non-RWDS members also save in the JBS, the JBS has had an impact on savings within entire communities.

Beyond Economic Empowerment

Participation in the groups of five and in the RWDS has changed the way in which women act and interact. In the past women typically were confined to their house or their village since they had few opportunities to venture out. Rural women were largely isolated in their farmsteads and had only periodic contact with other women, except for close neighbours and family members. Women in towns were to some degree less mobile than their rural counterparts because they were not involved in activities outside of the home, although they had greater opportunities to interact with other women because of geographic proximity. Malay Muslim women in Hambantota town, though not secluded, tended to keep to themselves due to an inability to speak Sinhalese.

Women's mobility has increased as a result of participation in the groups of five and RWDS. Now women leave the home and farmstead for RWDS meetings and to work with their group of five members, broadening their social contacts and increasing their physical mobility. An RWDS president living in Hambantota town recollects: 'We didn't use to go out of the house much, particularly at night . . . now we know each other in the area and meet to discuss our problems.' Younger Malay Muslim women who speak Sinhalese are facilitating older women's participation in the RWDS and are enabling Malay Muslims to become a part of the larger community.

Women have initiated strong group solidarity through the groups of five. The labour exchange among group members is very important because it addresses women's key constraints of time and labour. For rural women, assistance with crop harvesting and cooking during harvest time eases a large burden. As one woman notes, 'It is really a strength for us to have this assistance.'

Group solidarity is expressed not only in terms of labour exchange; women also discuss their personal and economic problems during the weekly group meetings. Many women commented on the importance of sharing problems with group members and what a relief it was to realize that they were not the only ones facing these difficulties. The group is also able to provide solutions to these problems. For younger women in the group, the older women play a mentoring role and share their experience and knowledge.

Before joining the RWDS, women had little chance to speak in public fora and to share their views and problems with a large constituency. The RWDS have on average 58 members, creating a more public forum for women than the groups of five. At the RWDS meetings, women present reports on the activities of their groups and discuss progress on savings and

136

the WDF's initiatives. Also, women are given an opportunity at the RWDS meetings to sing a song or read poetry that they have written, giving them a creative outlet that they never had before. Through participation in the RWDS meetings, women have learned how to conduct meetings and have gained public speaking skills. 'We are more articulate now,' notes one woman.

The groups of five, RWDS and WDF also provide opportunities for women to take leadership positions. At all levels there is a president who conducts the meetings. Since the president's tenure is for only one year, over time all of the members of the group of five will have filled this position within their small groups, and many will have served in officer positions within the RWDS. At the WDF level, the officer positions involve even more responsibility and time than at the lower levels, particularly as these women liaise with government officials. The WDF and JBS also employ a small number of women as staff. These are all new roles for women in this region since women do not serve in positions of authority within the local or regional government structure, and few have had formal employment. Furthermore, women's experience and visibility in these positions of responsibility may open opportunities for women to serve in such capacities in the governmental and private sectors.

Public speaking and leadership experience, as well as the solidarity of group membership, have made women more confident than before in dealing with authority figures. A financial officer for the Hambantota JBS notes that in the past women would have lowered their heads in the presence of government officials. They were shy when the district government agent spoke to them and seldom engaged in conversation with him. Now, they are more confident to discuss issues with authority figures. One of the WDF's staff even engaged a Member of Parliament in a debate about the future of the WDF, an act which not only indicates the strength of the woman but also the strength of the organization.

The success of the RWDS has made women confident about pursuing new ventures. When women began organizing themselves into societies there were many people in the community who doubted that these societies would be successful. One of early members of an RWDS remembers her qualms about the organization: 'At first we didn't think that we could build up such a society. Now that we have succeeded we are confident to take on many things.'

On a personal level, the ability to save money, borrow and pay back loans has increased women's self-confidence. Most women had little experience with formal banking institutions when they began saving money in the JBS. They were accustomed a demoralizing cycle of indebtedness with money lenders, and doubted that they could escape this cycle. By saving small amounts of money each week, women have begun to accumulate savings for future activities. Beginning with small loans of

Rs500, women have demonstrated to themselves and others that they can pay back loans in a timely fashion. As their confidence increases with repaying every loan, women like Babanona increase the amount that they borrow.

Women's position in the family has also changed due to their contributions to family income. While in many families the male head of household is still considered the principal income-earner, increasingly it is the woman in the household who is assuring family subsistence and security through her ability to save and access credit. Women, such as the wives of fishermen, who take loans to invest in their husbands' livelihood ventures have become the 'spark' for economic development in their families, raising their importance and influence in the family unit. Some women reported that their husbands now respected and solicited their opinions more than before because they recognized that their wives were largely responsible for the family's well-being. Women in leadership positions within the RWDS and WDF also have found that holding this position leads to more respect and influence within the family.

As women have begun venturing out of the home and participating in RWDS activities, men's attitudes about women's mobility have changed in some cases. Particularly in non-agricultural families, men were accustomed to their wives remaining in the home and tending to domestic duties. As one woman noted, 'Men wanted their wives to be at home when they [the men] left for work and when they returned.' Some men objected initially to their wives' participation in the RWDS because they thought their wives would neglect domestic work. Women's participation in the RWDS and groups of five has challenged these traditional roles for women, although women have had to negotiate this change with their spouses. Labour sharing among the group of five has enabled some women to free the time to spend on group and RWDS activities.

High rates of male alcoholism in the region have strained male-female relations and led to the impoverishment of some families. Some women, such as Somawathie, have been able to use economic leverage (and in a few cases, the threat of desertion) to encourage their husbands to stop drinking. However, the problem of alcoholism demands more than economic interventions for successful resolution. The WDF and RWDS have been working with women to address issues of male alcoholism and to identify men who are at risk of becoming alcoholics.

Through the programme to curb alcoholism, and other activities, the RWDS, JBS and WDF have become important in fostering a sense of community and community action among women. In many cases women joined the RWDS because they were approached by a neighbour who felt that they could benefit from the RWDS and JBS's programmes. Padma joined the RWDS after a member found out that she was taking large loans annually from money lenders and therefore would profit from participating

138

in the JBS's savings and credit programmes. JBS staff often take an interest in their clients' welfare and encourage them in their endeavours. While individual women certainly benefit from the RWDS and JBS's activities, women articulate that the family and community also benefit from these organizations and their activities.

The status of these organizations within communities and the district is symbolized by the high visibility of physical structures associated with the WDF and JBS. In front of the WDF building in Hambantota is an imposing sculpture of a woman which visually sets it apart from other buildings in the town. The JBS offices are in otherwise modest homes and buildings, but signs in front of the buildings indicate that these are locations of the banking societies. While these are minor points, they do indicate that these organizations have a physical and public presence in the district.

Sustainability of Organizations and of Impacts
The sustainability of benefits to the members of the RWDS, JBS and WDF and the sustainability of the organizations themselves are interlinked. All three organizations recruit their leadership and staff from within the membership. Since capacity-building on a continuing basis is emphasized by the organizations, the result has been a group of women with strong leadership, managerial and, in the case of the JBSs' financial and administrative secretaries, technical skills. For example, the WDF, rather than hiring educated women from outside of the district, has strengthened the capacity of local women to manage and administer the organization's programmes. In most cases, WDF leaders and staff have risen from leadership positions in the RWDS. By recruiting staff from within the membership, the JBS and WDF ensure that their staff are accountable to the members and have sufficient knowledge of the local area to manage programmes competently – two necessary criteria for a sustainable organization.

Aside from assuring their institutional sustainability, the JBSs and WDF also strive to become financially sustainable. Initially the JBSs use donor funds channelled through the WDF to pay the financial and administrative secretaries. Over a period of three years the banking societies take on the payment of these staff themselves, using moneys made in investments. At the present time half of the JBSs in the district are financially sustainable and pay their staff's salaries. At the WDF level, financial sustainability is also an important consideration; the organization uses earnings from its assets to pay staff.

The RWDS, JBS and WDF are aware that there are circumstances which could threaten their sustainability. For instance, changes in government policies on NGOs and banking societies, while not expected, could change the legal environment in which the organizations operate. The 'savings and credit culture' which the JBSs have established could be threatened if the next government decides to forgive loans taken from the state banks. Furthermore, the organizations have been particularly vigilant to avoid national and local politics from taking root in the RWDS, JBS and WDF. Since these organizations are intended to unite women across political lines, political divisions could significantly fracture the organization. To prevent this division from occurring, the leadership of the organizations is changed on a yearly basis through consensus, since formal elections could bring politics into the organizations.

There is evidence to suggest that the economic impacts of the organizations' programmes on women will continue. Savings and loan disbursements continue to grow. Between May 1992 and December 1995 total member savings increased by 54 per cent. During the same period the total amount of loan disbursements increased by 1695 per cent. The economic benefit of savings for individual women will continue to grow over time as interest accumulates in savings accounts. As women's capacity to use loans increases, they take larger and larger loans. The WDF is expanding its training programmes for women entrepreneurs to enhance women's income generation capacity. Since the popularity of the JBSs is in part due to the 'demonstration effect' of some women's successes with savings and loans, it is expected that women will persist in participating in the JBS and that new members will continue to join the RWDS to take advantage of savings and credit through the JBS.

The research indicates that the non-economic benefits of participation will extend into the future and expand over time. The greatest non-economic benefit women derive is the solidarity and mutual aid with fellow group of five and RWDS members. While the WDF social mobilizers have been responsible for assisting the groups of five with their activities, the WDF intends this position to be phased out over time when women members gain the capacity to undertake functions of the social organizers themselves. Even though the RWDS, JBS and WDF have fostered the establishment of the groups of five and provide their reason for being, the mutual aid and solidarity aspects of the groups of five could outlast these organizations (in part because they are based on an indigenous institution), and in this sense, are sustainable over the long term. Participation in the organizations has also made women visible in, and a vocal part of, their communities. Since this process is in motion it is probable that more and more women will become empowered to effect change in their households and communities.

In brief, this case study has shown that women have benefited greatly from the WDF, RWDS and JBSs' programmes. In Hambantota district, the monopoly of money lenders in credit provision has been broken, and landless households have been able to purchase land. As a result of group membership, women have gained access to savings and credit for investment and consumption; acquired leadership and managerial skills; and attained a sense of solidarity and community action. While these are only a few of the benefits of the organizations featured in this case study, they do indicate that through savings, credit, training and group work, the RWDS, JBS and WDF have put women on the road to sustainable livelihoods.

UNIONIZATION

Empowering Marginalized Workers: Unionization of Tobacco Workers by the Self Employed Women's Association in Kheda, Gujarat

SHARIT BHOWMIK and MEENA PATEL

THIS STUDY FOCUSES on the unionization process and the consequent economic and social change among female tobacco workers in Kheda District, Gujarat. The Self Employed Women's Association (SEWA) began its trade union activities in Kheda District in 1986 and has since become the major trade union in the district. Its total membership in the district at the end of 1994 was 14 500. The main strength in SEWA's organization lies in its ability to link up pure trade union activity of bargaining for higher wages with social security such as child care, health, savings, insurance with employment promotion measures. SEWA's efforts in Kheda District are a striking example of what women can achieve through combined actions, leading to empowerment.

Unionizing Tobacco Workers

SEWA's interest in organizing tobacco workers in Kheda District arose primarily because of its activities among *bidi* (hand-rolled cigarette) workers in Ahmedabad. The union has been organizing these home-based women workers for better wages and other facilities. It also played a significant role in getting the union government to pass the Bidi Workers' Act which grants protection and social security measures to this section of the working class. In fact *bidi* workers constitute the largest section of SEWA's membership. After unionizing women involved in processing the finished product, it seemed natural that the union would become interested in those engaged in manufacturing the raw materials.

The living and working conditions of the tobacco workers also attracted SEWA's attention. Kheda District is one of the richest districts in Gujarat State. However, it is also a district of great inequities. Alongside wealthy milk producers, cotton and tobacco growers and tobacco factory owners live impoverished and exploited workers who make up the majority of the district's population. Those working in the tobacco industry are employed as agricultural or factory labourers. Work in the tobacco fields includes sowing, weeding, and harvesting the crop. Workers are supposed to receive

143

Gujarat's agricultural minimum wage of Rs15 per day, the lowest statutory minimum wage for agricultural labour in India, but they may receive less than this if they have no union to protect them. In the factories, work is slightly better paying but more hazardous than in the fields. Women work long hours beating tobacco leaves, feeding leaves into machines and packing tobacco into sacks. They conduct these tasks, which often involve lifting large quantities of tobacco, while breathing in a thick pallor of tobacco dust. Women suffer from respiratory problems, in addition to physical fatigue and back ailments, from working in these harsh conditions.

Indiraben, one of SEWA's organizers in Ahmedabad, is from Chikodera village in Kheda. Before migrating to Ahmedabad with her family she had been a tobacco worker. She had experienced first-hand the exploitative practices, hazardous working conditions and low remuneration of tobacco workers. Working for SEWA had made her a confident union organizer, and she was keen to return to her district and use her experiences for organizing the rural women there. SEWA immediately agreed to her proposal and she was asked to function as the co-ordinator for SEWA's activities in Kheda. She began work in her home village.

SEWA's strategies in forming unions are significantly different from those of traditional unions (irrespective of their ideological moorings). Usually when a union tries to enter a new area it does so by framing a charter of demands (which should appear to be different from the demands of the existing unions) with the hope that this will attract the workers to their fold. After registering some members these demands are placed before the employers and if they are accepted the union gains credibility. If the employers refuse to entertain the demands, the union mobilizes the workers to agitate for their implementation. The union's objectives thus revolve around trying to wrest some gains for the workers. Such a strategy can be justified if one views trade unions as bodies which have been created only for economic gains. The major problem with this approach is that it depends on the union leadership for solving the membership's problems. The workers may be aware of the problems they face, but since the union's leadership formulates strategies for solving these problems, the workers have little input into these strategies.

SEWA, on the other hand, begins its activities by conducting a socio-economic survey of the area. This survey is conducted to give the organizers an idea of the problems that women face. The next step is making them aware of these problems and their likely solutions. Women learn their legal rights through worker's education programmes conducted by the organizers. These programmes aim to educate women so that they, and not the organizers, can decide on appropriate courses of action. Although this is a longer process than that adopted by most other trade unions, it attempts to initiate action from the workers themselves.

When Indiraben started conducting workers' education classes in the villages, she got very little response. The women were afraid that if they

144

participated in the classes, their employers would find out and victimize them. Many of them were cynical of such efforts because they felt that even if they became aware of their rights, they could never confront their employers with their demands as they would lose their work. The women also lacked the confidence to face the landlords and factory owners. Most women never dared to look their employers in the face. They would always cover their faces with their garment (*pallav*) and would bend their heads whenever their employers were around. The women were disempowered due to three main factors. First, their poverty made them dependent on the benevolence of their employers for work. The employers could refuse for the slightest reason to give them work, and the women were helpless in this situation. Second, the social distance between the women workers and their employers was reinforced by caste differences between the upper caste employers and lower caste women. Third, the inequality in gender relations prevailing in society adversely affected their status both inside and outside the household.

Their work was considered subsidiary to that of males, and they were made to believe that they should be content with whatever wages they were given. Low wages and low social status, coupled with the fact that they were women, made them helpless and unorganized. Earlier attempts by trade unions in unionizing tobacco workers were directed towards males. It, therefore, became extremely difficult to attract women into trade unions.

The breakthrough came when, while organizing a class in her own village, Indiraben found that some of the women present did not get work. They had worked in a factory for several years, but seventeen of them lost their work because they had complained to the Labour Department that the factory workers were not given minimum wages. This happened three years ago, and they had remained unemployed since then. This incident had also scared the other workers, as they felt that they would meet the same fate if they dared to speak out against their employers.

Indiraben decided to take their cases before the Labour Department. The factory records showed that the women had been regular workers for several years and no formal disciplinary action was taken before they lost their jobs. They were simply not called when the factory started production during that season. SEWA decided to fight the employer legally because it was not possible to take recourse to any other form of action at that time. However, the proceedings in the labour courts are time-consuming and would be expensive for the retrenched workers who would have to travel to Ahmedabad for the hearings. SEWA therefore decided to try another tactic. It organized the women to write a letter to the Chief Justice of the Ahmedabad High Court, a copy of which was sent to the legal aid cell of the court. Much to their surprise, the High Court reacted positively by treating the letter as a petition, and the Chief Justice ordered an investigation. The presence of investigators in the factory unnerved the employers. They had never expected that these impoverished workers would get any

145

redress. They immediately agreed to discuss the case with the union and come to a settlement. Most of the women were reinstated immediately, and those who were too old to work were given compensation. This incident had its effect on the other employers – both land and factory owners – who started paying their workers the statutory minimum wage.

Although SEWA was able to establish its credibility among the women workers in the region, there still existed an element of fear among them. One would have expected the union's membership to show a dramatic rise but this did not happen until a few years later, when in 1987 the membership increased from a few hundred to over 2000 members. In order for the union to be effective it had to have women members from several more villages.

The case of Rasnol village is illustrative of women's experiences in the villages where SEWA first started work in the district. Later, unionization became comparatively easier when SEWA was well established as a trade union.

Rasnol: A Case Study on Initiating Unionization

Rasnol has 250 SEWA members at present and is considered to have one of the strongest unions in the district. It was one of the first villages to be unionized by SEWA. The village has a child care centre run by SEWA, a savings group of 50 members, and over 70 women members in an insurance scheme. There is one tobacco factory in the village that normally would provide work to over 250 workers. The factory has not been functioning since 1993, and this has caused a fall in the wages for workers in agriculture as there is hardly any other source of work in the area. However, this has not affected the growth in membership of SEWA because the women realize that they need their union even more at this stage. The employers exerted a great deal of control over the workers when they were not unionized. For instance, the women complained that wages were frequently deducted arbitrarily. The workers got loans from the employers, which was one basis for this domination.

Indiraben initiated trade union activities here in 1986 by organizing workers' education classes. Through these classes, the unorganized, low-paid women workers learned their rights as industrial and agricultural workers. They were informed of legislation that grants them protection and regulates their working time. For example, an employer could not make them work for longer hours than those stipulated. They also learned that there were statutory minimum wages for the jobs they were performing and that the wages they earned were below the minimum wages. These classes served as a sound base for the union. The women learned what their rights were so that they could demand these from their employers. This meant that they could rely now on their own collective strength instead of depending on others.

Initially, the sailing was not very smooth for Indiraben. The women were afraid of attending the classes because their employers would be displeased. Indiraben had to make several visits to the village to convince some of the women to participate in the classes. At first, only the Christian workers joined. Indiraben was a Christian, and it was easier for her to make headway in her own community. After some time, women from the Naik community joined and soon others followed. The employers were naturally upset at the state of affairs. They saw in the union a loosening of their hold over the workers. They tried to dissuade the women from joining SEWA by explaining to them that they would be better off under their (the employers') patronage. When this failed, the employers started to taunt the women: 'Will your leaders pay you your wages when we throw you out?'

What the employers did not realize was that the union had by then helped to forge a bond among the women. The workers' education classes served not only as a means of making women conscious of their rights but also as a meeting place where women could exchange views and discuss common problems. The women soon realized that they were no longer helpless individuals, and they drew their strength from their collective. The Chikodera incident increased their confidence because they saw that there was a legal system in the country which could protect them.

The first action the women took through their union was to demand the minimum wage which was at that time Rs7 per day. The employers were paying them only Rs5 per day. The union leaders from SEWA met the employers and asked them to pay the correct wages. The employers readily agreed and even paid the workers at the rate of Rs7 on the next pay day. However, soon after the union leaders left they started deducting the additional amount from the workers' pay.

Such actions were common in the past. When labour inspectors came for inspection the employers made a farce of paying the minimum wages but recovered the excess amount from the workers after they left. However, the women were no longer willing to take this lying down. They now had a union and it was through this union, not through the efforts of a labour inspector, that they had forced the employers to pay the right wages. They immediately complained to their union, which informed the labour office. This time the labour inspector came with the union leaders to inspect the books. The employers realized that their ruse would not work any more. They agreed to pay the workers their due wages. Thereafter, the workers were able to increase their wages in agriculture and in the factory periodically.

Unfortunately, the factory closed down in September 1993, and the workers were laid off. The owners said that the costs of production were too high and it was necessary either to raise productivity or reduce the wage bill to make the factory viable. The only way of doing this was by introducing the piece-rate system of wages instead of the existing time-rate system. The women protested against this move and the employers retaliated by closing down the factory.

The union tried to persuade the employers to reopen the factory, and when all efforts failed, the women sat in a *dharna* (sit-down) outside the factory gates for six days. They demanded compensation for job loss. They were entitled to gratuity under the law, but the employers tried to avoid paying by claiming that this was a temporary shut down. The women also insisted that they had to be given work if the factory reopened. On seeing the mood of the workers the employers agreed to pay compensation which ranged from Rs1000 to Rs4000 per worker, depending on the years of service.

At the time of this study, the agricultural wage rate in this village was Rs16 per day, lower than that in other villages which had been unionized. This was mainly a result of the closure of the factory. Moreover, there were no other factories nearby where the women could go for work. SEWA, therefore, started other income-generating programmes under the government's Development of Women and Children in Rural Areas (DWCRA) scheme. This scheme was initiated to help women living below the poverty line. The women are expected to form groups and take up some income-generating activity. They are given an interest-free loan of Rs15 000 which serves as their initial capital. In Rasnol 14 women have formed a DWCRA group for starting plant nurseries. Each woman is given 10 000 saplings which she tends in her backyard and later sells to nurseries in Anand or Ahmedabad. The women grow fruit tree and eucalyptus saplings that fetch a price of around Rs3 per sapling. Part of this income is used for repaying the loan, and another part is kept as capital with the group for further development work.

The problems that Indiraben faced in unionizing women in other villages in the district are similar to those she faced in Rasnol. In Jharakia village, for instance, Indiraben went from house to house during the nights to explain to the women the need for a union. After a great deal of persistence she managed to convince a handful of women to attend a workers' education class. In Khambolaj village she started off by approaching Maniben, the president of the Mahila Mandal (village women's organization). Maniben readily agreed to help, but when she spoke to her members they expressed the same fear of their employers' reactions as women in other villages. Maniben, who is now the local leader of SEWA (*agevan*), managed to convince 40 women to attend a five-day programme. Here too after the union was formed the employers threatened not to help them with loans or provide regular employment in future. In Samarkha village, Indiraben also could not convince the women to organize a programme because they were afraid of the repercussions. She finally had to take them to

148

another village where the union had been established to show them the confidence the women there gained after they formed their union.

The consequences of unionization were also similar in the district villages. In all the villages we covered, we found that the women gained confidence in their collective strength after unionization. In all cases wages also started to rise. In 1986 wages were between Rs5 and Rs7 per day; by 1995, they had risen to Rs18 to Rs30 per day. The villages where the wage was Rs18 were those that did not have any factories. Villages having higher wages (between Rs22 and Rs26) were those that had a number of factories. Obviously, the bargaining power of the workers was determined by the extent not only of unionization but also of employment opportunities at the village level. However, what is significant is that in all villages the prevalent wage was higher than the statutory minimum wage notified by the government, namely, Rs15 per day.

Employers' Strategies and SEWA's Response

As SEWA's influence grew among the women, the factory owners became more and more uneasy. This was the first time that a union had been able to exist in this area for so long. There had been two earlier attempts at unionizing workers in this sector.

One union was a non-starter as the workers suspected it of having links with the owners. The other union was more militant, but the owners resorted to violence in curbing its activities. Its leader was severely beaten up and had acid thrown in his face. The SEWA union, however, continued to exist and grow, despite the factory owners' efforts to curb it. The owners soon realized that the SEWA union was firmly embedded in the villages and that the women workers were remarkably loyal to it.

Factory Owners' Association

The owners sought to develop new strategies to counter the union's influence. Since the women were uniting across villages and factories, it was necessary for the factory owners to show similar solidarity. In 1990 the factory owners formed their own association to enable them to take decisions on an industry-wide basis. Most of the workers we spoke to felt that the association had been formed mainly to unite the factories against the growing influence of SEWA. Why, the women asked, had the tobacco producers' problems not been felt earlier and why hadn't the producers formed an association earlier?

It would be incorrect, however, to assume that the factory owners' association has played a negative role vis-à-vis SEWA. The association has in fact helped reduce hostilities between workers and the employers in certain cases. In some cases it has acted as a mediating influence which has prevented escalation of conflicts between workers and factory owners. In

149

other cases, such as the crèche programme run by SEWA, the association has taken a positive stand by directing factory owners to provide financial support. At other times SEWA and the association have come together to highlight the problems of tobacco growers to the government.

Migrant Workers
There are other measures that the employers have taken to cut labour costs. The first step was to import labour from outside the area. The neighbouring state of Rajasthan has a large section of impoverished tribals who are without work. They are hardworking and willing to work for low wages. Many of the factory owners have been importing these people to work in their factories during the peak season when the demand for labour is high. The migrants are mainly from the Sirohi district of Rajasthan and are called 'Marwari' by the local population. The factory owners get their labour through agents who operate in the recruiting district. These agents contact families who are willing to go to Kheda for work and pay them an advance in cash, in a sense 'booking' them for the season's factory work. The factory owner provides the migrants with accommodation within the factory premises and weekly advances to buy food. The balance of their wages is given to them before they return home. Moreover, as the Marwari workers reside within the factory, the employers can make them work for long hours. They can also be kept isolated from the regular workers and the union activities. The employers are thus able to use these migrant workers to increase their bargaining position with the local unionized workers. It is quite significant that the import of Marwari workers has been increased substantially since 1991, the time when SEWA had established itself as the sole union.

Naturally, the women were upset over the import of migrant workers, as their presence served to reduce the bargaining power of the unionized workers. They had united to fight collectively for better wages, but the employers had countered their efforts by creating another section of workers who were willing to work for lower wages and who have, in effect, depressed wages. In theory, the best way to deal with the situation was to unionize the migrant women workers, but this was almost impossible under the circumstances. These workers lived within the factories and were under control of the owners. The migrants themselves were afraid that they would be sent back without any pay if they tried to associate with SEWA.

The union has therefore demanded that cheap migrant labour cannot be employed when local labour is available. It has been able to build up a fairly strong resistance to the impact of migrant labour and has sought the help of the Labour Department in this matter. The union's appeal to the Labour Department is based on the question of minimum wages. It has argued that migrant workers in a factory are paid wages which are lower than those paid to the local workers. Since the wages of the latter are based

150

on agreements signed by the union and the employers, paying lower wages to a section of workers would amount to violation of the agreements. The union has subsequently pressed for the formation of tripartite committees, composed of labour inspectors, representatives of the union, and of the employers, which would inspect the factories to ensure that proper wages are paid. In addition, regular workers should be issued with identity cards which would assure them regular employment. The employers can employ outside workers only when regular workers are not available for work. The employers have conceded both of these demands. Tripartite committees have been formed, and regular inspections are held. The employers have also agreed to issue identity cards to their regular workers. In this way SEWA has tried to ensure that the local workers are able to get work regularly, and that they are paid the proper wages.

Their plans have not been totally successful, as the problem of migrant workers pushing down the wage rate persists. At the time this study was conducted only around 1000 workers had been issued with identity cards. The tripartite committees were functioning, but in most cases the employers' representatives did not participate during the inspections. Perhaps a more effective way of dealing with the situation would be unionizing the migrants at their places of origin, namely their villages. SEWA apparently is not averse to trying this approach and one may soon find another branch of SEWA in Sirohi district of Rajasthan.

Piece-rate vs. Time-rate
Apart from bringing in migrant labour, the employers are trying to cut costs by introducing a system of wage payment through piece-rates. The prevalent system of wages is based on time-rates: if the wage in a factory is fixed at Rs20 per day, the worker is paid this amount after working for eight hours. Under the piece-rate system, the worker is paid according to output, and wages can rise or fall depending on the output of the worker. In tobacco factories the piece-rate wages are paid to a group of workers. The group is given charge of processing tobacco through the various stages of production. The employers pay the group a lump sum based on the amount of tobacco (measured in *maunds* – 35 kilogrammes) processed.

The employers are interested in replacing the time-rate system with the piece-rate system because it increases productivity through encouraging workers to produce more so that they can maximize their income. The migrant workers are usually employed on this basis. However, it is resented by the unionized workers because it invariably involves an increase in their work-load. Work in the tobacco factories involves a great deal of back-breaking activity, and any increase in the work-load would further strain women's health. The rate fixed under the piece-rate system is often so low that workers have to put in much more physical labour to earn even the existing daily wage; this is especially difficult for the older workers. In factories where the piece-rate has been introduced, invariably the older women had to opt out of factory work and take work in agriculture, as they were unable to cope with the work-load.

SEWA has opposed the piece-rate system because it increases women's work-load. The union demanded that, before imposing this system, studies should be conducted to compare the work-load and remuneration under the two systems. SEWA suggested that for the purpose of study, each factory should introduce the piece-rate system for a limited period of time. The production and wages paid during this period should then be compared with those under normal production. In many cases the employers tried to manipulate production so that there would be a big difference in output. In Rasnol village the women told us that a study was conducted before the factory closed down. The employers deliberately slowed down production during the period of time-rate so that the period under piece-rate would show an exaggerated difference in production. This happened in several other factories as well, and the result was that no conclusions could be drawn.

SEWA has laid down two conditions for introducing the piece-rate system. First, under no condition should the wage fall below the wage fixed under time-rate. Second, the workers must have a choice as to which system they would like: both systems must co-exist. This is necessary for protecting the interests of the older workers, as they are unable to cope with the enhanced work-load under the piece-rate system. The employers' association have accepted both conditions.

The employers find SEWA's influence over the women workers a deterrent to their plans of increasing production while decreasing costs. SEWA's presence in the district has protected these workers from the factory owners' exploitive practices. The women recognize the value of the union in protecting their interests, as can be seen from the sudden increase in membership. Since 1993 the piece-rate system has been introduced in nearly all the factories, while SEWA's membership has increased from 6713 in 1993 to 14 500 in 1994 and still further to 40 215 in 1995. Therefore, as the employers increase their exploitive methods the women find a greater need for a union to protect them.

Beyond Trade Unionism

SEWA's popularity as a trade union stems from the fact that it caters to the needs of women workers. Women form the overwhelming majority of the workers in the unorganized/informal sector, but most trade unions operating in this sector deal with problems relating to wages and work. They are also 'gender neutral' in the sense that they do not adequately address the specific problems of women workers. SEWA, on the other hand, stresses the need to find solutions to women workers' problems, both within and outside their place of employment. it tries to tackle these problems in a holistic manner and not in a segmented form, as most trade unions do.

For SEWA, the economic empowerment of women is seen not only as a process through which they gain greater access to employment and other resources but also as a means of achieving egalitarian relations within the family. SEWA's activities are, therefore, not restricted to increasing the bargaining power of women workers but extend to other areas of women's lives.

This section will deal with the type of activities conducted by SEWA among the tobacco workers. These include organizing crèches, savings groups, insurance, health, DWCRA groups and educational stipends. The data are from the villages surveyed. We will focus on the various problems SEWA faced in getting these activities implemented at the village level.

Child Care Co-operative
By unionizing women workers, SEWA was able to ensure better wages and improved working conditions. However, women faced many other problems, the most urgent of which was child care. Although wages had increased after SEWA's intervention, they were still not very high. As a result, all members of a family often have to work in order to cover the basic needs. In such situations, women with small children suffer as they are unable to give sufficient time to their work or to their children. Normally in an extended family child care is shared by other members, such as the mother-in-law or sisters-in-law. However, if all of these people are in the fields and factories during the day, the infants must accompany their mothers to the workplace. This often reduces the labour productivity of these women, and employers are reluctant to hire them. The problem is most acute for women with very small children since they have to be carried while their mothers work.

The children also suffer because there are health hazards associated with the work sites (tobacco fields or factories). In the factories, the fumes and dust have severe effects on the respiratory system, and in the field, the strong odour emitted from newly-cut tobacco leaves makes even adults nauseous. The only alternative to taking a child to the work site is having an older child look after the younger one. When this occurs the older child cannot go to school.

The government has a scheme for providing child care centres, known as *balwadis*, in every village, but these are meant for children above three years of age. There is no support system for those below three years of age. SEWA decided to initiate child care programmes in some of the villages. The main problem was to find funds to support the programme. SEWA was able to get financial support from the Aga Khan Foundation and from government agencies. There were other requirements besides finance for starting the

153

crèches, the most important of which was getting adequate space in the villages. Kheda's agricultural prosperity has made land a precious commodity, and getting even a couple of rooms or a tiny bit of land in the villages is a problem. The lack of space is the main reason why more crèches cannot be organized in the villages. In all the villages where crèches operate, the space (and sometimes the rent) has been provided by the village *panchayat* (local self-governing body). Seven crèches were started in the first year, and by the end of 1994, there were crèches in 37 villages. This scheme has not only provided child care services to women workers but in the process has developed women's self-confidence.

Managing the Child Care Programme
Like all of SEWA's organizing activities, the child care programme in Kheda District was started as an activity 'from below'. It not only grew out of the felt needs of the women but, from the beginning, SEWA insisted that it be managed by the women. SEWA would help them during the initial stages of establishing the programme and would guide them later. However, decisions about how to start the centres and the engagement of personnel had to be worked out at the village level by the women themselves. Although SEWA agreed to help finance the venture by arranging for grants from the various funding agencies, the women had to take the initiative of organizing all the other requirements.

The first problem was finding places to start crèches. The SEWA village-level leader (accompanied by others) had to approach the *panchayat* for this space. Such interaction between poor women and the *panchayat* had never occurred in the past. Even though the *panchayat* is an elected body, given the power relations in the villages in this district, it is invariably dominated by wealthy, upper-caste villagers. The tobacco workers are from the poor section of the village and belong mainly to the so-called lower castes. Hence, for these socially and economically marginalized women, approaching the *panchayat* for help was itself an experience. While doing so they realized that the *panchayat*, which had refused to redress their grievances in the past, was now willing to help them because of their collective strength.

After obtaining space for the crèche, the women selected the crèche organizers. These women were former factory or agricultural workers and had to be given some training before they could start work. Their wages were paid out of the grants received by SEWA, which also paid for the children's food and milk. Yet, as the number of crèches grew, the funds became insufficient. Each crèche has around 25 or more children and at least two organizers who mind the children. In 1994, the average cost of running a crèche was Rs4000 per month. Since the grants did not increase in the same proportion as the increase in the number of crèches, it became necessary to seek other funding sources. Women tapped various sources. In

154

some of the villages the women approached the factory owners for grants as they reasoned that the crèches are beneficial to the owners because they are spared the responsibility of establishing crèches inside their factories (as required by law). Many of the factory owners agreed to support the scheme. The women also negotiated with the milk co-operatives and the poultry farms in their villages to supply milk and eggs free, or at concessionary rates. In most cases the women were able to obtain these contributions.

The members of the *panchayats* and milk co-operatives, as well as the owners of the tobacco factories and poultry farms, are wealthy and belong to the upper caste. For lower castes to beg favours from such people is in keeping with local patron-client relationships between the upper and lower castes. The approach of the women in this case was different, as they were not seeking charity. They asked for grants and donations as a form of community service to the village. Their argument was that since they were members of the village community and workers in the factories, the *panchayat* and factory owners had obligations to them. This approach was significantly different from the subservient attitudes these women had displayed in the past. Union membership had changed their outlook and increased their self-confidence.

Apart from the programme's basic objective of providing support to mothers of infants, SEWA saw the child care programme as another way to help the women gain confidence in their capacities to manage their own affairs. In keeping with its policy of decentralization, SEWA decided that the child care programme should become independent of the union and a co-operative society should be formed to run the child care programme. The members would be the child care workers (there were 60 of them in 1994) and the district organizers of the union. The co-operative was registered in December 1994 under the name of Shri Saishav Mahila Bal Sewa Sahakari Mandal Ltd. (Shri Saishav Women Child Care Workers' Co-operative Society). The co-operative is an independent body affiliated to SEWA. All funds SEWA receives for running the child care programme are given to this body. The co-operative was formed mainly to ensure that the decision-making process in the programme would be democratic and the organization would be able to raise its own resources in the future.

Problems in Running the Programme
The child care centres were not always easy to establish. In a number of villages there were pressures from various quarters to close the programme. Even after the women were able to get their *panchayat* to sanction a place for the crèche, there were problems in retaining it. These problems centred mainly around caste issues. The upper castes often felt threatened by the fact that these women had been assertive enough to get what they wanted. In Rahatlav, where there was a shortage of space for

155

starting the crèche, the *panchayat* agreed to accommodate it in a room within the temple. This decision incensed the upper castes, who felt that the presence of lower caste children inside the temple would defile it.

However, the *sarpanch* (head of the *panchayat*) was firm about the decision and was able to deflect the problem for the time being. In the next election, the *sarpanch* lost and the leader of those opposing the crèche got elected. The crèche was closed soon after. The women retaliated by mobilizing support for restarting the crèche. Their efforts started gaining ground, which put the new *sarpanch* on the defensive. He finally agreed to provide another place for the crèche.

Women in Khambolaj village also had to struggle for crèche space. The *panchayat* refused to provide any space for the crèche, despite several requests from the women. Angered by their attitude, Luciaben, a local SEWA leader, decided to contest the next *panchayat* elections and won. Her sole objective in getting elected was to start the crèche and she was successful in doing this with the solid support of the women in the village. She is one of the three crèche organizers in the village. Her membership in the *panchayat* has helped women in other ways as well. She has been able to provide homestead plots to 120 poor women.

The major problem in expanding the number of crèches lies in the acute shortage of space in the villages. In Mehlav village, for example, the *panchayat* is willing to pay the rent for housing the crèche, but the women have not been able to find any place. The prosperity of the district has increased the value of land tremendously. The losers in this situation are the poor who find it exceedingly difficult to have access to any form of surplus land, either agricultural or village land. The plant nursery scheme under the DWCRA programme also faces the same difficulty. Unless some solution is found to this problem, the child care scheme will not be able to increase its activities. Perhaps one way would be to force the *panchayats* or the state government to requisition land in the villages for setting up crèches.

Women have benefited greatly from the crèche schemes. Their income has increased as they are able to work uninterrupted, and their children are well fed and cared for. This success has increased expectations in villages that do not have crèches. Moreover, the women now want the child care co-operative to start *balwadis* (centres for pre-school children) also. Since the crèches are being run efficiently the women feel confident that the *balwadis* would be run in the same manner if SEWA takes them over. However, *balwadis* are more expensive to run than crèches. In fact, paucity of funds is a major problem, and the union is trying to overcome this by raising its own resources. During the *agevan's* annual meeting held in December 1994, the *agevans* decided that each member should contribute Rs10 for setting up a core fund for the co-operative: this will amount to Rs140 000. In addition, the members would continue to approach the milk co-operatives and poultry farms in their villages for contributions.

Savings Groups
While the trade union has clearly contributed to the economic empowerment of women, another means of increasing this process is through savings. From its inception, SEWA has tried to link savings to its other activities. The members are encouraged to save a part of their earnings in banks. These savings can be used in the future for increasing their assets or for emergencies. Thus they need not fall prey to unscrupulous money lenders who charge exorbitant interest. SEWA's bank has played a key role in mobilizing the members' savings. Since it may not be possible for each woman to deposit her savings in the bank each month, women are encouraged to form savings groups for depositing their monthly savings. The group has a leader who is responsible for collecting money from each member (usually Rs10 each month) and depositing it in the bank.

Members can also avail themselves of loans from the savings groups. The group acts as the guarantor for the member and is responsible for collecting the dues. Each group can have its own guidelines regarding repayment and interest on loans. In Kheda, the savings group charges interest rates which are slightly higher than those charged by SEWA's bank. One part of the difference is kept by the group as its capital, another part is kept as an emergency fund, and the rest goes into the child care programme.

Women take loans for many purposes: repairing or extending their houses, buying cattle, releasing mortgages, and paying medical expenses. In most villages the women could not get loans in their own names from the banks because they do not own property and, therefore, could not provide collateral. In times of need they took loans from money lenders who charged very high rates of interest. The savings scheme has helped women get easy access to credit in times of urgency. Moreover, the women can use loans to purchase assets. Some of the women have bought cattle with the loans, while others have been able to redeem land which had been mortgaged.

In some cases the women have been able to set up small businesses with loans. We met one such person in Jhakaria village. She was from the caste of barbers and she was not familiar with agricultural work. After she joined the savings group she was able to get a loan to start a small provisions shop which she and her husband run in the village. In other cases, women have used their loans to pay for their daughters' education and to help their daughters pursue professional courses, such as paramedical training. The loans are repaid after their daughters find employment.

As loans are given only to women, the assets generated by the loans are in the women's name. The loan helps to increase the family's assets while giving the woman greater control over them. Similarly, if a loan is sought for redeeming mortgaged property, the title of the property has to be transferred to the woman (wife in most cases) before the loan is granted. In this way the savings groups encourage the process of economic empowerment of the women by giving them greater access to property. Apart from encouraging thrift, the savings groups give women confidence that they have direct control over their own resources since the savings and loans are in their own names. By contrast, women have some (but not total) control over their earned income, as this is pooled within the family budget.

In Jhaparia some of the women belonging to the land-owning sections approached SEWA to allow them to join the savings group. Normally this would not be allowed because the groups, like all the other activities of SEWA, are meant only for poor working women. However, on seeing their persistence the organizers decided to place their request before the members. The members readily agreed to accept the women in their group, and these women started contributing Rs10 every month which they saved from their household expenses. These relatively well-off women were very happy to be in the group because they felt that the money they saved, however little the amount, was their own. After a year, their husbands learned of this involvement, and they immediately stopped their wives from saving. The husbands did not understand why their wives, who could ask them for money at any time, would want to have independent savings accounts. The women's view was that they had joined the group to have independent access to resources instead of depending on their husbands.

By the end of 1995, there were 176 savings groups in the district with a total membership of 5690. The total amount of savings was Rs929 439, and Rs3 098 960 had been disbursed as loans. The repayment rate is 98 per cent.

Health Workers' Co-operative

SEWA's health support programme is run through a co-operative known as Lok Swasthya Sahakari Mandali Ltd. (People's Health Co-operative Society). This co-operative operates at the state level (unlike the child care co-operative which operates at the district level) and has health workers operating in villages and in the urban slums. The co-operative runs a few medical shops in municipal hospitals where it sells low-cost medicines and organizes training programmes for health workers and educational programmes for women (for example, on child care). Fees – which are placed in the co-operative's fund – are charged when these training programmes are offered to other organizations (NGOs or government agencies). The co-operative also charges fees for the services it renders to the clients, but these are very minimal. The fees charged and the profits from the medical shops are the main sources of income for the co-operative. The members of the co-operative are the health workers and other employees.

The health workers are selected from among the women workers. They are trained for the tasks they are expected to perform. Each health worker is allotted a few villages which she visits weekly. The health worker's duties include: supplying patients with low-cost medicines; immunizing children; promoting family planning; promoting maternal and child health care; and monitoring the health of the children in the crèches. She has to maintain records on each case for future reference. The clients are charged Rs2 per visit for children and Rs3 per visit for adults.

One of the major contributions of the health scheme is that it has made women conscious of their health and hygiene which, in turn, has reduced illness within their families, especially among their children. As a result women are better able to work and increase their income. Many of the women feel that the child care scheme and the health scheme have helped reduce a lot of worries for them. The morbidity rates in these villages have also declined, mainly because the women are now more aware of diseases and their causes, and medicines are easily available.

Other Support Programmes

One of SEWA's more popular schemes, developed in collaboration with the General Insurance Corporation of India, is the insurance scheme for the poor. Under this scheme, women take out insurance policies which cover their houses, health and accidents to a limited extent. The members have to pay Rs5 as a membership fee and Rs45 annually as premium. The women have benefited mainly from the insurance coverage on their houses. The monsoons in 1994 were especially severe in this district, and several members' houses were washed away by the heavy rains. The insurance has helped them recover major costs. The families of women who have died in accidents have also been compensated. In case of damage to property the survey to assess the damages is conducted jointly by SEWA's volunteers and the insurance officials. The scheme has become very popular among the women, and there are more members of the insurance scheme than of savings groups.

Apart from striving for improved living standards for its workers, SEWA is also trying to develop alternative forms of employment for the rural poor. One channel for doing this is the DWCRA programme.

In many of the villages, SEWA has been organizing the women to form DWCRA groups and start employment programmes through these groups. The most common scheme is plant nurseries. Plant nurseries have a great deal of potential in providing alternative or additional income to the rural poor as there is a good market for seedlings and saplings in the district. In Banaskantha, where this scheme is more extensively implemented by SEWA (as we have seen in the previous study), constraints to growing the better (and more expensive) varieties of plants are due to the local climatic and soil conditions. Moreover, the women in Banaskantha are totally dependent on the Forest Department for purchase of the saplings. These problems do not exist in Kheda. Because of better climatic, soil and market conditions in Kheda, the DWCRA groups are able to grow better varieties of plants and sell saplings at remunerative prices. However, the main constraint in Kheda is the limited availability of land. This factor has inhibited the expansion of this scheme to a larger number of poor women. None the

159

less, in places where it had been implemented, women have been able to increase their earnings.

SEWA has also tried to start other ventures under the DWCRA scheme besides plant nurseries. In Sinhoul village, it has used the DWCRA programme to encourage weaving. The weavers in this village had given up their profession because of impoverishment and had sought work as agricultural labourers in the tobacco fields. Although they have looms in their homes, they were unable to use them because they had no funds for buying yarn. SEWA unionized this village in 1992 and organized 12 women weavers into a DWCRA group. At first, SEWA negotiated contracts with the Khadi and Village Industries Commission to purchase coarse cloth, known as *Janata* cloth, which is sold at subsidized prices to the poor. However, the returns to the weavers from this variety of cloth were very low – lower than the wages they received as labourers. Recently SEWA has arranged for the Handloom Board to provide training for these women to upgrade their skills. The women are able to sell their improved products at fairly remunerative prices in the local market.

SEWA has also tried to help the workers' children to get education and learn new skills. Girls are encouraged to take up professional courses and, as noted earlier, loans from the savings groups are given for covering these expenses. Children of tobacco workers are entitled to receive stipends from the government for their education. These stipends are granted under the Bidi Workers' Act. The union helps the parents avail themselves of these stipends for their children. In 1995 it was able to get 150 stipends sanctioned.

The different schemes started by SEWA have helped improve the working conditions as well as expand employment opportunities for women. The crèche, savings and health schemes have contributed to improved working conditions but have also provided employment for women. For example, 60 former tobacco workers are now engaged as crèche organizers. If this scheme can be extended to other villages, more women workers will find alternative employment in the crèches. Similarly, the health workers' co-operative has provided employment to a number of women workers. Despite its limitations, the DWCRA programme has been able to provide employment for a number of women in the district.

Expanded employment opportunities, in turn, contribute to keeping the wage level stable. In a labour surplus situation, employers can keep wages low even when workers are unionized. The union recognizes that its bargaining position is weakened by surplus labour. Hence, withdrawing labour from the tobacco fields and factories into DWCRA schemes eases the situation in favour of the workers. The alternative employment created through SEWA's efforts may not be very widespread at present, but it is significant none the less. The women members are aware that employment can be created through means other than their employers, including their

160

own collective efforts. This basic lesson should encourage women to try alternative avenues of employment-generation in the future.

Impact of Economic Empowerment

In the preceding sections we have described the various strategies employed by SEWA in improving the economic conditions of the women tobacco workers in the district. Although the primary objective of SEWA as a trade union is to assure higher wages and improved working conditions by increasing the bargaining power of workers (*vis-à-vis* their employers and the state), SEWA links up various strategies to consolidate its activities. Most of the activities, whether or not explicitly economic, are linked to the central problem of increasing economic empowerment of the women. The union activities and the DWCRA schemes are focused directly on improving the economic conditions of, and creating alternative employment for, the workers. The other SEWA activities – such as insurance, savings, child care and health – serve a dual purpose of improving the quality of life of the women and their families, and thereby the productive potential of the women.

Drawing Strength from the Collective
SEWA's trade union activities have brought the women together as a group and made them aware that their strength lies in their unity. This change was brought about not through populist methods, such as mobilizing workers through emotional slogans and speeches. Instead, SEWA organized classes and study circles to raise the women's awareness of their rights and the need for unionization. SEWA's process is more painstaking and slow compared to the more standard methods adopted by other trade unions. Under the SEWA approach, a lot of groundwork has to be done before the union is firmly established. SEWA's approach has a deeper and more far-reaching influence on the workers because they begin to understand their rights, know the laws which protect them, and understand the importance of a union for defending their rights.

Another important feature of this process is that it helps workers gain greater confidence in their own capacities. They are able to understand and analyse their problems on their own instead of depending on outsiders. SEWA has deliberately chosen this strategy because of its policy of decentralizing decision-making to the grassroots level. SEWA has thus not only provided a union to fight for women's rights but has also given women the courage to speak up before their employers when their rights are violated. This aspect became very explicit when we interviewed the workers in the different villages. Time and again, we heard two words: *jagruti* (consciousness) and *sangathan* (organization). According to the women, they become aware (*jagrut*) of their rights

161

through their organization (*sangathan*). They told us that earlier they were afraid of and, therefore, docile towards their employers. They would never look at them face-to-face but would always cover their faces with their *pallav* (the end of their sari) in front of strangers. Now, they have discarded this veil as they are no longer afraid. Their *sangathan* has given them courage.

Many of the women had never been out of their villages, and the few who had travelled had never gone beyond Anand (the district headquarters). After joining the union, women started to leave their villages to attend union meetings. Many of them have now visited other districts and towns. The leaders (*agevans*) told us that earlier they were nervous and shy while speaking in front of strangers. They would never have imagined addressing large crowds, but now they could address large gatherings with confidence. They were no longer afraid to travel out of their villages. In almost all cases, women told us that they gained this sense of confidence through belonging to their *sangathan*.

Their new-found confidence gave women the courage to tackle other problems besides those of work and wages. At the village level, the women have been effective in intervening politically in the affairs of the *panchayats*. This is clearly seen in the establishment of child care centres in the villages. In most cases they were able to influence the *panchayat* to solve their problems. The women in Mehlav village told us that they now go to the *panchayat* office and sit on the chairs while talking to the *panchayat* members. Earlier, they used to cover their faces and sit on the ground with their heads lowered. Although they have not been able to start a crèche as yet, they have managed to get other demands met, such as the construction of a road near their homes and improved drainage.

The *agevan* of Jhakaria village narrated how she tackled the *panchayat* and the local police over a land dispute. When she was away from the village, the *panchayat* encroached on a part of her land to dig a well for a nearby upper-caste landowner to irrigate his fields. They even cut down seven trees on her land and took them away. On her return, she found that these people had filed a complaint against her with the police, accusing her of being a trouble maker. She told us that as soon as she heard of this, she went to the police and gave them a piece of her mind. She told them that she was from SEWA, that all the working women in the village were behind her, and that the police and the *panchayat* should realize that women like her are no longer ignorant and afraid. She even told the police officer (while sitting on a chair in front of him) that as a worker for SEWA she was rendering free service to the poor while the police were drawing salaries and doing nothing. Her barrage produced results, as the cases against her were dropped and she got back her land and her trees. She narrated this incident to us to explain how she had become bolder after she started working for SEWA. While she was speaking, another *agevan*, from

162

Gopalpur village, who happened to be present, told of similar experiences she had with the upper castes in her village. She too was able to confront them. In the other villages we visited we found the same attitude among the women. They said that they were no longer afraid of approaching district officials and the police when they faced problems. They explained that they understood their rights after attending the workers' education classes and that they lost their fear of those in authority after they realized their collective strength.

Changes in Gender and Family Relations
SEWA's work among the tobacco workers has had a very significant impact on gender relations. SEWA is the only trade union operating among the tobacco workers in the district. It organizes only women workers, and, as noted above, has played a major role in improving wages and working conditions. Male workers (not just female workers) have benefited from these measures, as their wages have also increased. The Equal Remuneration Act has abolished wage differences between the sexes, so when the SEWA union fought and secured better wages for its members the males also got similar increase in wages. It is important to note that women's struggles can benefit men, as usually they are perceived to be antagonistic to men.

The men recognize that whatever benefits they have gained are due to their wives, daughters or sisters being unionized. This has helped change the attitudes of men towards women within the working class. The women, realizing their strength, no longer comply with the subservient role that they were earlier expected to play within the family. For example, while discussing these issues with a group of women in Mehlav village, they told us that their husbands now share the housework, which they never did in the past. In many of the homes the men fetch water and firewood and help with cleaning. The women felt that their husbands respected them more now because they [the women] had become conscious and vocal. Their husbands, they add, had become more conscious than before mainly due to their activities.

Most of the women we interviewed told us that their family life had improved considerably after they had joined the union. The women felt more confident now and refused to be dominated by their husbands or their mothers-in-law. Wife beating by drunken husbands, which was very common in the past, has almost disappeared. In some of the villages the women told us that when such instances occurred they got together and told the errant husband to mend his ways.

SEWA's fortnightly magazine, *Ansuya*, is an important instrument for raising the consciousness of the women. The success stories of women published in the magazine are read out aloud in group meetings for the benefit of those who cannot read. Many of the women told us that the

163

magazine has helped them expand their horizons as they became aware of different issues concerning women.

After talking to the *agevans* and other women in the different villages, it became evident to us that there had been marked changes in family life; relations between husband and wife, between mother-in-law and daughter-in-law had become less repressive. What was more striking is that these changes did not occur through confrontations between the newly-conscious wife and the conservative/oppressive husband or mother-in-law. On the contrary, we found that the changes were a result of family acceptance of the new role the women played after forming their union. This again was largely due to SEWA's approach of laying greater stress on the family in the process of empowerment. The women were aware that the family was necessary for their own development but there had to be changes in the relationships within it.

In brief, we found that SEWA's programmes among the tobacco workers has had a significant influence in changing the lives of the women and their family relationships. The women have gained a great deal of confidence through their union and its allied activities. The changes, both economic and social, are deep rooted and are likely to continue. They are likely to be sustained due to three factors. Firstly, the institutions created, namely the union and the other support structures, are democratic bodies and they draw strength from the grassroots and not from the top. Secondly, most of the structures are financially independent (the union, DWCRA groups, saving groups and the health workers' co-operative) and those that are still dependent on external aid (child care co-operative) are likely to become self-supporting in the future. Finally, although these structures are independent bodies, they have strong links with each other, and therein lies their strength.

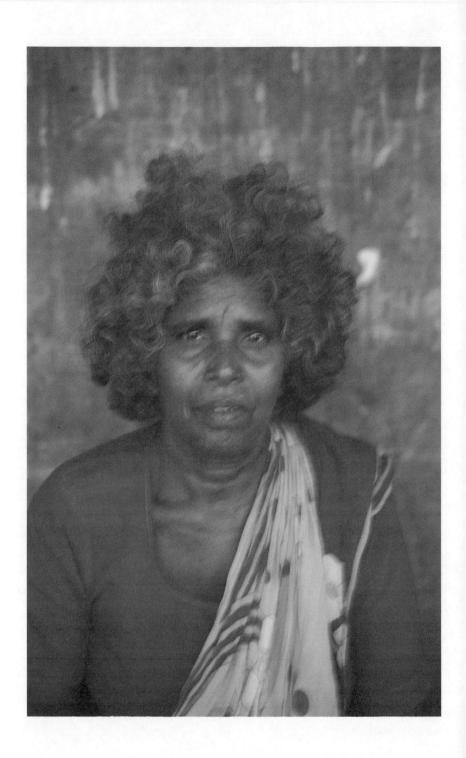

A Struggle within a Struggle: The Unionization of Women in the Informal Sector in Tamil Nadu

GEETHA RAMAKRISHNAN

We are the fighting force – not the deciding force

THE STRUGGLE OF unorganized labour in Tamil Nadu has persisted for over fifteen years. It began with construction workers fighting for better employment conditions, and spread to *bidi*[1] workers agitating for their rights. Women have been a critical force in all of these struggles. The number of women labourers in the unorganized sector in Tamil Nadu is estimated to be 7.8 million, with 2.5 million women participating as labourers in the construction industry alone, according to the 1991 census. Although these women constitute a large portion of the unorganized labour force, their worth as labourers has been inadequately valued. For example, the family incomes of unorganized women labourers range from Rs100 to Rs600 per month, placing them well below the official poverty line of Rs16 000 per year.[2] Inside the union movement, women have also had to 'struggle within the struggle' to get their voices and particular concerns heard. Some unions have failed to recognize or value the needs of their women members, leading to friction between the male leadership and female members.

Since union movement in the unorganized sector began with the construction industry, this will be the initial focus of this case study. The case study then will turn to the labour movement among *bidi* workers.

Unionization of Women Labourers in the Construction Industry

Women's work is essential to the construction industry. As the following section reveals, women are involved in many of the processes on sites and perform most of the heavy manual labour. However, labour conditions are poor and the rates of pay for women labourers are lower than those of their male counterparts. While there have been attempts, and successes, at organizing construction labourers since the 1930s, most unions have not recognized and advanced women's concerns as construction labourers.

---

[1] *Bidis* are hand-rolled cigarettes.
[2] Rs100 = US$3.30 as at July 1995.

Women in the Construction Industry

Women and child labourers, referred to in the industry as *chithals* (small persons), are on the lowest rung in the hierarchy of construction workers, receive the lowest wages, and carry out tough physical labour even in the sweltering heat of summer. The invisibility and exploitation of construction labourers, especially of women, occurs not only in the private house-building sector but also in government-financed construction.

Construction work normally starts by 8 a.m. and finishes by sunset. Construction workers typically labour for 9–10 hours a day but may work 12–14 hours a day, especially when laying concrete. No distinction is made between regular working hours and overtime work. Even though the Tamil Nadu Construction Workers Act of 1984 stipulates that the working day is nine hours, this act is yet to be implemented. Contractors often add a night shift in order to finish a piece of work to meet a deadline, but extra payment, if any, is arbitrary and very low.

Much of the work on a construction site is subcontracted and because of this the tendency to complete construction at break-neck speed is an inherent characteristic of construction work. The subcontractors are paid on a piece-rate basis, and their profits lie in the speedy completion of the construction project. They increase their profits by speeding up the work and increasing the length of the working day.

There is a gendered division of labour in construction work, as with most labour. Women do much of the heavy manual work on construction sites. Men typically dig the foundation holes and fill the baskets with mud, while women carry the earth and deposit it in the place allotted for it. Even though the digging is normally done by male workers, it is not uncommon to see women handling crowbars or spades. When laying a floor, women are employed in breaking rocks or bricks into small pieces, using a hammer.

Masonry work involves constructing walls with brick and mortar and then smoothing them as soon as the cement is applied. While both men and women prepare the mortar, women carry (headload) bricks, mortar, and water to the place where the mason is at work, often climbing ladders and scaffolding in the process. Women also assist masons in their work and clean implements and mortar trays after the work.

Curing work is mostly undertaken by women. As soon as the concreting is done, the floors, roofs and walls have to be continuously wetted with water. The water is allowed to stand on the floor in order for the mortar and cement to settle and dry properly. Curing has to be continued for a period of ten days.

Concreting work involves both men and women. The materials required for the concrete mixture are usually assembled near the machine by men, if this involves carrying bags of cement or sand. After the mixture is made, men and women form a human chain all along the scaffolding up to the place where the concrete is layed. In quick succession, the full mortar trays

168

are passed from one hand to another, as the work must be completed in a single day. On big sites, more women are employed to do only concreting work while in small sites, women do a combination of all types of work.

The physical difficulty of women's construction work cannot be overestimated. In concreting work, as much as 32 000kg of concrete mixture may pass through a woman worker's hands during a day. Women involved in masonry work will carry 9–12 bricks at a time, each weighing approximately 2.5kg. During an eight-hour shift of excavation work, women may carry up to 21 000kg of mud from the excavation site. The physical duress of women's work is exacerbated by the fast pace of construction work which often demands overtime hours.

Labour Conditions
There are two major groups of employers of construction labour: those in the private sector, and the government. In a survey of selected government construction sites conducted with the assistance of the Centre for Labour Education and Development,[3] the survey found that women labourers were recruited through subcontractors except in one case where they were recruited by the contractor.

In none of these sites was the minimum wage of Rs40 per day (1993) paid to unskilled workers. Women were paid between Rs20–25 per day, while male labourers doing the same unskilled work were paid Rs30–35. No employment cards or wage slips were provided for the workers, though many hundreds were employed on each site.

Child labourers were present in every government site and numbered 200 in the Telegu Ganga Project. Children generally played in the sand and at best were supervised by older children. At the Madras Harbour site there were 100 children below the age of five being watched by 60 older children.

The workers on the government sites were mainly migrants brought in from the drought-hit areas of South Arcot and Salem District and were housed in tiny low-built huts measuring 6′ × 8′ with no drinking water, toilet, or lighting facilities. At the Telegu Ganga site workers were bathing in a stagnant pool of dirty water for lack of washing facilities. Lack of drinking water at all the sites was also a problem. Since there was no canteen or even a tea shop at the Telegu Ganga site, workers had to travel miles just to get something to drink.

The workers employed in the construction of factories at the TAMIN sites were not provided with Employee State Insurance or Provident Fund. An accident that occurred in the construction of the Nehru Stadium

---

[3] See CLEAD Report on Government Construction, by E. Raman *et al*. The government construction sites surveyed were: the Madras Refineries, Manali, Madras Refineries Narimanam, Madras Harbour, Madras Rapid Transport System under Southern Railway, the TAMIN Factory Barugur, the PWD construction at Tirumayam and Barugur, and TAMIN (where the Tamil Nadu State Construction Corporation (TNSCC) was the contractor).

became an important issue in the agitation, even for payment of compensation. In short, the Minimum Wages Act, the Equal Remuneration Act, the Contract Labour Act, the Child Labour Act, and the Employees State Insurance Act – as well as numerous ILO conventions – were violated at all the government sites surveyed, even though each project cost millions of rupees.

For house building and medium-sized construction sites, workers are recruited either directly by *maistries* (masons who work as labour contractors) from slums and squatter settlements in cities and towns, or at marketplaces where they gather in the morning for work. There is fierce competition by *maistries* as well as workers to obtain work, and the most vulnerable are women. In Tamil Nadu, workers recruited in marketplaces in big cities like Madras, Madurai, and Coimbatore are paid minimum wages of Rs50 per day (1995), while the *maistry*-attached labour is paid between Rs45 and Rs50 per day. The number of working days ranges from 15 to 20 per month in the former case, while in the latter it is 20 to 25 days per month.

In the towns and villages the women's wages remain between Rs20 and Rs30 per day. There is no improvement in wages with experience. Moreover, women who start their working lives by age 10 find that due to physical duress, they must retire by age 50.

Women also face discrimination in the area of skill acquisition. Although some women have been trained in masonry, no promotional avenues exist for them. In the male-dominated *maistry* subcontracting system, even women with masonry skills may not find employment as masons.

The low wages paid to women workers have made their existence precarious. Between 30 and 50 per cent of women construction labourers are single women and shoulder financial responsibility for the family. Unexpected medical expenses, house rent and the education of children have become so difficult that indebtedness is a daily reality. With migrant labour, the added problem of moving from site to site and a lack of child care or educational facilities leads to child labour. Entire families of construction workers are bonded to the same industry from one generation to the next.

Chithals face a variety of serious health problems due to the nature of their work. Since they carry heavy loads and climb ladders, they complain of back pain, headaches and exhaustion, as well as breathing difficulties from inhaling dust and cement. Women work until the end of pregnancy and get back to work soon after delivery in order to make both ends meet. They often go into debt to meet childbirth expenses. Again, since they are not eligible for Employees State Insurance, every bout of sickness also plunges them into debt.

The majority of construction workers are homeless and live in slums or on pavements. The absence of basic amenities in these living conditions also increases the burden of housework for women, who may have to travel some distance for drinking water or toilets. Slum fires often lead to the

170

deaths of unattended children when their parents are at work on construction sites. Rather than improving slums and providing basic amenities, the Tamil Nadu State Government (in the name of 'Vision 2000' and various city beautification schemes) has enacted a vicious slum eviction policy of pushing slum dwellers to the outskirts of cities, forcing them to travel greater distances to reach their places of employment and to spend greater amounts from their meagre income on bus fare.[4] This city beautification scheme has promoted a form of neo-untouchability; unorganized labourers are required for the sustenance and growth of the state, but they are not allowed to live as citizens in the very cities they sustain.

Accidents and fatalities are an everyday feature of the construction industry. Fatal accidents have occurred due to open wells, electrocution, falling from roofs and scaffolding, earth cave-ins, and the collapse of walls. Protective measures are completely absent. Lack of proof of employment and total indifference on the part of a principal employer and contractor to assume liability are the major obstructions to getting compensation.

Struggles and Unionization in the Construction Industry

Although attempts at unionizing construction workers in the southern districts of Tamil Nadu were initiated during the nationalist movement of the 1930s and 1940s, such organizing was largely unsuccessful until the events of 1979 galvanized union activities in the construction sector. In 1979, cement scarcity and spiralling prices of building materials halted construction activities and led to widespread unemployment and starvation. In response to this situation construction workers spontaneously organized marches in Madras, with women construction workers at the forefront. They demanded the state to enact a control on the price of building materials, provide unemployment benefits for laid-off workers, and grant legal protection for construction workers.

Out of this struggle, construction workers formed a union, the Tamizhaga Kattida Thozilalar Madhya Sangam (TMKTMS). The union further defined the construction workers' demands to the state: the institution of a commission to fix minimum wages; provision of medical benefits through the Employees State Insurance Corporation;[5] crèche facilities; Rs10 000 relief for families of accident victims; 25 per cent reservation of houses constructed by Tamil Nadu Slum Clearance Board for construction workers; and free supply of work tools and implements. Neither the Tamil Nadu Government nor the

---

[4] As in the case of the Wallace Garden slum dwellers who were removed from their residence in central Madras and taken to a site 20km from Madras. See Kamala Visweswaran, 'Illegal Slum Evictions in Madras City,' *Economic and Political Weekly*. 21 October 1988.

[5] The Employees State Insurance Scheme is a compulsory health insurance scheme for all employees. Both employers and employees contribute to the scheme.

opposition parties responded to these demands, even after further demonstrations. However, the masons' guilds in different parts of the state responded to the agitation, and thus the union spread to the districts.

The charter of demands was submitted to the Government of India, and a delegation of construction workers visited Delhi in 1981 which led to the filing of a private member's bill on these demands. As a result, the Government of India issued a circular during the same year, extending Employee State Insurance medical benefits to construction labourers.

Finally, in 1982, the Tamil Nadu government responded to the union's demands and enacted the Tamil Nadu Manual Labourers' Act. This act provided for tripartite boards for various sectors within the construction industry which were listed in the schedule.

Crisis on the Union Front: Formation of the Second Union
In the early 1980s, the union leadership decided to field candidates for the BC/SC Front. When the union's membership register was sent to the Election Commission as proof of its membership pool, it came to light that its records had not been kept accurately. In particular, the union's membership, which was over 30 000 at the time, was shown in the records as numbering only 240. Poor accounting and the political alliances that the union leadership made for electoral purposes led to upheaval within the union. Many members felt that the leadership was concentrating too much on politics to the detriment of the union's democratic functioning.

In 1983 this upheaval resulted in the formation of a second union, the Tamil Manila Kattida Thozhilalar Sangam (TMKTS), with the aim of building a force of construction labourers on a non-party basis. The union continued pressing the government on issues of accident relief for workers' families, provision of housing and crèches, implementation of Employee State Insurance scheme for medical benefits, and non-payment of workers wages, to name a few. Legislation on these issues, the union felt, was necessary to protect construction workers, and government action was obligatory since the government was the largest employer of construction workers.

The union received some response to its demands in 1983 when the state government formed a Minimum Wages Commission to fix minimum wages for construction workers. In the same year, the government also introduced the Construction Workers Bill which extended existing labour acts to construction workers. This bill, however, was unsatisfactory to the union because it failed to consider the nature of employer–employee relationships in the construction industry. The union formed a committee and persisted in demanding that the bill be amended to include such measures as the registration of workers, accident relief and compulsory insurance. Although the amendments were communicated to the state government, the final draft of the bill did not include these amendments but contained certain provisions that were clearly gender-biased. For example, the bill

172

stipulated that women construction labourers would not be allowed to work after 7 p.m. Although this provision was meant to protect women workers, women union members felt that it would instead deprive them of employment opportunities. Women involved in laying concrete often work beyond 7 p.m. because this work must be done in one stretch without interruption. Concreting provides employment to large numbers of women, and if these women could not work beyond 7 p.m., their jobs would be taken by men. The women already worked in groups which afforded them protection after dark. The real issue for these women was the need for proper overtime wages.

The union also objected to the terms of a provision that extended the benefits of the Maternity Benefit Act to construction workers. Most women would not be able to collect such benefits as their employer and place of employment shifted too frequently. Furthermore, the legislation could make employers wary of hiring women.

The union continued to struggle for its demands and staged demonstrations to draw attention to its cause. Under pressure during the elections, the Tamil Nadu government issued an order providing Rs5000 for the families of fatal accident victims. Since the union's demands were for an accident relief payment of Rs10 000, and the Tamil Nadu Governor had previously announced that the government would pay this amount, the union was not pleased with the government order. It demanded that all of the election candidates give a written pledge to support the union's demands. Failing this, the union membership would boycott elections. As a result, candidates in 56 constituencies pledged their support for the union. Early in 1985, after the elections, the government increased the amount for accident relief to Rs10 000.

Despite this action, the new government was unwilling to implement the accident relief scheme. The union filed a writ petition in the Madras High Court, listing 32 cases waiting to be paid accident relief. Agitation by the union led the Revenue Department to begin implementing the scheme. However, the government instituted conditions for receipt of accident relief. In the case of Tamilarasi, who fell from the second floor of a building in Salem, the state government refused accident relief on the pretext that the family's income was above Rs3500 a year, since the wages of unskilled construction workers were over Rs10 per day. This and other cases prompted the union to press the government to issue an order for unconditional accident relief. Finally in 1989, Tamil Nadu government issued a modified scheme for accident relief as a government order.

National Campaign Committee for Central Law on Construction Labour
In response to persistent demands by unions, the Government of India set up a tripartite working group to examine ways and means of providing social security to construction labourers. The TMKTS had representation

on this committee. The union organized a national seminar in 1985 to develop a common strategy among construction workers' unions and to ensure that the Government of India would enact appropriate policies for construction workers. In order to take the struggle to the national level, the National Campaign Committee for Central Law on Construction Labour (NCC–CL) was formed at the end of the seminar to formulate a central bill. The salient features of the central bill were: the establishment of tripartite boards with 50 per cent workers representation (and proportionate representation of women); the compulsory registration of workers and employers; the recruitment of labour through rotational booking; the collection of a 2 per cent levy before sanctioning the plan; and the provision of Employee State Insurance, Provident Fund,[6] gratuity and monsoon allowance, maternity benefits, housing, skill training and crèches.

Subsequently, in 1988, the Government of India introduced the Construction Workers (Regulation of Employment, Conditions of Services) Bill which contained only safety provisions without any regulation of employment. The NCC–CL opposed the government's bill and gave a deposition to this effect before the Petition's Committee. The Petition's Committee recommended that the official bill be withdrawn and that comprehensive legislation, along the lines of the bill drafted by the NCC–CL, be enacted by the Government of India. The NCC–CL put forward a demand to all political parties before the election. Although the National Front, which included a bill similar to the NCC–CL's in its election manifesto, assumed power after the elections, the new government was dismissed before the cabinet consented to the bill.

State-wide Struggle for Tripartite Boards
While little progress was made on the national front, the TMKTS continued to struggle for construction workers' rights in Tamil Nadu. The NCC–CL drafted a model scheme for setting up Tripartite Construction Labour Boards under the Tamil Nadu Manual Workers Act and submitted this plan to the state government in 1990. The government actively considered the scheme but was dismissed before it could be enacted. With a new government and a new Labour Minister, the union began the process again. In 1991, the Labour Minister announced the government's intention to implement the Tamil Nadu Manual Workers Act and to extend statutory benefits to construction workers.

The implementation of the Tamil Nadu Manual Workers Act became the major focus of struggle for the Tamil Nadu construction workers, with

---

6 The Provident Fund is a statutory scheme under the Provident Fund Act. Every employer is required to deposit 16.66 per cent of an employees' salary with the Provident Fund. Of this, 8.33 per cent is contributed by the employer and the rest comes from the employees' salary or wage. When the employee retires or leaves the firm for any reason, she or he is paid the lump sum that has accumulated, including interest.

women militantly in the forefront, undaunted by police repression. Construction workers were well aware of unkept government promises, and indeed, this was the case with the act. By early 1992 the act had not yet been implemented and after union agitation the new Labour Minister made an announcement that the scheme would be notified in the official gazette by the end of September. The government did not keep its promise, and the union announced that a picketing programme would begin on November 30. Meanwhile, the Labour Minister said that the scheme would be notified by 14 January 1993. The union then postponed much of its picketing to see if the government would make good its promise. When it did not, the general council of the union decided to hold a peaceful *rasta roko* (roadblock) on 9 February 1993. More than one hundred thousand construction workers went on a one-day strike, and 25 000 were arrested, including 10 000 women. In Madras, the police *lathi* charged (beat with bamboo rods) women workers who squatted near the Secretariat, on Mount Road near the Labour Commissioner's office and on the Poonamallee High Road near the Madras City Municipal Corporation. Many women were seriously hurt.

The National Federation of Construction Labour (NFCL) in Bangalore and fraternal organizations in Delhi condemned this police violence. Significantly, however, women's leadership in the strike became a model for other groups wishing to have their grievances redressed. Medical college students struggling against the privatization of a medical college also adopted the tactics of *rasta roko* and pursued it many times later as well. Women construction labourers set a new precedent for political mobilization in Madras city and throughout the state of Tamil Nadu.

Upset by the government's indifference to the plight of construction workers, the union continued to pressure the government and called a three-day strike on all government construction sites, accompanied by processions and *dharnas* (sit-down strikes) in 29 districts. The Government responded with an amendment to the Tamil Nadu Manual Labour Act in April 1993, empowering the Construction Labour Board to collect a levy on all construction sites. As a May Day 'present' to the construction workers, the chief minister made an announcement that the Tamil Nadu Manual Workers act would be extended to all districts and that the Construction Labour Welfare Board would implement schemes for Employee State Insurance, Provident Fund, maternity benefits, pensions for workers over 60, crèches, worker identity cards, and accident relief.

The Third Phase of Unionization

The struggle for implementation and extension of the Tamil Nadu Manual Labour Act heightened major tensions within the union that were related to women's participation in the union. These tensions led to the formation of a

175

Tamil Nadu wing of the Nirman Mazdoor Panchayat Sangam (NMPS), a registered trade union with its headquarters in Delhi, formed with the objective of uniting construction labourers beyond differences of caste, religion, sex, and political affiliation. NMPS is also an important constituent of the NCC–CL.

The break in the TMKTS came about for several reasons. The first was the reluctance of the union's leaders to take radical actions as demanded by the membership, especially women members. During the struggle for implementation of the Tamil Nadu Manual Labour Act, members and part of the women's leadership believed that radical action, such as a non-violent *rasta roko*, was required since the government was notorious for breaking promises. The leadership was reluctant to take such an extreme step. When it was finally put to the vote, the union's General Council voted for the *rasta roko*. However, this incident created tensions within both leadership and the members. The reluctance of the male leadership actively to support women members' call for prohibition, and to take disciplinary steps against union officers who abused alcohol and women members of the union, contributed to this tension. Also, women who were mason trainees in a month-long training programme, launched by the union, were not paid for their labour due to the malfeasance of some male union officials. Although the matter was referred to the national Federation on Construction Labour (NFCL) for resolution, there was no action on the issue, and this further exacerbated gender tensions within the union. Finally, the union activists who joined the NMPS felt that the TMKTS's congratulations to Chief Minister Jayalalitha for announcing the implementation of the Tamil Nadu Manual Worker's Act was premature since the scheme was not yet law – a situation the activists have encountered before with respect to government announcements.

NMPS continued the struggle to get the act officially enacted. After the union announced its intention to organize a 15-day *padyatra* (march), the government issued a preliminary notification of the act. However, the act did not address certain grievances of the construction workers. The construction workers demanded that it be easier to get accident relief and that the act provide crèche facilities, Provident Fund, and Employee State Insurance to all workers, regardless of place and duration of employment. Both the Provident Fund and Employee State Insurance were guaranteed only to workers with permanent jobs. Since construction labourers are contracted seasonally and from job to job, they have no permanent work and were excluded from current provisions under the act. Finally, the scheme was limited to Madras, Madurai, and Kovai.

The union had additional demands that the act include provisions for elected representation of tripartite boards (with proportionate representation for women), the regulation of employment and wages, the registration of employers, and state-wide coverage of construction workers under the act. It held a mass hunger strike to press for the final notification. The final notification was not made until October 1994 and did not include the modifications that the union had demanded. The Construction Labour Welfare Board, which was to implement much of the act, was formed only in April 1995. It was formed in Madras, Madurai and Coimbatore. The NMPS is represented on the board and is active in registering workers.

On the national labour scene, the NMPS, through its membership in the NCC–CL, has pressed the Government of India to pass legislation for the provision of tripartite construction labour boards, employment regulations, compulsory registration of employers and workers, Employee State Insurance, Provident Fund, crèches, scholarships for children, housing, and unemployment allowances. The results of this struggle have again been disappointing. The government has introduced a bill that includes provisions for regulating working hours and working conditions (much like the 1988 bill) and additional provisions for temporary housing on site, and pensions. The NCC–CL was demanding amendments to this bill during the 1995 winter session.

Evaluating Empowerment

Union agitation and bargaining has resulted in an increase in women's wages. While women construction workers' wages in Madras were Rs15 per day in 1979, by 1993 they had risen to Rs50 per day. In rural areas wages have risen from Rs6 to Rs30 per day. However, these wage increases have been countered by rises in prices under the New Economic Policy. Despite this situation, women's increase in awareness and ability for collective action have given them a sense of security and confidence that they can effect social change.

Through the union, construction workers have been able to access compensation for accidents from the Chief Minister's Relief Fund or the Workmen's Compensation Act. As a result, compensation ranging from Rs20 000 to Rs100 000 has been granted for over 150 fatal accidents. Compensation for non-fatal accidents, when dealt with by the union, have provided quicker results than legal action.

One of the union's notable achievements is that gains made by the construction workers have resulted in gains by other occupational groups in the unorganized sector. After the intense struggles of construction workers between 1979–81 for legal protection, the Government of Tamil Nadu enacted the Tamil Nadu Manual Workers Act in 1982 which covered 15 different categories of workers, including construction labourers. The government order issued in 1989 to provide accident compensation covered a variety of occupations from agricultural labourers and municipal workers, to car drivers and palm tree climbers. Now, after the struggle for implementation of the Tamil Nadu Manual Workers Act, which resulted in the establishment of the Tamil Nadu Construction Labour Welfare Board, loading and unloading workers as well as agricultural workers have started articulating the demand for tripartite boards.

Women have been very vocal in the NMPS and at the village level but are not yet fully represented in the executive of the union. At the *taluk*, district and state levels, one of the five office bearers and at least three of the nine committee members are women. Women have continued struggling for equality in the union and to increase the wages of unskilled labourers. Women are also pressing for more skills training opportunities.

RUKMANI: STRUGGLING FOR CONSTRUCTION WORKERS' RIGHTS

Rukmani's story gives insight into the struggles and successes of women construction workers. Rukmani is a 55-year-old construction worker who lives in Chetput, Madras. She works to support her chronically ill husband, and her two surviving children. Rukmani has given birth to nine children, but seven have died due to lack of proper child care at her work sites. Her surviving boy was taken to all her work sites, while her girl was sent out for domestic labour.

'Since the children, as well as the construction labourers, need protection I joined the union in 1979. We have struggled, and I have gone to jail. Only now after our hunger strike has the government promised crèches, pension, and accident relief through the tripartite board. We have been struggling for a long time in the hope that, even if we don't benefit, our children will benefit.

'In 1979 my co-worker, Poonammàl, died in a building accident when she fell from the fourth floor while doing concreting work for the Madhavaram Telephone Exchange. Her dead body was left on our doorstep by the contractor who fled from the site. Those of us in the Chetput Branch of the union went to the headquarters and agitated in front of the GH. We got the hospital authorities to claim Poonammal's body for a post-mortem, and we registered a case in the police station. We all contributed money and conducted the funeral. But the Labour Commissioner said that neither the principal employer nor the contractor was liable for damages since there were no records of Poonammal's employment. The appeal is still in the High Court.

'After Poonammal's accident, we struggled to get Rs10 000 as compensation for fatal accidents from the Chief Minister's Relief Fund. We even boycotted elections to press our demands. Finally we succeeded in getting it raised to Rs20 000.

'My own work prospects have improved since I was trained in masonry two years ago. However, after the training programme, male contractors were unable to give me work as a mason. After the Appropriate Construction Group was formed I was able to get work, though irregularly. I earn Rs70 a day, since I am still only a half-mason.'

178

From Construction Workers to *Bidi* Workers

During construction workers' struggle for rights, the workers and the union leaders realized that this struggle cannot be isolated to one sector but must spread to other sectors of unorganized labour. The Centre for Labour Education and Development (CLEAD) was established to act as an catalyst for organizing unorganized labourers. Since *bidi* workers were living and working in the same slums as the construction workers, CLEAD undertook a study of *bidi* workers residing in slums of Madras and assisted in the formation of the Tamil Nadu Bidi Worker's Union. Women constitute the majority of union membership, and a women's committee has been formed in the union to foster leadership among women.

Conditions of Women in the Bidi *Industry*
There are over 500 000 *bidi* workers in Tamil Nadu with 50 000 working and residing in the Madras–Chengalpet District. Women form a large part of this workforce.

Bidi workers labour under a contract or subcontracting system. There is no direct contact between the *bidi* companies and the workers who labour at home from dawn until evening. Contractors or subcontractors provide the workers with a weight of tobacco leaves which must be returned as bundles of rolled *bidis*. When the leaves are of bad quality (which is the norm rather than the exception), the number of *bidis* will be fewer than the number stipulated by the contractor, who will then deduct an amount from the workers' wages.

There are three steps in *bidi* making. First, the leaves are soaked in water and cut to size, using a metal plate and scissors. Then the leaf with tobacco inside is rolled into a *bidi*. Finally, the top is closed and the bottom is tied. In some areas there is a gender division of labour in *bidi*-making with children closing the tops, women cutting the leaves and men rolling the *bidis*. Older male children may be trained in rolling *bidis*, as this is a skill acquired in childhood.

There are three factors that have influenced *bidi* industry wages in Tamil Nadu. First, the current minimum wage fixed by the Government of Tamil Nadu is below the minimum wages fixed in Kerala and Andhra Pradesh. For this reason Kerala *bidi* companies operate across the state border in Tirunelveli District, Tamil Nadu; and the Andhra Pradesh companies operate in Chingleput District, Tamil Nadu. Secondly, the variable Dearness Allowance[7] (DA) is two paise for one point in the price index for *bidi* workers. While in the construction industry the DA is four paise for each

---

[7] Most minimum wages have an in-built Dearness Allowance which indicates how much the wage will increase in proportion to the increase in the price index that in turn indicates price fluctuations.

179

point and the minimum wages are Rs49 per day, in the *bidi* industry the minimum wage is Rs35.90 with a 'bonus' and Provident Fund contribution deducted from what has already been deducted for bad leaves. Thus, Rs25 is the actual wage for rolling 1000 *bidis*. Finally, although each of the three steps in *bidi* making is carried out by a different person, the Government of Tamil Nadu has fixed the minimum wage for rolling a thousand *bidis* under the assumption that the work is done by one person during an eight-hour work day. In reality, different wages are given for each process. For eight hours of work, a leaf cutter receives Rs6, the individuals closing the *bidis* get Rs4, and the *bidi* roller earns Rs15.

This wage structure is unsatisfactory for *bidi* workers. The law defines the 'minimum wage' as the amount of money required by a unit of four (two adults and two children) for the basic requirements of food, clothing, rent, education, and health. The minimum wage for *bidi* workers takes into account neither basic needs nor the division of work prevailing in the *bidi* industry. The result for most *bidi* workers is exploitation at the hands of contractors, poverty, malnutrition (due to eating only one meal a day) and a perpetuation of child labour. Women *bidi* workers, who typically are involved in the cutting operation, make less than half of what the mainly male *bidi* rollers earn, leading to a gender differential in the wage structure.

Although the employee's Provident Fund is available to *bidi* workers, the system is often abused by employers. Taking advantage of the *bidi* worker's poverty, unscrupulous owners suggest that workers close their accounts to get a lump sum payment; they then reopen the accounts in false names and collect the worker's money. Moreover, it is only the person who collects the leaves and tobacco from the subcontractor and then returns the *bidis* who is registered for the Provident Fund, while the workers who cut the leaves (mostly women) and close the tops receive no coverage. There are also employers who collect the Provident Fund contribution and do not pay up.

The Bidi Worker's Welfare Fund has been constituted by the Government of India out of a levy on the sale of *bidis* at the rate of four paise per *bidi*. The Fund contains millions of rupees. From this fund, *bidi* workers should receive medical facilities, maternity benefits, housing loans, stipends for children's education, and welfare cards. In some locales, these services and benefits are not available. For example, thousands of *bidi* workers (the majority of whom are women) live in the Madras areas of Washermanpet, Royapettah and Triplicane. However, no hospitals have been built in these locales. There are only mobile dispensaries, staffed by one doctor and inadequately stocked with medicines. Because of their low living standards and the work they do, *bidi* workers complain continually of tuberculosis, asthma, anaemia and backache.

The Tamil Nadu Bidi Worker's Union

The Tamil Nadu Bidi Worker's Union continues to struggle for minimum wages. In 1993, when it put forward a demand for parity in DA with the construction sector, no other union was willing to raise this issue. Earlier, the unions were only signing settlements for the minimum wage already fixed by law. But during 1995 all unions had raised the demand for variable DA. The *bidi* worker's union has also demanded that the government fix fair wages for leaf cutting, rolling, closing, and labelling work. The DA was raised from one paise to two paise, but the union did not sign the settlement. It conducted a *dharwa* (sit-down strike) to focus the public and government's attention on the following demands: appropriate calculation of minimum wages; the issuing of identity cards to all workers; access to Provident Fund by all workers; removal of conditions for education stipends; and provision of housing schemes and hospitals.

Action by the union has resulted in *bidi* workers accessing education stipends for their children available under the federal Bidi Workers Welfare Act. In the first year, all the applications received stipends, but in the second year, many applicants were rejected on the basis of the children's poor progress in school. *Bidi* workers' children attend school only irregularly and may be engaged in *bidi* work themselves. The union has argued that merit should not be the basis for providing children's scholarships. The stipend is an incentive for sending the children to school and contributes to the elimination of child labour in the *bidi* industry. The union has posed these arguments to the authorities many times, but to no avail.

The union has also been instrumental in obtaining welfare cards for *bidi* workers, and continues to struggle for housing schemes and hospitals. Housing is a critical issue for *bidi* workers, since it is not only their living quarters but also their workplace. *Bidi* workers encounter the same housing issues as construction workers do because both occupational groups live mostly in the slum areas of Madras and other urban centres in Tamil Nadu. The major problem of slum dwellers is the constant threat of eviction. They must also contend with unsanitary living conditions and a lack of drinking water, which is particularly a problem for women who must go in search of drinking water each day. Slum fires and the flooding of slum areas during the monsoon are annual problems. The *bidi* workers' union has been pressing the Department of Labour to provide decent, safe housing, worksheds and services in the slums. Together with construction workers and other slum dwellers, the *bidi* workers formed the Tamil Nadu Slum Dwellers and Residents' Association in 1992 when there was a series of evictions under the Tamil Nadu State Government's 'Vision 2000' programme. This association continues to struggle against evictions and for clean drinking water, sanitation, and fireproof housing, among other issues.

MANIMEGALAI: WORKING TO EDUCATE HER CHILDREN
The benefits of union membership are well-illustrated by the experience of Manimegalai, a 35-year-old widow living in Mangadu Village (Poonamalee) with two daughters. She was one of the first members of the Tamil Nadu Bidi Worker's Union and works as a leaf cutter, earning only six rupees a day. Once the union was formed the first activity was to get welfare cards for all *bidi* labourers, including leaf cutters and closers. The mobile dispensary was also brought to Mangadu once a week. In spite of her low wages, Manimegalai has sent her children to school. However, the quality of education in the government school is so low that she wondered if it was worthwhile sending the children to school. However, because she received an educational stipend for her children from the Bidi Worker's Welfare Fund, she felt that the children's schooling should continue. She is proud of the fact that she was able to organize private tuition for her children so that they would be able to study and pass their yearly exams.

Toward the Future of Unionization in the Unorganized Sector

As the cases of the construction workers and *bidi* workers demonstrate, women labourers in the unorganized sectors face many difficulties in their day-to-day lives. They have struggled to get their concerns addressed by both the federal and state governments. While women are indeed the 'fighting force' in these struggles, they have not been the 'deciding force' as they have had to confront the patriarchal attitudes of male union leaders and government officials.

The Centre for Labour Education and Development (CLEAD) is assisting women labourers in their struggles for rights and better working conditions. CLEAD was formed in 1992 to document and monitor labour conditions in the unorganized sector. Since it was formed, CLEAD has been involved in a number of initiatives with women labourers. CLEAD, along with the National Commission for Women, organized conferences in Madras, Nagappattinam, Madurai and Tuticorin involving female labour in agriculture, construction, fisheries, domestic work, weaving, match making, *bidi* making and cigar making sectors. In December 1995, National Commission for Women, with CLEAD's assistance, organized a two-day Public Enquiry on Women in the Unorganized Sector, in Tamil Nadu. Women selected during the conferences, as well as officials from state and central government departments, gave depositions before this public enquiry which was conducted by eminent jurists and women leaders. This effort has evolved into a Women Labour Co-ordination Committee which is demanding the implementation of legal rulings and recommendations of the public enquiry.

These efforts by CLEAD, and the determination of the women labourers themselves, will continue to carry the union movement forward in a manner which accommodates the interests and concerns of the millions of women in the unorganized sector in Tamil Nadu. As one woman labourer noted: 'Some ask whether by the sound of a "hen", dawn will come. This they say to deter us [the women union members] from being active. But we will not rest until we win.'

Lessons Learned

MARILYN CARR, MARTHA CHEN, RENANA JHABVALA

Overview

THERE ARE OBVIOUSLY a great many lessons to be learned from the experiences of the organizations contributing to this volume, and the purpose of this chapter is to provide an analysis of the case studies within the context of the key questions which the research was designed to address. Before beginning the more detailed analysis, however, it is useful to look at some findings of general interest.

First, one cannot help but be struck by the sheer size and rapid growth of the organizations involved. The more mature organizations such as BRAC and Proshika now have respectively one million and almost a half million women members, and their numbers are growing at ever increasing rates. For example, in the last 12 months alone, BRAC records 120 000 new women members. The numbers of women reached by some of the other organizations look small by comparison, but these figures are still impressive if consideration is given to the relative youth of the organizations compared to BRAC, and their geographical location in areas less densely populated than Bangladesh. For example, in the 11 years since AKRSP assisted the first women to form an organization, 29 000 women have become organized in 857 groups. In the study area in Andhra Pradesh, CDF has assisted 12 500 women to form 235 thrift and credit groups in a five-year period. And in Sri Lanka, the Women's Development Federation, which came into existence in 1989, now has 25 900 women members in a district which has a total population of only half a million people.

Second, it is apparent that the structure of many of these organizations is at once very complex as well as being highly participatory. In all cases, there are primary groups (women's groups/societies/unions) and, in many, these have become federated at the secondary, tertiary or even higher levels. For example, SEWA's 220 000 members are consolidated into 362 producer groups and 72 co-operatives at the primary level; and seven federations and one national union at the secondary level. WDF's membership of 25 900 belongs to 466 rural women's development societies which are consolidated at the secondary level into 67 rural banks and at the tertiary level into the Women's Development Federation. The 425 581 women members of Proshika belong to 25 940 women's organizations

185

which join with the village organizations to form 3485 village coordination committees (VCC), 343 union co-ordination committees (UCC) and 48 *thana* co-ordination committees (TCC).

Third, while women's empowerment, rather than material gain, is the ultimate goal of all organizations, it is worth mentioning the role these organizations have played in mobilizing savings and assets over which women have control. Women received 75 per cent of the loans disbursed by BRAC up to 1995 (a total of US$115 312 500) and account for a major share of the total members' savings of US$15 600 000. In Proshika's case, women have received US$12 950 000 which amounts to 52 per cent of all loans disbursed. SEWA Bank has 55 000 depositors with a total in savings and shares of US$3 million.

Fourth, several of the case studies show that, while not all organizations paid special attention to women in their early years, they have learned through experience the value of helping women to establish their own organizations alongside those of men. For example, CDF, which was established by the farmers' co-operatives in 1982 to assist its members, found that women were being excluded because they did not own land. In 1990 CDF started to help women to form their own thrift and credit groups which did not have land ownership as a basis for membership. AKRSP began forming VOs (local village organizations) in 1982, but over time women recognized that these did not address their needs adequately. In 1984 one group of women broke off from a VO to form their own WO and asked AKRSP to assist them. In Tamil Nadu, unions were formed as early as the 1930s, but women were not involved. In 1979, because of women's involvement in protests, the construction labour movement developed from the masons' guilds (a purely male skilled workers' organization) into a trade union movement with women in the forefront of the struggle. And in BRAC, which started to put strong emphasis on reaching women in the late 1980s, the membership of women rose from 61 per cent in 1989 to 80 per cent in 1995.

Fifth, the organizations, because of their participatory approach to development, are starting from where the women are and with what they say are their priorities. It is clear from the case studies that there is a recognition of the fact that, in most cases, women are workers rather than simply housewives, and that they work long and hard hours for little remuneration. When asked, they give the need for work/employment/income as their priority even though the organizations may feel that their priorities lie elsewhere. For example, although AKRSP originally identified labour-saving technologies to relieve women's work burden as a key programme area, these did not address women's main concern. What women really wanted was a means of earning income. Similarly, when BRAC experimented with the approach of organizing the poor to resist village power relations versus that of delivering credit and training, the latter was the most popular with village

186

organizations. Sometimes women have taken their own initiatives in empowering themselves through economic means. For example, the women's groups in Sri Lanka decided that health and nutrition was not their priority need and was, therefore, an insufficient reason for their existence. Access to credit and related services was a priority for them, and they took the initiative first to start savings and credit schemes and then to establish a network of rural banks. Clearly, women have been active participants in the development process, and not merely passive recipients.

Sixth, most organizations believe that economic empowerment means bringing women into the mainstream of economic activity, thus reducing their dependence on NGOs and increasing the likelihood of sustainable gains. For example, AKRSP has gone from being a provider of inputs and securer of markets for the relatively immobile women of northern Pakistan to linking women with merchants who supply inputs and enabling them to negotiate directly with merchants, marketing co-operatives and truck drivers. BRAC has created linkages between women poultry/egg producers and government extension workers so that chicks and other inputs, and services and advice are available on a sustained basis without further recourse to BRAC itself.

Seventh, advocacy has become an important component of most organizations. For example, CDF's advocacy work has led to a change in the co-operative laws in a way that improves the environment for co-operative activities. SEWA is active in lobbying the Forest Development Corporation to issue licences, widen sales channels, and raise official prices for gum to help the women gum collectors in Banaskantha to overcome the adverse effects of trade liberalization on their incomes. The trade unions in Tamil Nadu have numerous successful experiences in advocating changes in policies and laws to benefit informal-sector workers. Proshika has advocated a change in forestry policy to enable women members to gain legal entitlement to profit from forestry maintenance, and BRAC has successfully advocated changes in government policies with respect to poultry production, sericulture and health. In all cases, the organizations have drawn on their years of micro-level experience to advocate change at the macro-policy level. The case studies present a strong argument for the need to work at both the micro and the macro level if significant and sustained change is to be realized.

Eighth, the case studies show a marked trend toward creating employment opportunities for women through providing services needed by other women in the community. For example, AKRSP has trained local women to be 'master trainers' who train others in their communities in improved techniques. BRAC has set up a system of 'barefoot' vets and 'barefoot' lawyers who respond to women's needs in these areas, and SEWA has trained women to be health care and day care providers who are then organized into health care and day care service co-operatives. In all cases,

187

communities are responsible for payment of fees for services, thus ensuring the sustainability of livelihoods and quality of services through accountability to the community. These paraprofessionals also take on some of the responsibilities of the NGO/PO, thus ensuring the sustainability of service delivery without dependence on the NGO/PO.

Ninth, most of the case studies refer to the fact that while empowerment of women means that the *status quo* in the family, the community, the workplace and the economy are being challenged, there is a need to try to reduce conflict and to bring men along with developments.

Finally, and perhaps most important of all, while the agencies and women's organizations in the case studies represent a variety of original approaches, they have moved towards a common understanding of how best to organize women for empowerment. The key to this common approach is that the most effective entry point is economic empowerment. This, in its turn, has been achieved in a variety of ways depending upon the circumstances of the women involved.

Sources of Women's Disempowerment

As mentioned in the Introduction to this book, a key to poverty alleviation and the empowerment of women is the understanding of the sources of women's lack of power. The case studies vividly point out the complexities of women's lives and, thus, the complexity of the strategies needed for their empowerment.

Although the concrete details of women's lives differ across the eight settings, the case studies all tell a similar story. Women face unequal power relations in virtually all their day-to-day interactions: not only (or even primarily) in their families but in all local institutions. The local institutions – each with its own institutional rules and norms – which dominate women's daily lives include: the marriage and kinship system; the household and extended family; lineage, kinship, and caste groups; local community associations; patron–client relationships; and local elected bodies (such as slum or village councils).

Few women are active participants in any of these institutions, other than the household. Rather, these institutions serve as mediating structures between women and the wider world and interact in such a way as to restrict women's access to resources, to markets, and to government. The case studies do not examine these institutions in any detail but offer clues as to how they structure women's lives.

Marriage and Kinship Systems
With the notable exception of Sri Lanka, where many communities follow a bilateral system of inheritance, most of the communities studied in this volume are patrilineal. The key elements in the patrilineal system – which

188

affect virtually all women to varying degrees – are patrilocal residence; patrilineal inheritance; a gender division of labour; and norms of female seclusion. In all patrilineal communities women face restrictions on where they can live and whether they can inherit property. Typically, women leave their parental home at the time of marriage to join their husband in his home, and return to their parental home – or move to a third locale – only under dire circumstances. And typically, few women inherit land from their husband, and when they do they are seen to have use-rights not full ownership-rights. Still fewer women inherit land from their fathers. In some patrilineal communities, such as some Muslim and upper-caste Hindu communities, women are kept secluded and are prohibited from seeking gainful employment. The net result of this patrilineal system is a structured dependence of women on men: that is, women are conditioned to be economically and socially dependent on male kin and have limited direct independent access to resources and markets.

In all of the areas studied, few women own land in their own right, with the notable exception of one or two who were able to buy land after investing a series of loans in profitable activities. When asked about recent changes in their lives, members of BRAC-sponsored WOs report that a number of husbands have recently willed land to their wives.

In northern Pakistan and Bangladesh, when AKRSP and BRAC first started working, many women had not worked, or even moved about, outside their homes. Even now, when AKRSP initiates activities in new areas, women often have to seek their husband's permission to join the local women's organizations.

Household and Extended Family
Within their own marriages and their immediate families, many women have limited power to bargain for their rightful share of property, maintenance, health care, or even food and to resist beatings (and other forms of maltreatment) by their husbands. All of the case studies report cases of alcoholism and wife-beating by husbands. In Sri Lanka one woman whose husband was an alcoholic began secretly saving money and eventually used the money to begin a new business and to persuade her husband to stop drinking. In rural Bangladesh and Pakistan women also face the likelihood – with little chance of recourse – that their husbands might take a second wife, file for divorce, or simply desert them.

Within their husband's extended family women have even less bargaining power. Yet under the rules of patrilocal residence women have few options other than to continue to live with, or near, their husband's family if their husband deserts them or dies. But few women can bargain effectively with their in-laws for maintenance or for a share of their husband's land or other property. Among those communities – Muslim and high-caste Hindu communities in India, Bangladesh, and Pakistan – which do not allow women to

189

work outside their home, the predicament of widowed, divorced, or deserted women often becomes intolerable. Each case study features at least one single woman who has defied local norms and customs to fend for herself. Anwara, a community leader of a WO organized by Proshika, refused to live with her in-laws – who expected her to observe *purdah* – took up tailoring to earn an income, and lives alternately with her two brothers.

Patron–Client Relationships

Many low-income men and women depend on – and thereby get locked into client relationships with – local patrons: wealthier residents of their village or slum who provide them with employment (for low wages), loans (with high interest), advice and arbitration (often in the patron's interest), or political protection (in return for political support). Women are often particularly dependent on patrons for access to credit and employment because they lack direct independent access to formal financial and labour markets. If they are single, with no male kin to support them, women are often unable to resist harassment and other forms of exploitation by their patrons. In southern India, according to the Co-operative Development Foundation, women often have to pledge their future produce to local merchants at less than market prices in order to get loans. In Dhaka and Madras, women are subject to harassment and violence by slumlords and liquor barons. However, the BRAC case study indicates that single women who belong to local WOs are less likely to turn to wealthy patrons as the WO offers an alternative source of support.

Community Groups and Local Councils

Most community groups and local councils are dominated by the local élite. Unfamiliar with the law or with their rights as citizens, the poor often lack voice and representation in local institutions. As a result, the poor – particularly women – often rely on these groups for advice or counsel, for arbitration of local conflicts, for representing their grievances or demands to local government, and for extracting goods and services from government. Some of the case studies report instances of women turning to the local élite to settle quarrels among themselves or to resolve land and other disputes. However, the local élites are themselves often the sources of local corruption or exploitation. In the Proshika case study, local élites – in collusion with local Forest Department officials – were responsible for illegally felling trees in one forest area, and local slumlords – in collusion with local municipal officials – were responsible for forced evictions in one urban slum.

Wider Economy and Markets

In the wider economy or markets, women face other forms of unequal power relations: some generic to the poor, some specific to women. In addition to limited employment or economic opportunities, the poor face low wages as well as exploitation (in the form of bribes, fines, high prices, and wage deductions) by employers, the police, slumlords, shopkeepers, and others. The net result is that the poor often pay unusually high prices for raw materials, electricity, fuel, and food. The urban poor are also subject to threats of (or actual) evictions by the government or slumlords.

To compound these forces women often have limited direct access to employment or economic opportunities outside the home due to norms of female seclusion and dependency. Because they do not own property to offer as collateral, women have limited access to loans from formal financial institutions and are charged particularly high interest rates in the informal financial markets. In Sri Lanka, the Women's Development Foundation reports that women remain indebted to money lenders and pawnbrokers who charge more than 200 per cent interest per year. Another feature of the informal financial markets that works against women is that what is generally pawned to pawnbrokers is what is seen as women's property: namely, jewellery and utensils.

Further, many labour markets are segmented along gender lines so that women who work outside their homes are often in the lowest-paid and most insecure jobs. In Madras, women (and children) comprise the lowest rung in the hierarchy of construction workers: both female and child labourers are called *chithals* (small persons). If women try to move up the hierarchy (to take up more skilled jobs), they face resistance and harassment by male masons and by the male trade unionists: both the masonry subcontracting system and the construction workers' union are male dominated.

From this brief analysis, illustrated by examples from the case studies, we get a picture of the various contexts, roles, and relationships in which women lack power. To help us understand this complexity, the sources of women's disempowerment which are reported in the case studies are presented in Table 1. These sources have been divided into two broad categories. First, there are those which arise because women are members of low-income households, or disadvantaged groups but which women, because of their gender, experience more intensely than the men of those same households or groups: what we have called *women-intensive* sources. Second, there are sources which arise primarily because of women's gender or, in other words, because of gender stratification rather than other forms of stratification (such as caste or class): what we have called *women-exclusive* sources. Within these categories, the reported sources of women's lack of power have been grouped according to whether they arise in the social, political, and economic spheres of women's lives. Of course, none of the compartments in this matrix is watertight or mutually exclusive.

In summary, the lack of power of low-income women in South Asia arises from a conjunction of two primary systems of stratification – class

Table 1   Sources of Women's Disempowerment

	Women – intensive	*Women – exclusive*
Social	Dependence on élite Dowry Poor housing Poor infrastructure Class violence Social isolation	Dependence on male kin Divorce or desertion Patrilocal residence Gender division of labour Gender violence Norms of seclusion Limited bargaining power/ mobility
Political	Lack of consciousness Lack of representation Lack of organization Lack of voting rights Limited bargaining power Anti-poor policies	Male-biased policies
Economic	Limited asset base Limited access to resources Limited employment High interest loans Indebtedness Limited bargaining power Imperfect markets Unfair or high prices Environmental degradation Exploitation	Patrilineal inheritance Male-biased recruitment Limited access to loans Gender-stratified markets Gender exploitation

and gender – which interact with, and mutually reinforce, one another through local social, political, and economic institutions. A third axis of stratification is also quite pronounced: namely, social status as institutionalized in the caste system among Hindu communities, and parallel social class systems in other communities. One key dimension of the status of different social groups is the 'behaviour' of their women. In India, the norms of female seclusion – including the ban on work outside the home – are more rigidly enforced in upper caste/class groups than in lower caste/class groups; whereas in Bangladesh and Pakistan the norms of female seclusion are more widely enforced across most caste/class groups.

Women experience a lack of power, and must fight subordination in multiple roles or identities: as workers in securing jobs or livelihoods; as members of poor households in meeting basic needs: and as women in negotiating gender relations. Which source of disempowerment and which of their roles is of primary significance to specific women (or specific groups of women) is a matter of personal judgement, either by the women themselves or by others. Clearly, daily reality as experienced by low-income women living in villages or slums is often quite different from the way in which that reality is interpreted by outsiders (whether by policy makers, by a 'parent' NGO, by men, or by other women). The practical implications of this difference in understanding are that if a process of empowerment is externally induced – as in some cases by the 'parent' NGO – it should be internally directed. That is, the direction and pace of the process should be in women's control in order to be responsive to their expressed needs and interests as well as to be sustainable into the future.

Most of the organizations documented in this book have allowed women to determine the direction and set the pace of change. In response to the local context and the expressed needs or interests of local women, some organizations working in relatively prosperous areas where many women are in the paid work-force – like the Construction Worker's Union and SEWA in the Kheda area – have focused primarily on helping women in the paid work-force by organizing them into a trade union to make demands and negotiate secure higher wages or better jobs. Others working in poorer areas with limited economic opportunities – like AKRSP, BRAC, Proshika, and SEWA in the Banaskantha area – have focused primarily on helping women increase the productivity and marketability of their subsistence activities by linking them up to markets and services. Still others working in areas where there appear to be sufficient economic opportunities – like the Co-operative Development Federation and Women's Development Foundation – have focused primarily on helping women to meet the basic needs of their families, by providing credit on favourable terms. In all cases, whatever the primary focus, individual women and the women's organizations have fought unequal power relations in their families, communities and local markets.

Organizing Women for Economic Empowerment

Reasons for Organizing
Because of their emphasis on women's control over their own lives, the case studies give insight into the organizing principles upon which women's empowerment is based. It is very clear that, in the South Asian context, women's economic empowerment and overall empowerment cannot come about without organizing. There are several reasons for this.

Women living in poverty have very few financial resources or assets. However, when they pool what little resources they have, this can have significant impact. In most of the cases recorded, women have been able to pool their savings as a means of acquiring credit for productive purposes. In some, such as Proshika, they have pooled their savings to acquire essential items such as tubewells, and in others, such as Banaskantha, they have pooled their labour to undertake tasks such as starting nurseries which would have been difficult to do on an individual basis.

193

Further, in most of the organizations studied, the women's group has acted as the collateral for individual women's loans who would otherwise have been denied access to credit because of their lack of ownership of land, property and other assets. The organization makes this happen in two ways: through offering the group as a mutual guarantee and through using the group savings at its disposal to offer collateral.

Women's organizations often enable women to gain increased access to markets. In Banaskantha, for example, women came together to bypass middlemen and to access urban garment markets which increased their earnings by 300 per cent. Similarly, the Khyber women's organization in northern Pakistan was able to access the potato market through group action, and basket weavers in Sri Lanka were able to access export markets through their involvement in the Women's Development Federation.

Women's organizations also provide an ideal medium through which essential services such as credit, training and health and child care can reach women living in poverty. All of the case studies record in one way or another how NGOs/WOs have effectively delivered services to individual women through their community-level organizations.

Some of the case studies show how unionization strategies have enabled women to come together in an organization to co-operate with each other, rather than compete for jobs, and thus bargain for increased wages and better working conditions. The unions in Kheda and Tamil Nadu most clearly demonstrate this strategy with women being able to raise wages and argue for better working conditions. In Kheda, women's actions led to a rise in men's wages as well as their own. Even when women's organizations are not actually registered as unions they can still raise their bargaining power and hence their income through co-operating rather than competing with each other. In the Lucky Mohila Samiti, for example, women embroiderers set a joint rate for their work below which all of them agreed not to sew. In the case of AKRSP, the women in the Khyber WO were able to set a price for potato seed below which none of them would sell to merchants.

Other case studies demonstrate how organizing has enabled women to make their joint voices heard by policy makers, and to change laws and macro-economic policies in their favour. Examples include: the struggle of the women in the informal sector in Tamil Nadu to bring the Construction Workers Act into existence; the ability of the women in rural Bangladesh to alter the policy of the Forest Department in their favour; the changing of policies in Gujurat in favour of women gum collectors; and the work of the co-operatives in Andhra Pradesh in changing co-operative law.

Finally, and perhaps most importantly from women's own perspective, the studies show how women lose fear and gain confidence when they come together in solidarity. Alone, they were unable to face exploitation in the home, in the workplace and in society. Together, however, they lose some of their vulnerability and their oppressors lose much of their power. At the household level, there are many cases of group support for members who are being beaten by their husbands, with a resulting decrease in incidents of violence against women. At the community level, women have found the confidence to oppose village élites and other oppressors. For example, women in the Jamuna Mohila Samiti fought with village elders to be able to come out of *purdah* to protect their forests, those in Kheda fought with the elders to gain access to land on which to build a crèche, and those in Lucky Mohila Samiti have been able to fight the *mastans* and slumlords who oppress them in the slums of Dhaka. And in the workplace, women workers in the tobacco factories in Kheda no longer cover their heads and bow to their employers but confront them on a range of issues.

Barriers to Effective Organizing
While the case studies show that the benefits of organizing are very worthwhile for women, and that organizing is clearly necessary to women's economic empowerment, they also demonstrate that the process is not an easy one and that many difficulties are encountered along the way. These relate both to the weak position from which women are starting and to the opposition encountered from those who are likely to lose power and control through women's organizing activities.

One of the most powerful barriers to organizing is that of fear. Women have been brought up in fear of their men, their employers, and their communities. They live in constant fear of losing their livelihoods, of starvation, of losing their children to illness and of being thrown out of their houses. Traditional attitudes towards women, which result in a lack of mobility, a lack of value of women's worth, and a position of deference to male opinions, compound this problem. All of this leads to a sense of helplessness among women, which must be overcome before they can begin to take their lives into their own hands. Women have also grown up in a world in which they are constantly cheated by others and they are, therefore, distrustful of the motives of organizations which claim that they wish to help them. Gaining women's confidence and trust can be a long process for NGOs seeking to organize women, but it is one which must be gone through. A further barrier to organizing is women's lack of knowledge or skills. As was seen in many of the case studies, a low level of literacy among women has often made it difficult for them to take on full responsibility for the management of their own organizations. Thus, many NGOs/WOs have introduced literacy training or adopted other strategies (such as encouraging younger, better-educated women to join groups) to overcome this obstacle.

Since organizing, if done effectively, leads to a shift in power between women and men, and between poor and rich, it is hardly surprising that much resistance is encountered from vested interests in the home, the community and the workplace. Opposition takes many different forms. It can be violent, as in the case of Lucky Mohila Samity in Dhaka, where the *mastans* opposed women's organizing activities and used force when the women confronted them. It can use established power structures, as in the case of the Jamuna Mohila Samiti in Bangladesh, where the village élite persuaded forestry officials to register false cases against women members. Other strategies include attempting to cause distrust among women through, for example, accusing leaders of dishonesty (as in the case of WO Hussaini in Pakistan), or inciting men to oppose women's activities by telling them that it is wrong to let their women move around freely. Counter-organizing can also be used, as in the case of Kheda, where factory owners formed their own association to fight the union of women factory workers. Kheda also provides an example of one of the most potent forms of opposition, displacing women from work.

Autonomy and Sustainability of Women's Organizations
Before leaving this section on organizing, we need also to look at the important issue of the sustainability of women's organizations and the related issue of their autonomy, for there is little point in investing time and energy in organizing women if their organizing structures are incapable of standing alone in the long term. As we have stated earlier, there has been a general tendency in South Asia to underplay the role of the women's organizations and to concentrate instead on the work of the NGOs that have helped women to establish such organizations. The case studies show, however, that there is a very complex relationship between NGOs and women's organizations, which has been hitherto little recorded, but which is central to our understanding of women's empowerment. Either explicitly or implicitly, all the organizations included in the study recognize that women's empowerment is much more likely to be achieved if women have total control over their own organizations which they can sustain both financially and managerially without direct dependence on, or subsidies from, others.

The case studies record a variety of ways in which autonomy is being achieved. In the case of AKRSP, BRAC and Proshika, village organiza-tions/women's organizations were deliberately created by the 'parent' NGO in order to facilitate delivery of services essential to women's eco-nomic empowerment. Over time, these VOs/WOs have begun federating among themselves and in some cases the federations are beginning to take over some of the services previously offered by the 'parent' NGO, thus reducing dependence on it. In northern Pakistan, WO members reported 'At first, AKRSP staff used to do everything for us. Now we are doing more and more for ourselves'. In Sri Lanka, the women's groups at the village level were originally started by government, primarily for non-economic purposes. However, women's need for access to credit and sustainable livelihoods led them to transform their groups which took on an autonomy and drive of their own and came together to create the Women's Development Federation which provides advice and assistance to its membership. The Co-operative Development Federation is an NGO which was established by farmers' co-operatives to provide advice and assistance to its membership. In turn, CDF has promoted the creation of women's thrift and credit societies which have become federated into an autonomous regional co-operative. SEWA is a trade union promoted by another bigger trade union (Textile Labour Organization) which, in its turn, promotes other autonomous women's organizations such as the Banaskantha Women's Association and the Child Care Co-operative. And in Tamil Nadu the construction workers' organization grew out of a previous union (Masons' Guild). In its turn, it promotes other unions such as the Bidi Workers Union and has been instrumental in setting up CLEAD, an NGO which works on behalf of informal-sector workers in general.

While the case studies point to a strong trend towards autonomy on the part of the women's organizations, we obviously also need to ask whether they will be able to survive in the long term. There are three ways in which we can measure sustainability: financial, in the sense of surviving without external funds; managerial, in the sense of day-to-day management being handled by women stakeholders themselves or by someone hired by them; and linkages, in the sense of having sustained access to markets, government services, and infrastructural support essential for continued functioning.

Given these definitions, we can see that most of the women's organizations are well on their way to achieving sustainability. Financially, WDF and CDF are able to cover the majority of costs involved in running their secondary- and tertiary-level organizations, and the unions rely on membership fees to cover their expenses. Service programmes such as child and health care tend to remain dependent on external funding, although in some cases, such as SEWA, there is a move towards making these self-reliant too through members paying for services provided by other women.

Managerial sustainability is an explicit goal for many of the organizations and the case studies show that much headway is being made in this respect. In northern Pakistan, women's organizations, which used to depend on NGOs or male community members for day-to-day management, are increasingly taking over these responsibilities as a result of management training, provision of literacy skills or inclusion of younger better-educated women in group membership. And in Bangladesh, under the BRAC developed textile and garment programme, village women are supervising production and quality control in the production centres and sub-centres.

Finally, many of the NGOs/POs are promoting the sustainability of women's organizations by encouraging and facilitating linkages with the private sector and with government services. For example, AKRSP has helped the WO Khyber to establish linkages with markets for their potatoes. WDF has established a market information service for its members which helps them to find potential buyers for their produce. And BRAC has linked women's poultry enterprises with government services that provide inputs such as chicks and vaccines.

The case studies demonstrate that as women's organizations become increasingly sustainable and more autonomous, their relationships with NGOs change in nature. In general, when women's organizations take on greater responsibility for day-to-day activities and for the provision of economic inputs and services to its membership, this enables the NGO to concentrate more on macro-economic issues and lobbying activities at the national level which, as yet, are still beyond the capabilities of the WOs. Increasingly it is the women's organization which identifies issues of importance to its members, and it seeks assistance from NGOs and elsewhere as required.

Empowerment Strategies

As we have seen, although each organization places major emphasis on women's organizing, and can be categorized according to the major organizing principle to which they subscribe, within this, they adopt a variety of empowerment strategies with specific economic and broader economic support goals in mind. While the emphasis in all cases is on economic empowerment, clearly there has often been a need to operate in the political and social arenas to bring this about. The dichotomy between economic and political empowerment is a false one. Both forms of empowerment constantly feed into and off each other.

Specific Economic Strategies
Specific economic strategies of the organizations described in this book fall into five basic categories. These are:

○ financial interventions (increased access to credit)
○ enterprise development (increased access to skills/business/management training and improved technologies/production packages)
○ marketing strategies (increased access to markets)
○ bargaining (for higher wages/better working conditions/job security)
○ socio-political strategies.

Financial Interventions With the exception of the informal sector unions in Tamil Nadu, all organizations have been involved in some sort of financial intervention. In cases such as CDF and WDF, access to credit has actually formed the base for organizing women for empowerment. In most of the others, it has not been the primary focus, although considerable amounts of

198

savings and loans have, nevertheless, been accumulated and dispersed. For example, by 1995 BRAC had disbursed US$180 million and Proshika had dispersed US$13 million in loans to women members.

The way in which savings and loans are handled varies between organizations. In the case of CDF and WDF, the women's organizations are very much in charge of their own affairs and, once established, handle most 'banking' arrangements themselves. In both cases, the NGO and PO provide initial training in accounting and other necessary skills and then provide advice and assistance when requested. AKRSP has also left the women's organizations to handle their own savings and credit arrangements, although in this case the low level of literacy among women has often meant that they have had to hire a literate man to handle finances. Younger women are more educated than their mothers and are increasingly taking over these roles. BRAC and Proshika, on the other hand, facilitate members' savings and credit schemes through their extensive network of field staff and branch offices, which also handle all accounting. BRAC now has 235 Rural Credit Project branches set up specifically for this purpose.

One interesting aspect of the financial strategies employed is the extent to which 'banks' have been created in areas where none existed before. CDF set out with the explicit intention of enabling women eventually to own and manage their own financial institutions, and it is making progress towards this end. WDF was established to co-ordinate the savings and credit activities of the Rural Women's Development Societies in Hambantota, and shortly after initiation became the umbrella organization for a growing network of rural banks into which the savings clubs were consolidated. AKRSP, while not intentionally helping women's organizations to start 'banks', has noted that in some cases the WO has become the 'bank' for the entire village – serving both women and men.

Enterprise Development While access to credit is usually a necessary condition for women's involvement in productive activities in the informal sector, it is rarely a sufficient one. Normally, a range of other services are required to assist women to absorb the credit in a productive manner – especially if it is to be used for purposes other than the most traditional activities at the household level.

With the exception of CDF and the informal sector unions in Tamil Nadu – which link their women members to other organizations to provide skills and business training and access to improved techniques and technologies – all organizations included in the book provide their members directly with integrated enterprise development packages of various types. Some of these are quite innovative and make every effort to take account of women's particular needs. For example, AKRSP provides both subsistence and graduated packages so that women can start off by improving their existing subsistence-level household activities and graduate on to commercial production. Having experienced difficulty with collective production packages, the NGO adapted to women's preferences by introducing individual packages. Another interesting strategy adopted by AKRSP is the use of 'master trainers' – women from the communities who are trained to provide advice, guidance, training and inputs to other women. This is especially useful in remote areas and where *purdah* is prevalent, thus limiting women's mobility and contact with male trainers. BRAC has also introduced some highly innovative models for women's enterprise development. The example of poultry production described in the case study shows how a properly developed sub-sector programme, which takes all forward and backward linkages into account, can provide income opportunities for thousands of rural women. It also shows how an NGO can help poor women through persuading government to take over a development model, and provide services which were previously unattainable.

While most of the initiatives in the case studies relate to provision of services which help women to engage in productive self-employment, there are one or two examples of NGOs/WOs directly providing jobs for rural women. For example, the BRAC handloom and embroidery production centres and sub-centres directly employ almost 2000 women and provide attractive working conditions in a safe and non-exploitative environment. Similarly, there are several examples of organizations creating jobs for women through the provision of services to other women in their communities. These include the 'master trainers' and barefoot accountants in the AKRSP; 'barefoot' doctors in SEWA's health programmes; and 'barefoot' vets, doctors and lawyers in the BRAC poultry, health and legal literacy programmes. Although it is the community which pays the 'wages' in these cases, it can still be seen as a form of employment-creation by the NGO or WO.

Market Strategies A common problem with programmes that promote women's self-employment is that insufficient attention is given to market trends and to the marketability of the produce of women's labour. Market constraints can be of two types. First, the product may be one for which there is no effective demand because the market is flooded. Second, even though there may be a demand for the product, women may not be able to sell it because they either do not know where the markets are, or they have no access to the market.

The NGOs and WOs in this book have found solutions to both of these problems. In the case of flooded markets, Proshika, BRAC and AKRSP have all assisted women to move from traditional activities, which have few or no barriers to entry, into non-traditional activities which demand improved technical skills and increased amounts of capital but which provide

200

higher profits because of greater market demand. Examples include sericulture, tailoring, weaving and brickmaking. The NGOs often have internal technology development capacity which is used to provide improved technologies to help diversify the range of enterprise options open to women.

In the cases of market information/access to markets, there are also good examples of effective strategies. WDF has helped several of its members to find markets for their produce by supplying them with market information in general, or by linking them directly with a prospective buyer. AKRSP has linked its women's organizations with merchants, marketing cooperatives and truck drivers to assist their access to markets for their potatoes down-country in Pakistan.

Bargaining In many parts of the region, women's means of livelihood is through casual wage labour, rather than through self-employment. As several of the case studies show, this tends to be related to agriculture or agroprocessing in the rural areas, and to a variety of activities, including construction work and *bidi* making in the urban areas. In general, remuneration is below minimum wage rates, working conditions are hard and often hazardous, and there is little or no job security involved.

NGOs/WOs have attempted to help women trapped in these circumstances in two ways. First, some have introduced the financial/enterprise development/marketing strategies mentioned above so as to assist women to move out of casual labour in the informal sector, and into self-employment. This aims at benefiting the women themselves, but also reduces the supply of wage labourers, thus driving up the wage rates for those women still needing work. For example, in the case of WDF, both men and women report increases in the agricultural wage rates since the impact of the rural 'banks' has begun to make itself felt.

Second, other organizations – mainly those with a union background – have assisted women workers to organize to bargain for their rights. The SEWA experience in Kheda is a powerful example of this type of strategy, as are the various experiences of the informal sector unions in Tamil Nadu. Even organizations which are not thought of as being involved in union activities have turned to bargaining strategies when appropriate to do so. For example, this strategy was used by Proshika to assist women to protect their rights of access to forest resources in rural Bangladesh and to protect their homes and workplaces in the slums of Dhaka.

Socio-political Strategies Finally, although the NGOs and WOs in this book all see their main aim as achieving women's empowerment through economic empowerment, there has often been a need to work on social and/or political constraints to this. As we have seen from the case studies, once economic empowerment has been achieved, overall empowerment is much easier for women to acquire. However, in order to achieve economic empowerment in the first place it is often necessary to adopt one or more socio-political strategies.

As we have seen, a major set of constraints to women's economic empowerment lies in well-entrenched customs and mores, such as the observance of *purdah*; traditional religious and cultural attitudes towards women; and power relationships within the family and larger community, all of which aim to maintain the subordinate position of women. A variety of strategies have been used by NGOs and WOs to help women overcome these constraints. Many refer to the need to ensure that men are 'brought along' with attempts to organizing women. This can be done by starting with a small number of women from pockets of least resistance who can act as a demonstration to others of the value of a women's organization. AKRSP has been using this strategy with effect. In the case of CDF, the organization built upon the fact that it had a long-term working relationship with men in the community and was trusted by them. In all cases, organizations have counted on the visible income benefits resulting from women's group activities to drive home the demonstration effect.

Another set of socio-political constraints facing women's economic empowerment relates to legal barriers and adverse policy measures. NGOs and WOs have found strategies to deal with these also. For example, the fact that women in Andhra Pradesh could not join co-operatives because they have no land rights led CDF to set up special thrift and credit societies which had no such requirements. The trade liberalization policies in Gujarat, which led to great hardships for women gum collectors facing cheap imports of gum, were tackled by SEWA directly confronting the Forestry Department to introduce compensatory changes in their purchasing regulations.

Broader Economic Support Strategies
As can be seen in the case studies, most of the NGOs and WOs have become involved in activities which, although they do not lead directly to women's economic empowerment, are an essential complement to those activities and strategies which do. They include the provision of: child care; health and family planning services; life and health insurance schemes; accident relief; literacy skills; scholarships for children's education; housing loans; environmental education programmes; and legal aid.

How these are provided, and in what form, varies from organization to organization. For example, child care can be provided through a special co-operative or sub-group of women set up to perform this service for all group members (Kheda); through bargaining with government for access to state assistance (construction labour welfare board in Tamil Nadu); or through informal co-operation between group members (Proshika).

Similarly, health services can be provided in a number of ways. BRAC and SEWA have trained cadres of 'barefoot doctors' who provide basic health care to communities. WDF has trained volunteers from the membership of the Women's Societies to monitor health conditions. AKRSP, BRAC and SEWA/BWA link women's organizations to existing health and family planning services.

Life and health insurance schemes have proved popular with women, and tend to be financed through members' contributions. SEWA, which charges a membership fee of Rs5 and an annual premium of Rs45, reports that its insurance scheme was appreciated by women who lost their houses in flood conditions. The Women's Regional Association of Thrift Co-operatives in Andhra Pradesh runs a Death Relief Insurance Scheme which operates off interest on withheld bonuses, and which writes off all loans outstanding against a member at time of death.

Literacy skills are provided directly by BRAC and CDF; and both SEWA/Kheda and the Unions in Tamil Nadu have helped tobacco and *bidi* workers to gain access to stipends for their children's education through negotiations with government bodies.

The Economic Empowerment of Women

In the Introduction we defined economic empowerment as 'economic change/material gain plus increased bargaining power and/or structural change which enables women to secure economic gains on an on-going and sustained basis'. Here, we look at whether these empowerment gains have been realized and try to define the economic and non-economic benefits of the empowerment strategies used, in the words of women themselves.

Material Gains/Economic Change
The research did not set out to *measure* change, but to *understand* change – both the process and the impact of change – from the perspectives of the women who belong to the organizations studied and the people who work for those organizations. When and where the case studies provide data on, or examples of, material change, they do so to illustrate the *type* of change that occurs rather than to measure the *amount* of change. As such, this study offers some qualitative rather than quantitative insights on the changes in women's lives as well as on the process of change.

The case studies suggest three broad types or levels of economic change – direct tangible results, indirect tangible results, and less tangible outcomes. A summary of these is presented in Table 2. In the rows we have listed the broad categories of economic strategies: financial services; enterprise and marketing strategies; organizing; and support services. In the columns we have classified the different types of results/outcomes – direct

203

Table 2 Types of economic change

Strategy	Tangible results		Less tangible outcomes
	Direct	Indirect	
Financial	low interest rates high savings rate ability to buy in bulk	increased income increased assets safety net	increased control of resources increased credit-worthiness reduced reliance on money lenders
Enterprise Marketing	upgraded skills improved knowledge introduction of non-traditional skills access to better quality inputs reduced costs increased production improved market links	increased productivity increased income	expanded awareness improved image increased bargaining power increased mobility increased self-confidence
Organizing	increased wages improved working conditions collaborative production collaborative marketing	increased income improved health improved well-being	job security increased bargaining power increased access to markets
Support services	released time improved health improved housing reduced risk	increased productivity increased income	

tangible, indirect tangible, and less tangible – that typically result from these strategies.

Direct tangible results are those which are most immediately observable and measurable following the implementation of a particular strategy, and are most easily related to it. They are, however, usually a means to something else – increased income or well-being – which often takes longer to achieve and which has less direct linkages with the intervention. These in their turn may eventually result in less tangible (measurable) outcomes such as expanded awareness and increased bargaining power. Typically, these are excluded from assessments of 'conventional' economic programmes and projects which aim simply to increase women's incomes.

Direct Tangible Results As described above, all but one of the programmes studied provided financial services (of one kind or another) to women

204

members, which means that most women members now have access to more capital at less cost (i.e., at lower interest rates) than before. Further, all but two of the programmes studied provide inputs, training, and technology to women, which means that many members now have better quality inputs at lower costs and improved skills and knowledge which, in many cases, leads to increased productivity. The net result of these interventions is that many of the women members enjoy higher net profits from their enterprises; profits which they can use for consumption, savings, or investments. In regard to investment, BRAC, Proshika, WDF, CDF, AKRSP, and SEWA/Banaskantha all report that many women have expanded their chicken rearing and animal husbandry activities; some women have expanded their agricultural activities (by leasing or buying land); and some have expanded their small trading operations or small shops.

Several of the organizations have also helped women move into non-traditional economic activities – activities in which men were traditionally engaged, or activities new to a given region. BRAC, for example, has helped hundreds of thousands of women take up non-traditional activities, such as agriculture (including managing deep tubewells); sericulture (including working as mulberry tree guards); weaving, dyeing, and tailoring; running restaurants; carpentry; improved poultry rearing (including running chick rearing units); shrimp culture; and brick-making. It has also trained thousands of women to become paraprofessionals who deliver health, veterinary, and legal services to BRAC members and other villagers. Because many of these activities generate higher profits than women's traditional activities, they help women to move beyond subsistence levels.

In some areas the organizations have helped women to fight for improved working conditions; not only for increased wages but also for less hazardous conditions and for worker benefits (such as accident or life insurance). Most notable in this regard have been the two trade unions, SEWA and the construction workers union. Women tobacco workers, unionized by SEWA, became so united and effective in bargaining for improved working conditions that the factory owners formed their own association to negotiate with them. To provide a fall-back position to the women – in the event of owner backlash or job loss – SEWA helped develop alternative employment and economic opportunities for them. The women construction workers in Tamil Nadu have been able to fight for, and get, higher wages, accident compensation, stipends and scholarships for their children's education, and mobile on-the-worksite health care facilities.

Several organizations including SEWA, BRAC and Proshika have recognized that women may be unable to take advantage of credit and training programmes if their domestic responsibilities leave them with little

205

time to invest in productive activities. In the absence of sufficient government resources to supply child care facilities, health and other services which assist women to play their dual role, the support strategies devised by NGOs and women's organizations have made a significant difference.

Indirect Tangible Results In terms of indirect tangible results – that is, those which occur as a result of low interest rates, upgraded skills, reduced costs, etc. – all eight case studies report increases in women's incomes, savings, and assets. Most of the cases also report changes in consumption and expenditure levels in the households of women members. The evidence cited in the case studies includes concrete figures for a few individual women and anecdotal evidence for larger numbers of women. Nevertheless, they do give some feel for the increased benefits realized by women in the study areas.

With respect to income, the AKRSP case presents net profit figures for two women. Bibi Zinaba is able to earn a net income of Rs19 000 per year after only three years involvement in AKRSP's individual and collective production packages; and Bibi Rahnuma earned a net profit of over Rs20 000 in the first year from her poultry hatchery. After investing Rs9000 and vacating two rooms of her house to expand her operation, Bibi now nets over Rs30 000 per year. In the case of savings, AKRSP reports an average savings of Rs60 per week per member or Rs3150 per year per member. Members of the Thrift and Credit Groups in Andhra Pradesh save Rs10–20 per month which amounts to a total of over Rs5 million in savings, as of March 1995.

It is clear from several of the case studies that women's assets have increased. In the Proshika groups most women now own more or higher quality personal assets than before, such as jewellery, beds and metal sheet roofs; they also own productive assets such as sewing machines, embroidery workshops, small shops, rickshaws, goats, cows and land. The BRAC case study cites examples of women who have used their earnings to purchase jewellery, tools and improved housing – one woman reports proudly that she paid for the entire family house with her savings and investments. And the WDF case study cites examples of women members who have purchased fishing boats and nets for their husbands and have leased land so that they have become cultivators rather than landless labourers.

With respect to changes in consumption and expenditure, most of the programmes report that many women have now bought additional home furnishings and clothing for themselves and their families. As one woman from Andhra Pradesh puts it 'if I want to buy a sari or something else, I now do it straightaway'. Many women also refer to the use of savings and profits for children's education – especially that of girls. One woman in Bangladesh reports that because she earns an income she is able to send her daughter to school. Without her income she is not certain whether her husband would have done so.

It is evident that women see this self-earned income as an essential safety net – something they can fall back on if household resources are, or become, unavailable through their husbands' attitudes or because of loss of employment, desertion or death of a spouse.

Less Tangible Outcomes Almost all the organizations – albeit to varying degrees – have sought to improve, upgrade, or expand the skills, knowledge base, and awareness or consciousness of women. Through a variety of interventions designed to increase women's knowledge and awareness, they have brought about palpable and remarkable changes in the women's self-image and self-confidence. Equally important to the women as this type of personal empowerment is their collective empowerment as members of an organized group. Many women testified to the mutual trust, self-help, and solidarity they have gained through their own organizations.

It is these types of outcomes of economic interventions which contribute to our definition of empowerment, and which are examined more closely in the following sections.

Increased Bargaining Power

As we discussed earlier, women in South Asia face unequal power relations in virtually all their day-to-day interactions: within their own households and with their husband's extended family; within their own communities and with the local élite; within local labour and financial markets and with local government officials. Indeed, women's daily lives are structured and determined by the complex interactions of unequal power relations between men and women and between different classes and castes. The key determinant of women's empowerment is whether (or not) women gain bargaining power in their day-to-day relationships. The case studies report increases in women's bargaining power, as follows:

Within the Household and Extended Family It is clear that the programmes documented in this book have – in various ways and to varying degrees – helped women to gain control over resources and finances, earn independent income, and participate more actively in the outside world. Moreover, through participation in local women's organizations, women have gained access to alternative support structures, and to institutions outside the family. As one woman in southern India states: 'this *sangham* is like my mother's house'. By this she means that she can always go to her thrift and credit group for financial and other support and assistance – something which is important when women are often isolated geographically from their own family after marriage.

207

As they gain independent support, connections, knowledge, and resources, women's relationships within their households and with their husband's extended family begin to change. Many women report that as they have gained increased consciousness and assertiveness, their husbands and other male kin respect them more. One woman in northern Pakistan reports that 'ever since my involvement in the WO, especially my father-in-law asks and respects my opinions on all matters'. As women are given greater value and respect within their households and extended families, they are able to negotiate a more equal sharing of responsibilities and resources and to resist maltreatment and violence within the home. In the BRAC case study, several women reported that their opinions on household financial matters are increasingly solicited and valued by their husband and other male relatives. In the SEWA-Kheda case study, several women reported that their husbands now share in housework, cleaning, and fetching firewood and water. In the Proshika case, several women reported that, due to their independent incomes, their dependence on their families has reduced and their relationship with family members has improved. For example, some women said that their husbands do not yell at or beat them as much; others have said that their husbands now 'fear' them a bit. The Co-operative Development Foundation and BRAC, among other cases, reported that many local women's organizations try to mobilize community opinion against husbands who beat their wives and that, with the backing of their organizations, women are able to shift the balance of power within their household.

Within the Community In most communities in South Asia, community elders set social norms and settle all matters relating to community social behaviour. Generally, all community or caste elders are men, whose rules and decisions place women in restricted and vulnerable positions. However, as women gain power through their local organizations – particularly through group linkages with markets and other institutions outside their community – the community decision-making process begins to alter to include women and their concerns. For women, access to community decision-making is extremely important; they tend to use their improved bargaining position to negotiate change in community rules and norms. The local councils which define and reinforce social rules are different in different places: in rural India, caste *panchayats* (councils) play this role for each caste community; in rural Bangladesh, local *shalish* (judicials) play this role in each village. Traditionally, only men belonged to and attended these councils. Zahera from BRAC reported that she now attends the *shalish* in her village. 'Our men go to the *shalish* as members of the *shalish*. We are asked as members of the *samiti* (women's organization).' In other words, when Zahera or other women are invited

208

to attend a village *shalish*, they are invited to represent their *samity*. The *samities* are being recognized as important institutions in the village.

In Banaskantha, the Aahir women are struggling with their caste *panchayat* over the issue of women's mobility. Earlier, according to local social norms, women were supposed to remain within their homes and homestead. After organizing, however, the women began moving out of their homes and going to other places such as Ahmedabad (the state capital) and even Delhi (the national capital). In an attempt to control the women, the caste *panchayat* strictly reinforced the rule that women could not go out of their homes. In response, the women began mobilizing support against this rule. They mobilized the men of their own families, especially the younger ones; they made formal petitions to the caste *panchayat* (both directly and through SEWA); and they broke the rule several times without being sanctioned or criticized. In the end, they were able to get the rule relaxed to allow them to move about as far as the local district headquarters. Currently they are lobbying for complete relaxation of the rule. Similarly, they are mobilizing support against the caste *panchayat* rulings which discourage the education of girls.

With Local Élites Solidarity, alternative employment, access to markets and support structures considerably increase the bargaining power of women with local élites, including their patrons. Women in Kheda and Tamil Nadu could bargain for higher wages and better working conditions once they had been unionized. Women in Bangladesh could fight to protect the forests and to confront the slumlords because of their strength in numbers. Most importantly from the women's perspective, they have even earned the respect of the local élite. As Hasina of BRAC put it, 'Powerful villagers – those who are involved in *shalish* and judgements – now know us and respect us. I have also become acquainted with many people in the village whom I would not have had occasion to meet if not for our activities through the *samiti*.'

Within Markets As they develop knowledge, skills, better products, and solidarity, women's access to, and bargaining power within, local markets increases. WO Khyber in northern Pakistan could improve their bargaining power both with middlemen and truckers for the marketing of vegetables, thereby improving their earnings considerably. 'They come to us, so we tell them what we will sell at. If they don't accept, there are many more buyers.' Access to their own savings funds and ownership of assets improves women's bargaining power with money lenders, leading to greater access to loans at lower interest rates. As one woman in southern India reports 'previously we used to borrow at high rates of interest and face a lot of difficulties, but now we are able to meet our needs easily'.

With Government Structures In all the case studies, because they are now members of their own local organizations, women are better able (both individually and collectively) to deal with – and voice their demands to – government institutions and officials. For example, the women unionized by SEWA in Kheda now approach government officials and the local police to address their problems. Because of their increased bargaining power, the women's organizations (either directly or through the 'parent' NGO) have even been able to change government policies. And because of their strength in numbers, women's organizations have been able to field their own candidates, or otherwise influence local elections.

A Mutually Reinforcing Process As we have seen in the case studies, the women's organizations and NGOs intervene at many levels – household, community, markets, government – and in all spheres of life – social, economic, political. For the women, increased access and bargaining power at one level or in one sphere becomes a lever for increased bargaining power in other spheres or at other levels. To illustrate, bringing more income into the family gives women added bargaining power with their husbands; more respect and freedom within the household allows women to give more time and commitment to their local organization; increased solidarity within their local organization gives women increased bargaining power in their community; backing from a local community council gives women added leverage in dealing with government officials; and support from government institutions, as well as group solidarity, gives women greater access to, and bargaining power in, local markets.

One strength of the strategies described in these case studies is that they are multi-layered, multi-level interventions in support of women's empowerment. Another strength is that they recognize, promote, and build upon the centrality and power of economic resources. Access to economic resources gives women a bargaining power that often the men within their own families do not have which, in turn, gives them bargaining power with the men who control their communities, local markets, and local government. As we have seen, this bargaining power takes many forms: the ability to make demands, to seek redress, to resist exploitation or violence, to defy custom, to negotiate fair treatment or equal access to resources. As many women testified, they no longer feel weak, subservient, or acquiescent.

Structural Change
The case studies give ample evidence of material gain and of increased bargaining power. By far the most important component of economic and overall empowerment, however, is that of structural change, for without this, strategies and interventions – however successful in the short term – may fail to lead to long-term and sustained benefits for women.

210

Perhaps one of the most valuable contributions of the research undertaken in preparing this book is the documentation of cases in which the organizations involved have been able to bring about structural changes as a result of the implementation of their empowerment strategies. With respect to economic empowerment, such changes have occurred at the levels of policies, institutions, infrastructure/services and markets and, in all cases, they have brought about transformations which promise sustained access to the means of livelihoods for thousands of women. Of particular interest is the fact that socio-cultural/political barriers have inevitably been encountered on the path to economic empowerment, which must be, and have been, overcome. In addition, socio-cultural/political changes – many of which are far-reaching and structural in nature – are often an important outcome of women's economic empowerment. There is clear evidence that economic and political empowerment are inextricably linked – with each feeding into and off each other.

Policy Changes The ability of NGOs and WOs to have any impact on macro-economic policy, or on laws affecting women's full participation in economic development, is frequently questioned. The case studies included in this book do, however, give us some concrete examples of how this can be done. In the Banaskantha study it was shown that SEWA has been able to interact with the Forestry Department on behalf of women gum collectors to help them deal with trade liberalization policies which were affecting their source of livelihood. Measures include issuing of licences to women, and loosening of purchasing regulations which will allow women to sell to the highest bidder rather than having to sell to government at a fixed (low) price. In Andhra Pradesh, CDF has been able to change the co-operative laws in such a way as to make the environment for women's co-operative activity more supportive.

Institutional Changes The case studies also give evidence of how empowerment strategies have led to institutional changes. For example, in Sri Lanka the women's organizations in Hambantota have directly facilitated the setting up of rural banks in an area where these did not exist, and where there was no access to credit either for women or men. Similar changes are happening in the case of AKRSP where the savings and loan schemes run by some of the WOs are taking on the shape of village banks serving men as well as women. And in Andhra Pradesh, CDF is working towards enabling women to run their own financial institutions.

Institutional change of a different kind has occurred in a number of cases through a change in the way in which infrastructure and services are delivered to women. For example, BRAC has developed a whole new support structure for women poultry rearers and persuaded the government to take over and maintain such support. In addition, BRAC, AKRSP, SEWA and

211

WDF have changed the whole nature of service delivery through the promotion of 'barefoot' workers, whereby women within communities are trained to supply veterinary, health, legal and child care services and skills training to members of women's organizations in return for a fee. Besides creating much-needed employment for the 'barefoot' workers, these schemes have also played an important role in women's empowerment, especially in Pakistan and Bangladesh, where women's mobility and contact with men has previously restricted their access to services and training.

Market Changes Other changes have occurred in the economic sphere which, although less striking than those described above, have nevertheless had a significant and lasting impact on women's ability to earn a living. These relate to changes in marketing structures, interest rates and wages. For example, in the case of AKRSP, women who were once isolated within the household are now trading in regional and national markets through Punjabi traders and negotiating prices on their own behalf. In Andhra Pradesh, the interest rates charged by money lenders came down because they lost their monopoly on lending after the formation of women's thrift and credit groups. And in Sri Lanka, wages for agricultural labourers (both women and men) rose after the formation of rural banks because many of the women used loans to lease paddy lands, thus reducing the numbers of labourers available for hire.

Socio-cultural Changes While the organizations included in this book have all seen economic empowerment as the basic principle around which women are organized, most have found that it is necessary to address various socio-cultural and local political constraints before this aim can be achieved. For example, the issue of *purdah* has had to be addressed in the case of the Pakistani and Bangladeshi organizations before women have been able to acquire the degree of mobility required to participate in meetings, access markets and interact with males outside of their household. The AKRSP, BRAC and Proshika case studies all show how this socio-cultural practice has been changed in the course of adopting economic empowerment strategies. The same organizations have also been able to bring about a breakdown in the traditional division of labour within the family, with women taking up traditional 'male' occupations such as tailoring and provision of veterinary services, and taking on the financial and managerial aspects of their own organizations.

By starting with those women who, by nature and/or circumstance, are the most likely to be prepared to take risks and to challenge the *status quo*, most of the NGOs and WOs have been able to demonstrate the value of women's organizing activity to the community as a whole, to overcome prejudices on the part of male relatives and village élites, and to pave the way for the greater involvement of women in the economic sphere. This in turn has led to significant socio-cultural and political changes and to women's greater overall empowerment. Recorded changes include decreased dependence on male relatives; reduced dependence on patron-client relationships; greater participation of women in decision-making within the family; changes in property relationships; greater participation of women in local politics; increased respect for women as economic actors; and increased mobility within the community and beyond.

While economic empowerment is the source of these far-reaching changes, it is interesting to note that in many cases women refer not to economic gain as a benefit in itself, but to the other things – awareness, knowledge, respect, recognition, unity, increased mobility, confidence to handle problems outside of the family, and the ability to speak out – which have occurred because of it.

Toward a Broader Perspective on Women's Empowerment

The experience documented in this book suggests the need for a broader perspective on women's empowerment. This broader perspective should contextualize the concept in everyday lived reality; move beyond the (often) false dichotomies posed between economic versus political processes, and between individual versus collective power; offer concrete strategies for addressing everyday structural issues; and, most importantly, move beyond the perspective of outsiders to incorporate the perspective of grassroots women.

Everyday Forms of Women's Empowerment

The case studies suggest a broader perspective on women's empowerment which is grounded in everyday lived reality. There are two dimensions to understanding empowerment in everyday terms: to understand empowerment we need both to *concretize* and to *contextualize* what happens in women's lives. To begin with, empowerment has to be understood in terms of concrete everyday experiences. If empowerment is the ability to exercise power, then everyday forms of women's empowerment are the ability of women to exercise power in the social institutions that govern their daily lives: the household and extended family; local community councils and associations; local élite; local markets; and local government. In addition, empowerment has to be understood in context, that is, the concrete everyday reality of women's lives differs from place to place. If everyday forms of women's empowerment are the ability of women to exercise power in the social institutions that govern their daily lives, then the nature, norms, and rules of local social institutions in given contexts need to be understood.

As noted earlier, Schuler and Hashemi (1993) have studied empowerment as envisioned and experienced by women members of BRAC and

213

Grameen Bank in rural Bangladesh. From their discussions and interviews with women who belong to both programmes, Schuler and Hashemi argue that there are six specific components to female empowerment in Bangladesh: sense of self and vision of a future; mobility and visibility; economic security; status and decision-making power within the household; ability to interact effectively in the public sphere; and participation in non-family groups. In their subsequent study of empowerment as envisioned and experienced by urban members of SEWA, Schuler and Hashemi found that one of these components – mobility and visibility – was far less important than others. The urban members of SEWA put more emphasis on women's interaction in the public sphere and collective actions to confront discrimination than the rural members of BRAC and Grameen Bank. One conclusion is that SEWA's approach is more collective and political than the BRAC and Grameen Bank approach.

However, Schuler and Hashemi (1993) note an important difference between the members of SEWA's urban programme and the members of the rural programme of BRAC and Grameen Bank; namely that the urban members of SEWA are (and always have been) relatively visible, independent, and mobile workers in the urban informal sector, who interact daily with traders, middlemen, or policemen; whereas the rural members of BRAC and Grameen Bank are (and used to be even more so) relatively invisible, dependent, and immobile workers in the rural subsistence sector, with few links to the market economy. Such fundamental differences in the context of women's lives suggest that a fundamentally different approach to women's empowerment might be required in different contexts.

This point was borne out when SEWA started working in rural areas after its initial successes in urban areas. As the two case studies of SEWA's rural programme in this volume illustrate, SEWA has been able to transplant its political approach – what SEWA calls 'struggle' – in one rural area: a relatively prosperous district (Kheda) where the women are active and visible in the paid labour force. However, it has had to adopt a more economic approach – what SEWA calls 'development' – in the other rural area: a relatively poor district (Banaskantha) where low-income women are not as actively engaged in the paid labour force, and where there are far fewer economic opportunities.

What is clear from the SEWA experience is that the everyday process of women's empowerment – the domains in which it occurs and the pace at which it is enacted – is largely determined by the environment in which women live and work; and that it is important to understand women's needs and interests in each specific context from the women's own perspectives and experience. Indeed, one important way to compare different approaches to promoting women's empowerment is to determine who takes the decision as to what domains of women's disempowerment to

214

address, in what sequence, and at what pace, rather than simply to compare what domains of women's disempowerment are being addressed. What is also clear from the SEWA experience is that our analysis and conceptualization of women's empowerment needs to be context-specific. Where women have been secluded and have not been active in the paid labour force or in the market economy – such as in rural Bangladesh and Pakistan – economic empowerment involves defying strong patriarchal kinship norms and entering markets (capital, labour, and product markets) with relatively few skills, and even less experience. Where women have been active in the paid labour force or in the market economy but where there are few economic opportunities – such as in Banaskantha district, (Gujarat state) or in Warangal and Karimnagar districts (Andhra Pradesh state) in India or in Hambantota district in Sri Lanka – economic empowerment involves building alternative economic opportunities as a base from which to negotiate better terms and conditions in existing opportunities. Where women have been active in the paid labour force or in the market economy and where the economy is strong and dynamic – such as in the Kheda district (Gujarat state) or in Madras city (Tamil Nadu state) in India – economic empowerment involves organizing women to demand better terms and conditions of work, or better jobs.

The Economic is Political

Many theorists interested in women's empowerment have argued that there is a false dichotomy between the personal and the political: that, in fact, the personal *is* political; in other words, that personal relationships between men and women reflect a power relationship between them. However, they continue to argue that there is a dichotomy between the economic and the political. But, as the case studies documented in this book illustrate, the economic (like the personal) *is* political. Most economic transactions or interactions are political in nature (involve a power dynamic) and most so-called economic approaches to women's empowerment are political in nature (involve challenging or changing that power dynamic). In brief, economic empowerment involves changes in power relationships in both the economic sphere (as an input) and in the social and political spheres (as an output).[1]

The organizing of women in most of these cases has been oriented more towards meeting women's practical needs rather than their strategic interests; that is, the organizations have been oriented more toward the solution of immediate survival problems than restructuring the social order. But the

---

[1] While recognizing the false dichotomy between economic and political approaches, we use the term 'economic empowerment' in this book as a shorthand phrase for an approach to women's empowerment which focuses primarily (or at least, initially) on women's disempowerment in their economic lives.

215

actions taken have been political in nature; have involved gaining and exercising power. In defending the rights basic to their lives – such as food, housing, education, health, water – the women have had to fight political battles not only (or primarily) against their husbands or male kin but also against community leaders, local élite, shopkeepers, slumlords, money lenders, employers, police, and local government officials.

Some scholars and practitioners concerned with fighting for women's socio-political rights or, more broadly, with promoting democratic societies, may not be aware that organizing women around their economic concerns can contribute to women's power more generally, as well as to democratic values.[2] But clearly, as the case studies illustrate, organizing women for economic empowerment can serve to promote shared knowledge, mutual trust, self-help, reciprocity, and solidarity among women which, in turn, can lead to increases in women's participation and bargaining power in local institutions. In short, what is not strictly political action can have political outcomes.

As the case studies illustrate, organizing women for economic empowerment involves increasing the bargaining power of individual women in their everyday economic transactions – in the daily distribution of food and other resources within their families, in their daily encounters with shopkeepers, money lenders, officials, and customers – as well as developing the strength and solidarity of women's organizations. Furthermore, transactions cannot be neatly separated from their personal and collective political power. This is because women experience both economic and political power (or the lack thereof) in the same set of institutions: the family; the kinship, caste, or other social group; local councils and judicials; patron-client relationships; local markets; and local government.

As the case studies suggest, there are two dimensions to making these local institutions more open and responsive to the interests of low-income women: including low-income women as players in these institutions; and changing the rules or norms of these institutions which constrain women's lives. If making local institutions more democratic is an important building block in promoting more democratic civil societies, then understanding how these institutions exclude and constrain women's lives is a critical first step. From different parts of South Asia, the case studies in this book suggest a range of institutions – such as local slum or village councils – from

---

[2] In the literature on building democracy, the concept of social capital – defined variously as the reciprocity, norms, or trust that arise from participation in local associations and that facilitate joint action by, or promote civic-mindedness among, participants – has gained increasing attention (Coleman, 1988; Putnam, 1993). As the case studies in this book suggest, organizing women for economic empowerment can lead to trust reciprocity, and solidarity among women which, in turn, often translates into joint or collective action for common objectives by women. In other words, organizing women for economic empowerment can generate social capital.

which low-income women are excluded and a variety of norms – most notably, the seclusion of women – which constrain women's lives.

Personal and Collective Power

In the literature we also found a dichotomy posed between individual empowerment and collective empowerment. Most of those who would classify the experiences documented here as economic (rather than political) approaches would also classify them as individualistic (rather than collective) approaches. Yet all of them involve organizing women into local organizations or groups. And all of them involve one or more collective strategies – collective borrowing, collective production, collective marketing, collective bargaining – as well as mutual support and solidarity. Among the examples of collective empowerment and action, the case studies report instances of women's groups taking action against the husbands of group members who either beat or divorce their wives, of women's groups taking part in local judicials (*shalish*), of women's groups fielding their own candidates and voting their own minds in local elections.

What the case studies suggest is the need to consider in any given context the following questions: When are individual or collective strategies important or appropriate? What forms of collective action might be appropriate? In northern Pakistan, after finding limited demand for, or satisfaction with, collective production schemes, AKRSP dropped most of its collective production schemes in favour of individual self-employment. However, in the same area, local women's groups later developed a collective marketing strategy which linked women to markets which they could never reach individually. Other forms of collective action include: joint management of credit operations (CDF and WDF); bulk purchase of consumer goods (WDF); and reciprocity and exchange (labour exchange, marketing within women's organizations).

The case studies also suggest that individual and collective strategies should not be seen as alternatives. Rather, women need both types of strategies just as they need both personal power (from within) and collective power (from solidarity with other women or men). In fact most of the organizations report an iterative – mutually reinforcing – empowerment process which shifts from acts of individual resistance, to acts of collective resistance, to occasional public protests, and back again.

Speaking Out

The case studies suggest that if women are organized – or better still, if women organize themselves – to contest discrimination in day-to-day economic transactions or to demand access to local economic resources, or simply to manage their economic activities better, they will lead the process of empowerment in directions which are appropriate to their own needs, interests and constraints; and that what may seem like simple shifts in women's status within their family, community or village often represents significant shifts in women's consciousness, perceptions, security and power.

Perhaps one of the most common expressions of significant change from the women's own perspective is their new lack of fear and their new-found ability to speak out at all levels so as to share problems, make demands, negotiate and bargain, and participate in public speaking and decision-making.

Self-confidence and overcoming fear is mentioned along with 'speaking out' many times and in many ways. Bibi Safida of the WO Hussaini states: 'even if someone opposes me I can reply with confidence'. Bibi Azida adds 'Now I am going everywhere and am no longer afraid'. Others in northern Pakistan relate 'Before we organized ourselves in a Women's Organization we used to believe everything and agreed with everything our men told us. Now, we have learned to state our opinions and views . . .' A woman in southern India says 'Previously, I never spoke to anyone on any subject. Now the strength of the members gives me the strength to speak to anybody.' The women in the construction workers' union (NMPS) report 'We do not fear authority. We can talk to officials, even police, because of the union.'

Most women have found the strength to face husbands, families and village and community leaders. As one group explained its confrontation with village leaders: 'we do benefit . . . and you don't know. Now those who opposed us are silent.'

REFERENCES

Batliwala, Srilatha (1994) 'The Meaning of Empowerment: New Concepts from Action,' in Adrienne Germain, Gita Sen and Lincoln Chen (ed.) *Population Policies Reconsidered: Health, Empowerment and Rights,* Cambridge, Mass.: Harvard School of Public Health, pp. 127–138.

Calman, Leslie J. (1992) *Toward Empowerment: Women and Movement Politics in India.* Boulder, Co.: Westview Press.

Chen, Martha A. (ed.) (1996) *Beyond Credit: A Subsector Approach to Promoting Women's Enterprises.* Ottawa: Aga Khan Foundation Canada.

Coleman, James S. (1988) 'Social Capital in the Creation of Human Capital,' *American Journal of Sociology* 94 (supplement): S95–S120.

Farrington, John and David Lewis (ed.) *Non-governmental Organizations and the State in Asia,* London and New York: Routledge.

Mayoux, L. (1995) *From Vicious to Virtuous Circles? Gender and Micro-enterprise Development.* UNRISD Occasional Paper No. 3, Geneva.

Mitter, Swasti and Rowbotham, Sheila (1995) *Women Encounter Information Technology.* London and New York: Routledge and UNU Press.

Mustafa, Shams and Ara, Ishart (1995) *Main Findings Report of the RDP Impact Assessment Study.* Dhaka: Research and Evaluation, BRAC.

Ng, Cecilia and Kua, Anne Munro (ed.) (1994) *New Technologies and the Future of Women's Work in Asia.* Maastricht: UNU/INTECH.

Omvedt, Gail (1986) *Women in Popular Movements: India and Thailand during the Decade of Women.* Report No. 86.9. United Nations Research Institute for Social Development, Geneva.

Putman, Robert D. (1993) *Making Democracy Work: Civic Traditions in Modern Italy.* Princeton, NJ: Princeton University Press.

Schuler, Sidney R. and Hashemi, Syed M. (1993) *Defining and Studying Empowerment of Women: A Research Note from Bangladesh.* John Snow International Working Paper No. 3, John Snow International Research and Training Institute, Arlington, VA.

United Nations Development Programme (1995) *The Human Development Report.* New York: Oxford University Press.

United Nations (1995) *The World's Women: Trends and Statistics.* New York: United Nations.

ABOUT THE CONTRIBUTORS

Sharit Bhowmik is Professor, Department of Sociology, University of Bombay. He has conducted several research studies on tea plantation worker co-operatives in India and has published extensively on this topic.

Marilyn Carr is Chief of the Economic Empowerment Section of the United Nations Development Fund for Women. She is a development economist with over 20 years experience in Asia and Africa and specializes in the fields of small enterprise development and technology choice and diffusion, particularly with respect to rural women. Before joining UNIFEM, she was Senior Economist with the Intermediate Technology Development Group in the UK. Dr Carr has written and edited 10 books and several articles on rural industry, technology choice and rural employment.

Martha Alter Chen is Director, Program on Non-Governmental Organizations, Harvard Institute for International Development, and Lecturer, Kennedy School of Government, Harvard University. Dr. Chen has specialized in and written extensively on gender and development, poverty and alleviation and non-governmental organizations. She has long-term resident experience in Bangladesh and India.

Chitrani Dhammika was President of the Women's Development Federation in Hambantota, Sri Lanka.

Renana Jhabvala has been working with the Self Employed Women's Association (SEWA) since 1977. She was elected Secretary of SEWA from 1981 to 1994. At present she is looking after SEWA's national and international activities and its research and development. She is also Secretary of the National Centre for Labour (NCL). She was awarded a Padmashri (Indian National Award) in 1989.

Sandra Kalleder worked as an intern for the Aga Khan Rural Support Programme (Pakistan) in 1994–95. She holds a Master's degree in rural development from the International Development Studies Programme at Sussex University. She is presently pursuing post-graduate studies in Germany.

220

W.M. Leelasena is Senior Advisor for the Royal Norwegian Embassy in Colombo, Sri Lanka. Formerly while Senior Officer in the Sri Lanka Planning Service, he held a number of key positions in planning and managing development programmes. As a founder and director of one of the first integrated rural development programmes in Sri Lanka, he played a key role in developing local-level planning with a special focus on mobilizing resources of the poor for their self-development.

Abinta Malik is Head, Policy and Research Section, Aga Khan Rural Support Programme (Pakistan). From 1994–95, she was Programme Manager, Women in Development Section and previous to that worked as Women in Development Monitor in the Monitoring, Evaluation and Research Section. She holds a M.Phil. from University of Cambridge in Economics and Politics of Development.

Meena Patel has worked with the Self Employed Women's Association (SEWA) since 1987. The focus of her work has primarily been on union activities, legal work and policy campaigns. She has represented SEWA on several national commissions and international labour organizations.

Geetha Ramakrishnan is Secretary of the Centre for Labour, Education and Development in Madras, India.

Lamia Rashid is Research Associate in the Policy Research Department of Proshika's Institute for Policy Analysis and Advocacy. She has been working in the development field in Bangladesh for the last five years.

Nandita Ray works as a consultant for socio-economic programmes in rural areas. She has undertaken numerous evaluations of women's co-operatives and other programmes in Andhra Pradesh and Madhya Pradesh. She sits on the board of trustees of the Co-operative Development Foundation.

Gul Rukh Selim was Senior Researcher, BRAC Research and Evaluation Division, during 1993–1995. She is currently Research Associate at the Centre for Society, Technology and Development (STANDD) at McGill University. She has extensive field research experience on gender and development in Bangladesh and Zimbabwe.

Md. Shahabuddin is Deputy Director (Programme), Proshika. He has worked in the NGO sector since 1976. Mr. Shahabuddin is currently overseeing the Urban Poor Development Programme, Impact Monitoring and Evaluation Cell and the Policy Research Development of Proshika's Institute for Policy Analysis and Advocacy.

D. P. Vasundhara is Manager (Advocacy), Co-operative Development Foundation in Hyderabad, India.

GLOSSARY OF NON-ENGLISH TERMS

agevan SEWA village leader.

ana old unit of currency before the taka was converted to decimal units, each taka consisted of 16 annas.

balwadis centres for pre-school children.

bari a group of usually kin-related homesteads organized around common courtyards.

bidi hand-rolled cigarettes.

bou bride or daughter-in-law.

chena rainfed highlands, originally cultivated under shifting cultivation.

chithals small persons.

crore ten million.

dai midwife.

daktar literally, doctor. BRAC health workers or Shebikas are known as daktar in the village.

dharna sit-down strike.

dheki wooden mortar and pestle operated by hand or foot used for husking, polishing and pounding rice and other grains.

haram sin.

jagrut to become aware.

jagruti consciousness.

Janata cloth coarse cloth.

kanthas embroidered quilts.

khas land public land owned by the government.

lakh one hundred thousand.

lathi bamboo pole.

maistry (maistries) skilled masons.

mandal group.

mastans thugs or racketeers paid for by powerful, local patrons.

nakshi kantha embroidered quilts often using folk motifs to tell stories of village life.

Nath caste council of the Aahir.

paan leaves containing a sweet paste, betel leaves and a mixture of spices.

padyatra march.

pallav end of sari worn over the shoulder.

panchayat local, self-governing body.

para village government.
purdah female seclusion.
rasta roko road block.
samaj literally, society. In Bangladesh villages, samaj refers to mosque-based societies that function as social units during ceremonial and religious occasions, such as marriage and funerals.
samiti association, local term for village or women's organizations in Bangladesh, India and Sri Lanka.
sangathan organization
sangham association.
sarpanch leader of panchayat.
shebika health worker
seer unit of weight measurement equivalent to 0.9 kilograms.
shalish community court or judiciary.
taluk sub-unit of a district (India).
thana sub-unit of a district (Bangladesh).
union administrative unit composed of villages (Bangladesh).
VO village organization.
WO women's organization.

LIST OF ACRONYMS

AKFC Aga Khan Foundation Canada
AKRSP Aga Khan Rural Support Programme
BDWA Banaskantha Development of Women and Children in Rural Areas (DWCRA) Women's Association
CDF Co-operative Development Foundation
CLEAD Centre for Labour Education and Development
DWCRA Development of Women and Children in Rural Areas
FAO Food and Agriculture Organization
FTCA Federation of Thrift and Credit Associations
GAMA Gilgit Agricultural Marketing Association
GWSSB Gujarat Water Supply and Sewerage Board
IDPAA Institute for Development Policy Analysis and Advocacy, Proshika
IPCL Indian Petro-Chemicals Limited
IRDP Integrated Rural Development Programme
JBS Janashakthi Banking Society
NCC-CL National Campaign Committee for Central Law on Construction Labour
NFCL National Federation of Construction Labour
NMPS Nirman Mazdoor Panchayat Sangam
PG primary group
RWDS Rural Women's Development Societies
SEWA Self Employed Women's Association
TMKTMS Tamizhaga Kattida Thozilalar Madhya Sangam
TMKTS Tamil Manila Kattida Thozilalar Sangam
WID Women in Development
UNDP United Nations Development Programme
UNIFEM United Nations Development Fund for Women

ANNOTATED BIBLIOGRAPHY

Selected Studies on Women's Empowerment

SOPHIA LAM

Acosta-Belén, Edna and Christine E. Bose. 'From Structural Subordination to Empowerment: Women and Development in Third World Contexts.' *Gender & Society,* **Vol. 4, No. 3, September 1990, pp. 299–320.**
Intended to introduce a collection of case studies on women organizing for change, this article presents an interpretative framework that conceptualizes 'women as a last colony'. The authors argue that the subordination of women in the Third World is very much a result of colonialism; as much as colonialism established power relationships between the colonizers and the colonized, it established similar relationships between women and men. Men have colonized women by isolating them in the domestic sphere, by devaluing their contributions to the economy, and by controlling their sexuality. These power relationships have endured, as evident in more recent development policies and programmes that rely on women's unpaid or underpaid labour for capitalist development. Although the word *empowerment* is not actually used in the body of the article, the authors seem to suggest that the processes of empowerment and *gender decolonization* are closely linked. There is a pressing need, the authors argue, for a 'focus on a worldwide process of gender decolonization that calls for profound reformulations and restructuring of the power relations between women and men at the domestic and societal levels, free of all hierarchies'. The concept of women as a last colony is thus a 'compelling metaphor of liberation'. As documented in the accompanying case studies, women are indeed adopting innovative strategies to overcome gender inequality and to resist new forms of subordination.

Adams, Alayne and Sarah Castle. 'Gender Relations and Household Dynamics.' Gita Sen, Adrienne Germain and Lincoln C. Chen (eds). *Population Policies Reconsidered: Health, Empowerment and Rights.* **Boston, MA: Harvard School of Public Health, 1994.**
This article examines the impact of intrahousehold dynamics on women's reproductive decisions and outcomes in rural West Africa. The authors contend that between-gender relations and within-gender relations (specifically, relations among women) in the household determine women's degree of control over material and non-material resources which influence reproductive options and outcomes. Between genders, the authors noted that while West African women have considerable economic

225

independence, which gives them autonomy over reproductive matters concerning children's health and nutrition, they may not have the same degree of control over fertility decisions. These decisions are largely constrained by a prevailing patriarchy system. Among women, power relations influence inequalities in access to, or control over, non-material resources, such as health information and labour. Moreover, women's relationships beyond the household – in other households, in the community, and in the economy – also affect reproductive decisions. Finally, a woman's status is influenced by the social and economic power and prestige that comes with a particular role in her life cycle. As a mother-in-law a woman exercises more power in the household than as a daughter. Policies and programmes which aim to empower women in reproductive decision-making need to consider these complex power relations that structure women's lives.

Antrobus, Peggy. 'The Empowerment of Women.' Rita Gallin, Marilyn Aronoff and Anne Ferguson (eds). *The Women and International Development Annual.* **Boulder, CO: Westview Press, Inc., 1989.**
In this essay the author discusses the 'problematic' concept of empowerment by exploring three aspects of empowerment: the co-option of the empowerment strategy, the definition of empowerment, and the ways in which privileged professionals who work in the field of international development can contribute to women's empowerment. The author begins by asserting that the strategy of empowerment is being co-opted by international agencies to conceal structural adjustment policies; these policies threaten women by decreasing their access to income and services, while increasing the demands on their time to fill the gaps created by reductions in social services. Then, in defining *empowerment*, the author deconstructs the concept of *power*, distinguishing between role power (or power *over*) and personal power (or power *for*); she focuses on the potential of personal power – the strength within each person to act – to empower women. Political activism is central to the author's concept of empowerment; this is reflected in the definition that she cites from Sandra Morgen and Ann Bookman's editorial volume *Women and the Politics of Empowerment*: empowerment is 'a spectrum of political activity ranging from acts of individual resistance to mass political mobilizations that challenge the basic power relations in our society'. Finally, the author contends that privileged professionals can contribute to the empowerment of poor women only by first empowering themselves. This requires 'critically examining, resisting, and challenging policies and programs which are inimical to women's strategic gender interests'. It also requires adopting a stronger feminist position, one which supports women to do their own gender analysis.

Ashford, Lori S. 'Gender Equality and the Empowerment of Women.' *Population Bulletin (New Perspectives on Population: Lessons from Cairo).* **Vol. 50, No. 1, March 1995, pp. 17–22.**
This volume summarizes the discussions of, and goals articulated at, the International Conference on Population and Development (ICPD) in Cairo, in September 1994. An overarching theme of the conference is the role of women in achieving population and development goals. The new thinking endorsed in Cairo is one of which the objectives of stabilizing population growth and enhancing development efforts require the advancement of women. Indeed, the goal articulated in Cairo is to 'bring about more equitable relationships between men and women, and empower women to participate more fully in development'. Therefore, a broad policy to be pursued by the 180 countries represented in Cairo is the empowerment of women. Education is the prime avenue for empowering women; with more education, women have greater access to employment opportunities and increased ability to secure their own economic resources. Legislation which protects women from discrimination and promotes gender equality also needs to be enacted by governments. In addition, cultural and religious barriers to the advancement of women need to be tackled.

Batliwala, Srilatha. 'The Meaning of Women's Empowerment: New Concepts from Action.' Gita Sen, Adrienne Germain and Lincoln C. Chen **(eds).** *Population Policies Reconsidered: Health, Empowerment and Rights.* **Boston, MA: Harvard School of Public Health, 1994.**
Based on a study of empowerment programmes in South Asia, this article explores the concept of empowerment, beginning with the debates that led to its emergence in development theory. According to the author, the notion of empowerment has its roots in the interaction between feminism and 'popular education'; the 'empowerment approach' was first clearly articulated in 1985 by Development Alternatives with Women for a New Era (DAWN). Empowerment is defined as 'the process of challenging existing power relations, and of gaining greater control over the sources of power.' Further, 'The goals of women's empowerment are to challenge patriarchal ideology . . . to transform the structures and institutions that reinforce and perpetuate gender discrimination and social inequality . . . and to enable poor women to gain access to, and control of, both material and informational resources.' Externally induced, the empowerment process begins from women's recognition of the forces that oppress them; this eventually leads to action. However, in order for the process to lead to *sustained* changes, *collective* action must occur. The author identifies three approaches to women's empowerment: the integrated development approach, which focuses on women's survival and livelihood needs; the economic development approach, which aims to strengthen women's economic position; and the consciousness-raising approach, which organizes

women into collectives that address the sources of oppression. To be effective, empowerment strategies must simultaneously address women's practical gender needs as well as strategic gender needs. Finally, an
undemocratic environment and a fragmented understanding of the concept
and process of empowerment will hinder experiments in empowerment.

**Berger, Iris. 'Gender, Race, and Political Empowerment: South African
Canning Workers, 1940–1960.' *Gender & Society*, Vol. 4, No. 3, September
1990, pp. 398–420.**
This article, based on a study of women workers in the South African
canning industry during the 1940s and 1950s, explores the structural conditions that fostered women's active participation in the trade union and in
political organizations concerned with gender and racial issues. It also
raises the question 'to what extent is women's empowerment a product of
favorable circumstances and to what extent a result of skilful organizing?'
Although many characteristics of the women labour force in the South
African canning industry are found in today's world market factories, such
as low wages and least-stable work, there were a few unique characteristics
that may have made organizing South African women relatively easier. For
one, the climate during this period was more amenable to trade unionism
than that in many authoritarian regimes. Another feature may be that the
social gender gap in South Africa was relatively smaller than that found in
many developing countries. In explaining women's high level of empowerment in the union, two structural conditions were important: women's
predominance in seasonal labour; and communities in which women, men,
and children worked in the same factories. Union policies responded to
these conditions by addressing a wide range of community issues, which
maintained women's involvement during the off-season; and by translating
gender concerns into family issues, which helped women minimize the
tension between their working lives and their household responsibilities.
Thus, women became active supporters of these favourable union policies.
Finally, an active political movement to dismantle apartheid contributed to
women's political activism.

**Bhasin, Kamla. *Towards Empowerment: Report of an FAO-FFHC/AD
South Asia Training for Women Development Workers*. New Delhi and
Rome: Freedom From Hunger Campaign/Action for Development (FAO),
1985.**
In order to empower the rural poor, especially the women, female development workers must first empower themselves. This is one of the key mes-
sages in this report of a training workshop held in 1983 and participated in
by 15 female development workers representing 14 major organizations
involved in rural development in Bangladesh, India, Nepal, Pakistan and
Sri Lanka. In addition to the rural poor and the participants themselves,
the workshop also aimed to empower South Asian initiatives that address

rural poverty as well as ideologies and strategies which support women and workers. In empowering each other, the workshop participants shared their experiences, insights and ideas; learned from each other and from other organizations; made linkages between their personal lives and their professional lives as change agents; and found strength in participatory analysis and collective action. The report also highlights some of the successful initiatives of South Asian NGOs, such as the Self-Employed Women's Association in India, Gonoshasthaya Kendra in Bangladesh and Participatory Institute for Development Alternatives in Sri Lanka.

Bhatt, Ela. 'Toward Empowerment.' *World Development,* **Vol. 17, No. 7, 1989, pp. 1059–1065.**
This article describes the plight of self-employed women in Gujarat, India, and the struggles of the Self-Employed Women's Association (SEWA) to demand worker's rights and to overcome injustice. Established in 1972, SEWA is a trade union that gives political strength to, and creates economic opportunities for, more than 40 000 poor, self-employed women. For SEWA, central to the empowerment process are the strategies of *struggle and development;* struggle entails fighting for one's rights and interests through the trade union, while development involves building alternative economic structures such as co-operatives. Organizing is crucial to these strategies. As the author explains, 'To organize means to bring people together to think through their common problems, to agree on their common issues, to decide on common action, and to forge common ideologies.' Because injustice exists at various levels, the author argues that to be effective it is therefore necessary to wage the struggle at corresponding levels. This includes taking direct action, filing complaints with government departments, and influencing policies to make them more responsive to the needs of the self-employed. The author illustrates these tactics by describing the struggles of home-based producers and vendors and hawkers.

Blumberg, Rae Lesser, Cathy A. Rakowski, Irene Tinker and Michael Monteón (eds). *Engendering Wealth and Well-Being: Empowerment for Global Change.* **Boulder, CO: Westview Press, Inc., 1995.**
This collection of case studies illustrates how women in the developing world have been most negatively affected by structural adjustment, and how they have been empowered through their responses to these economic challenges. Specifically, as the author of the introductory article asserts, women are empowered through an increasing control of economic resources, especially income, and through education. The premise of this argument is that women's control of economic resources relative to that of men is the most important factor affecting the degree of gender equality. In addition, the cases explore the ways in which economically empowered women contribute to the wealth and well-being not only of their families, but also of their nations. Women's important contribution to wealth and

well-being at both micro- and macro-levels – through their productive activities and through the consequences of their education – have shifted the view of women as victims to one of women as the key to sustainable development. The cases are drawn from Latin America, Africa, Eastern Europe, China and the Islamic nations.

Calman, Leslie. *Toward Empowerment: Women and Movement Politics in India.* **Boulder, CO and Oxford, UK: Westview Press, Inc., 1992.**
This book documents the women's movement in India. It traces the political and structural crises that led to the emergence of the women's movement; examines the resources that made it possible; evaluates the achievements and failures of the movement; and speculates on the promises and problems its future holds. In characterizing the structure of the Indian women's movement, the author outlines two ideological and organizational tendencies: one, the 'rights wing', focuses on issues of rights and equality; and the other, the 'empowerment wing', stresses personal and community empowerment of poor women. The former is primarily urban-based, while the latter is both urban- and rural-based. The author acknowledges the complex interplay of various types of power – economic, political, social and psychological – integral to the empowerment process, but cannot identify which one prevails. She also argues that the empowerment of women in the household is necessary before women can participate in public life; women must have some control over their own lives and enough self-confidence before they can engage in politics. Thus, empowerment movements may be the best channels to draw poor women into mainstream political life. Looking into the future, the author argues that the effectiveness of the Indian women's movement depends more on empowerment groups which tap into essential resources by co-operating with the state, than on those that oppose, wherever possible, any state co-operation.

Karl, Marilee. *Women and Empowerment: Participation and Decision Making.* **London and New Jersey: Zed Books Ltd, 1995.**
Aimed to build awareness and promote the empowerment process, this sourcebook provides an overview of women's participation in politics and society. It contains analytical frameworks, discussion questions, cross-country statistics, and lists of organizations and resources. The sourcebook evaluates the extensiveness of gender discrimination in society and describes how women are participating in the life of their communities and in society. Specifically, it explores forms of participation (i.e. household, economic, social and political), obstacles to political participation (e.g. lack of education, the double burden of work), channels of participation (e.g. electoral politics, public life, NGOs and movements), and organizing strategies that women around the world are using, both at the grassroots level and at the international level, to gain political control. Political participation is central to the empowerment process. Specifically, the empowerment

230

of women involves the interplay of four interrelated and mutually reinforcing components: collective awareness-building, capacity building and skills development, participation and greater control and decision-making power, and action to bring about greater gender equality. The author also presents other approaches to empowerment, including the Women's Empowerment Framework used by UNICEF.

Mahmud, Simeen and Anne M. Johnston. 'Women's Status, Empowerment, and Reproductive Outcomes.' Gita Sen, Adrienne Germain and Lincoln C. Chen (eds). *Population Policies Reconsidered: Health, Empowerment and Rights.* **Boston, MA: Harvard School of Public Health, 1994.**
This article explores the complex relationships between women's work, education, status, empowerment, and fertility. Empirical evidence shows that women's educational level is correlated with fertility; the more education a woman has, the more likely that she will delay marriage, desire a smaller family, and use contraception. However, studies on the links between women's non-domestic work and fertility have not shown any simple correlation. The authors argue that policies that rely on increasing women's educational and work opportunities to reduce fertility are insufficient. What is crucial are 'strategies for women's empowerment that lead to their increased autonomy and decision-making power, providing them with an alternative power base that is independent of the domination of men.' In conceptualizing women's status and autonomy, three dimensions of inequality are commonly considered – inequality in prestige, in power, and in access to, or control over, resources. A woman may experience greater gender inequality in one dimension, in one location, such as the social unit, or at a particular stage in her life. The authors contend that if employment is to empower women, employment programmes must satisfy at least three conditions: they must reduce women's total work burden; they must ensure that women have access to, as well as control over, income; and they need to increase women's access to non-kin support, information, and outside contacts. Finally, empowerment strategies are likely to be effective if they support women to mobilize peer groups and community resources.

Mayoux, Linda. *From Vicious to Virtuous Circles? Gender and Micro-Enterprise Development* **(Occasional Paper 3). Geneva: United Nations Research Institute for Social Development (UNRISD), May 1995.**
With reference to studies, theories and trends, this paper provides a critical overview of gender and micro-enterprise development in developing countries. The author evaluates past and current experiences in micro-enterprise development – such as training credit and group production programmes – and argues that most programmes have not made a significant impact on the incomes of poor women. One cannot assume, therefore, that micro-enterprise programmes reduce gender inequality. The author

contrasts two approaches to gender and micro-enterprise development: the market approach, 'which aims to assist individual women entrepreneurs to increase their incomes'; and the empowerment approach, 'which aims not only to increase the incomes, but also the bargaining power, of poor producers through group activities.' Both approaches, she asserts, contain a number of inherent tensions and contradictions. For example, within the empowerment approach, there are potential economic and social costs to co-operative production; they include the costs in terms of time outside the home and spent in decision-making. Highlighting the diversity of the small-scale sector on the one hand, and the complexity of the constraints posed by gender inequality and poverty on the other, the author contends that devising a 'blueprint' for successful women's micro-enterprise development is unlikely. Furthermore, the success of micro-enterprise development for women depends on transformations in the wider development agenda.

Mazumdar, Vina. 'Women's Studies and the Women's Movement in India: An Overview.' *Women's Studies Quarterly*, **Vol. 22, No. 3–4, Fall–Winter 1994, pp. 42–54.**
This article describes the impact that women's studies in India have had on the Indian women's movement, and examines the efforts that the movement has made to empower women. In the mid-1970s, the focus of women's studies in India shifted toward the concerns and priorities of the non-privileged classes. This shift has contributed to the revival of the women's movement. As the academic arm of the women's movement, women's studies have actively contributed to policy-oriented research on the marginalization and exploitation of women in the economy, in the political process, in the education system, and in the media. More broadly, women's studies have challenged traditional notion of *development* and have promoted development strategies that are sensitive to egalitarian and gender concerns. The growing number of women's organizations, the increasing frequency of conferences and workshops, and the emergence of networks over the past decade and a half demonstrate the active, though not entirely cohesive, efforts to strive for women's empowerment. The author argues that 'The concept of empowerment of the most deprived groups of women to enable them to enjoy their constitutional rights has given way to the understanding that empowerment is mutual. Women at the grassroots, when they are organized, emanate a kind of energy and determination for change which galvanizes all those who work with them.' Thus, the strength and sustenance of the women's movement will depend on the effective marshalling of women at the grassroots.

Moser, Caroline O. N. 'Gender Planning in the Third World: Meeting Practical and Strategic Gender Needs.' *World Development,* **Vol. 17, No. 11, 1989, pp. 1799–1989.**
Gender planning, a planning approach based on the rationale that women and men play different roles in society, and therefore have different needs, provides a conceptual framework and a methodological tool for incorporating gender into development planning. In this article the author provides the rationale for gender planning, illustrates the potential and limitations of different interventions to meet gender needs, and evaluates development policy approaches from a gender planning perspective. To be effective, development planning for low-income women needs to recognize gender needs; specifically, planners need to distinguish between *practical gender needs*, which refer to what women require in order to fulfil their roles and tasks, and *strategic gender needs*, which refer to what women need to overcome their subordination. As the author describes, the empowerment approach utilizes 'practical gender needs as the basis on which to build a secure support base, and a means through which more strategic needs may be reached.' Indeed, the author points out that the most effective women's organizations have been those which started out addressing practical gender needs, such as health and employment, but which have used these concerns to meet particular strategic gender needs. The potentially challenging character of the empowerment approach is evident in a few struggles that the article describes.

O'Connell, Helen. *Dedicated Lives: Women Organizing for a Fairer World.* **Oxford, UK: Oxfam UK and Ireland, 1993.**
The stories of eight women's lives and efforts to work for equality and social change are told in this book – one which in fact reflects the will of many women with whom Oxfam works to overcome gender-based constraints. Women and their organizations have adopted different strategies to end gender discrimination and to empower women; however, common to these strategies is a focus on education for consciousness and collective action. The eight women also agree that women's organizations must be independent in order to be effective. Among the stories told is one of Vigi Srinivasan, whose work with the NGO Adithi in Bihar, India has given her insights into strategies to empower poor women. She believes that there are certain things – such as the religious and cultural perceptions of women and entrenched political structures – that are impossible to change at present because women's groups are not strong enough. Thus, her two-pronged strategy for empowering women focuses on 'alternative employment and alternative power structures at the local level achieved through building and strengthening women's groups.' Adithi is introducing women to non-traditional skills, such as carpentry and pottery, with the aim to increase women's income and their control over it. It is also working with dairying

women and fisheries women to access resources from the government. Gaining access to land (for example, leasing land with fish ponds from the government) is one way that women's groups are challenging the local system of land ownership.

Raheim, Salome and Jacquelyn Bolden. 'Economic Empowerment of Low-Income Women Through Self-Employment Programs.' *Affilia*, Vol. 10 No. 2, Summer 1995, pp. 138–154.
In this article the authors argue that self-employment programmes which use empowerment principles offer a viable alternative to traditional approaches to promote economic self-sufficiency of low-income women in the United States. Studies have shown that conventional social welfare policies, advanced in such initiatives as welfare-to-work programmes, have not been effective in promoting women's economic self-sufficiency; this is largely because they do not address labour market conditions which keep women unemployed or in the part-time and low-wage job pool. Self-employment programmes specifically designed for low-income women, however, can overcome these market limitations. In addition, they can reduce the barriers to entrepreneurship by increasing women's access to credit and capital, technical expertise, business management training, and information and support networks. Furthermore, self-employment programmes provide the flexibility that women need to manage child care and family responsibilities as well as increase women's self-confidence that comes from learning to manage one's business. The authors point out that while self-employment strategies are consistent with American entrepreneurial ideals, ironically they also subvert the patriarchy system and the state. Indeed, female entrepreneurship has the potential for women's empowerment, and this undermines male control in the home, in the workplace, and of the social welfare system.

Rowbotham, Sheila and Swasti Mitter (eds). *Dignity and Daily Bread: New Forms of Economic Organising among Poor Women in the Third World and the First*. New York, NY: Routledge, 1994.
This anthology of case studies documents women's experiences of creating new forms of economic organizing that addresses the inequalities of gender, class and race, and that recognize the actual conditions of poor women workers. To this end, the case studies also highlight the constraints within which these women operate. For example, one case study looks at the 'struggle and development' strategy of the Self-Employed Women's Association (SEWA) in India. SEWA's strategy combines trade unionism with co-operative production, and has organized thousands of poor women around labour concerns as well as health and welfare issues. Another important element of SEWA's strategy is the provision of social services which maintains participation. New organizational structures, including trade unions and women's organizations, have also emerged in free trade

zones of Malaysia, Philippines and Sri Lanka where young women workers make up most of the labour force. These structures make links between work and social networks, and consider not simply women's working lives, but also their lives in the boarding-houses and in the community. The case study on Bombay's cotton textile industry before 1940 reveals that the marginalization of women by factory-based industrialization is not a recent phenomenon. Together, these case studies highlight the importance to women's organizing efforts of building alliances. Historically, working-class women's alliances with supportive middle-class women and male workers have strengthened their working status.

Samarasinghe, Vidyamali. 'Puppets on a String: Women's Wage Work and Empowerment among Female Tea Plantation Workers of Sri Lanka.' *The Journal of Developing Areas*, Vol. 27, No. 3, April 1993, pp. 329–340.
This study, based on a field survey of the tea plantation sector of Sri Lanka, describes women's subordinate position within the tea plantation system and outlines factors which prevent their economic independence. The author contends that women's economic independence, a necessity for women's empowerment, requires not only women's access to resources, but also women's *control* of their own income. In Sri Lanka, despite the fact that female tea plantation workers bring home relatively higher re-muneration than their husbands who also work at the plantations, their economic independence has not improved. The author probes the house-hold power structure and the patriarchal controls within the tea plantation system which, combined, effectively prevent women from gaining more control over their incomes. For example, because male workers normally collect their spouses' earnings, they have almost exclusive control over total household incomes. An important lesson can be drawn from this study: development strategies which simply increase women's access to resources do not necessarily ensure their empowerment.

Schuler, Margaret, (ed.) *Empowerment and the Law: Strategies of Third World Women*. Washington, DC: OEF International, 1986.
This collection of case studies highlights the problems women face in the developing world and the strategies that they are using to overcome them. In the introductory article, the editor proposes a conceptual framework, what she calls Women, Law and Development (WLD), to analyse and address the major legal issues which concern women. The WLD frame-work emphasizes strategies; specifically, it outlines strategies aimed at using or challenging the three components of the legal system: structural, substantive, and cultural. At the core of WLD strategies is the goal of empowerment. Empowerment refers to the capacity to mobilize resources to produce beneficial social change. Three critical dimensions characterize the empowerment process. The first level is individual consciousness-raising; the second is the development of collective consciousness; the third

– mobilization – builds on the previous two levels and is where collective skills and resources are translated into political and legal action. It is within the WLD framework that the 55 case studies drawn from the experiences of women from 32 countries are presented.

Schuler, Sidney Ruth and Syed Mesbahuddin Hashemi. *Defining and Studying Empowerment of Women: A Research Note from Bangladesh.* **JSI Working Paper No. 3, Arlington, VA: JSI Research and Training Institute, April 1993.**
Based on research in rural Bangladesh, this paper describes an approach to exploring women's empowerment and presents individual-level indicators of empowerment. The authors contend that because women's subordination is part of a cultural system, the process of empowerment must ultimately weaken the systemic basis of women's subordination. An approach to study the empowerment process, then, is to focus on the village community as the locus of social change, and on the individual woman as the primary unit of analysis. Based on surveys on the attitudes and experiences of Grameen Bank, BRAC and other credit programme participants, the authors identified six domains in which women have traditionally been subordinated, and in which empowerment is believed to be taking place: sense of self and vision of a future; mobility and visibility; economic security; status of decision-making power within the household; ability to interact effectively in the public sphere; and participation in non-family groups. The order of the domains suggests a linear process of empowerment whereby a woman's individual consciousness leads to increased mobility, greater likelihood of engaging in a wage employment, more decision-making power in the household and, eventually, higher levels of community participation. In rural Bangladesh, however, the process of empowerment is generally not as linear as outlined above. Survey indicators associated with these domains are presented.

Sen, Gita and Caren Grown. *Development, Crises, and Alternative Visions: Third World Women's Perspectives.* **New York: Monthly Review Press, 1987.**
The empowerment of women is crucial to fulfilling the alternative development visions articulated by Development Alternatives with Women for a New Era (DAWN), a network of activists, researchers, and policymakers. In this book, which captures the conditions and struggles of women worldwide, the authors critically examine the development policies and strategies that have proven to be damaging to women. In rejecting these strategies, they offer an alternative approach that is rooted in a vision of feminism which 'has at its very core a process of economic and social development geared to human needs through control over and access to economic and political power'. Not only women, but women's organizations also need to be empowered, since they are central to strategies for

social change. The authors evaluate the strengths and weaknesses of six major types of organization, and suggest ways in which they can be more effective in pushing for positive change. For one, women's organizations must strengthen their organizational capacity. Finally, empowerment of women and organizations requires not only resources and leadership formation, but also democratic processes, dialogue and participation.

Sharma, Kumud. 'Grassroots Organizations and Women's Empowerment: Some Issues in the Contemporary Debate.' *Samya Shakti*, Vol. VI, 1991–92, pp. 28–44.
Using experiences from India, this article examines the debate on the dynamics and role of grassroots organizations in empowering women, particularly poor women. The author first acknowledges that there is general agreement on the vital role that grassroots organizations of poor women workers play in women's economic and political empowerment, but concludes, after looking at the debates on the concepts of *grassroots* and *empowerment*, that there is no agreement on the usage and ideological underpinnings of these terms. This is because the search for empowerment makes contradictory demands on grassroots organizations; they have to confront the forces that disempower women, but at the same time stay in the 'mainstream' to ensure access to governmental resources. Nevertheless, the author offers a definition of empowerment: 'The term empowerment refers to a range of activities from individual self-assertion to collective resistance, protest and mobilization that challenge basic power relations. For individuals and groups where class, caste, ethnicity and gender determine their access to resources and power, their empowerment begins when they not only recognize the systemic forces that oppress them but act to change existing power relationships.' The author also examines the responses of the Indian government, intermediaries, such as research organizations, and NGOs to women's mobilization, and how these responses have contributed to the debate on women's empowerment. Finally, the author argues that simply documenting organizational efforts and strategies would not advance the women's movement in India. More rigorous analysis of the meaning, parameters, strategies and process of empowerment is necessary.

UNDP (Dhaka). *UNDP's 1994 Report on Human Development in Bangladesh: Empowerment of Women*. Dhaka: UNDP, March 1994.
Despite the biases that Bangladeshi women face in the household and in the economy, their contribution to the growth and modernization of the country is substantial. The experiences of such NGOs as BRAC and the Grameen Bank, as well as recent economic trends such as the expansion of the (women-laboured) garment industry, suggest that empowering women could create enormous benefits for women, their families and the entire society. This third in a series of reports by UNDP, Dhaka on human

development in Bangladesh focuses on the empowerment of women. Empowerment is defined as 'a process which enables individuals or groups to change balances of power in social, economic and political relations in society . . . In the Bangladeshi context, empowerment should give the vast majority of women the freedom of choice for self-fulfilment and self-development as well as equal access to domestic and community resources, opportunities and powers.' Development interventions should empower women through electoral and legal reforms, education and economic opportunities. Efforts to improve the conditions of Bangladeshi women are noteworthy, but much more needs to be done. The report urges governments, donors, NGOs, and other development agencies to take more strategically visioned and planned affirmative action to ensure women's empowerment. Finally, the report offers a list of actions which may be included in a strategy for empowering women.

Westergaard, Kirsten. *People's Empowerment in Bangladesh – NGO Strategies.* **CDR Working Paper. Copenhagen: Centre for Development Research, November 1994.**
Most development organizations in Bangladesh share an ideological approach that focuses on grassroots development, collective action and empowerment. Specifically, they follow a two-pronged strategy which provides credit and other services on the one hand, and strives for empowerment on the other. *Empowerment*, in this paper, refers to the enabling of poor people to decide upon the actions which they perceive to be key to their development. Empowerment is concerned with organizing people to gain more control – political and economic – over resources and institutions, and with tackling the root causes of poverty. This paper reports on a field study that examined the different empowerment strategies adopted by six development organizations, mainly NGOs, in Bangladesh. Some organizations, such as the Bangladesh Rural Advancement Committee (BRAC), follow the strategy of credit/services provision and empowerment, while others, such as Nijera Kori, focus on conscientization and empowerment. Based on the field data, NGOs with economic development programmes have improved the economic situation of their members. Moreover, greater economic independence has increased group strength and solidarity; it has also led to increased self-esteem of its members, especially among the women. This is revealed in women increasingly challenging social norms that discriminate against them, and becoming politically more active in their communities.